No Laughing Matter
Race Joking and Resistance in Brazilian Social Media

Luiz Valério P. Trindade, PhD
Department of Sociology
University of Southampton, UK

Series in Sociology

www.vernonpress.com

In the Americas:	*In the rest of the world:*
Vernon Press	Vernon Press
1000 N West Street,	C/Sancti Espiritu 17,
Suite 1200, Wilmington,	Malaga, 29006
Delaware 19801	Spain
United States	

Series in Sociology

Library of Congress Control Number: 2020939004

ISBN: 978-1-64889-095-6

Also available: 978-1-62273-796-3 [Hardback]; 978-1-64889-080-2 [PDF, E-Book]

Cover design by Vernon Press using elements designed by Zlatko_Plamenov / Freepik.

Table of Contents

List of figures and tables

Figures

Tables

Foreword

Studying race relations in Brazil represents a particular challenge, especially for black researchers. The myth of 'racial democracy' has been ideologically disseminated within our borders as an epistemological project that has served (and continues to serve) the hegemonic financial and academic power both within Brazil and in the international context. If in Brazil racist beliefs of colour-blindness, or racial neutrality, have postponed the effective understanding of contemporary power and exploitation relations, outside the country past renowned intellectuals have contributed to disseminate the fallacy that racism in Brazil would be a mild force when compared with the scenario found in other Afrodiasporic countries.

Nonetheless, the reality regarding Brazil's racial groups has always been quite different from the picture drawn based on the principles of the so-called 'racial democracy'. Starting from interpersonal relations and advancing towards what can be measured in the micro and macro-economic level (e.g., employment level, access to fundamental rights, exercise of full citizenship, and including the right to life itself). In effect, despite the effort fostered by Brazilian elite to disguise or even hide the country's ingrained racism, it does not pass fully unnoticed thanks to numerous social science studies and the distinctive role played by social activism, as this book unveils.

Finding that in Brazil we live in a sort of twofold or threefold society, paraphrasing the intellectual and *quilombola* Beatriz Nascimento, reflects and coalesces first with W.E.B Du Bois' concept of the 'second veil', and second with Charles W. Mills' epistemology of white ignorance, among other parallels found in the critical production of counter-hegemonic intellectuality of other black thinkers, indigenists, feminists, and anti-colonialists. Thus, unveiling the explicit and implicit connections between the manifestations of humour and language with the relations of power and oppression in contemporary digital communication platforms is a necessary endeavour.

However, as it has happened and continues to happen in other areas of everyday social interactions, the knowledge about the social dynamics on the internet in general, and on social media in particular, also suffers from a particular form of racial blindness, fuelled with an aggravating factor: the perception that this digital technology is neutral. The loss of the political facade of digital technology has led techno-utopians to strongly believe in the web's revolutionary aspect. From the defence of a libertarian utopia in John Perry Barlow's 'Declaration of the Independence of Cyberspace' that mistakenly believed that cyberspace would not reproduce geographical borders, patriarchal societies, racism and classism (although it was already dominated by white male American) to how the GAFAM oligopoly (Google, Apple, Facebook, Amazon and Microsoft) defines itself as the utmost symbol of freedom on the web (at the same time that they give in to and support local authoritarianism, from the US to China), the criticism of technocentric essentialism on the web as if it was somehow detached from the reality in the offline context needs to be done.

Having said that, what I call double opacity comes into play: how hegemonic discourses make both the social aspects of technology invisible and the debates about the primacy of racial issues in different spheres of society - including technology, recursively.

Thus, I can notice that Luiz Valério P. Trindade has challenged this double opacity throughout his extensive track record of publications, from the analysis of the social representation of black Brazilians in printed pieces of advertising to the construction and dissemination of racist discourses on social media. The combination of this solid scholarship now converges in *No laughing matter: race joking and resistance in Brazilian social media*, which represents an essential study that innovatively explores specific aspects of vicious racist humour in the daily lives of many black Brazilians, and women in particular as the predominant target of this pernicious practice.

The supporters of the social media 'filter bubble' (as coined by Eli Pariser), tend to believe that what composes each user's virtual environment is determined solely by who you are and what you do (i.e., your interactions). But it fails to take into consideration that behind user's interactions, powerful algorithms are determining and managing these 'filter bubbles', as I advocate in my publications. In effect, social media platforms help in creating online communities, but they also enable the clash of distinct world views, ranging from social transformation to the inhuman horror of racism. The myriad of viewpoints in some cases is separated by a big gap of humanity. That is to say, certain social groups who are unable to accept the social advancement of the 'other' because such achievements might offset their own privileged social position.

The increase of racist hate speech on social media in Brazil, as reported and skilfully analysed by Trindade in this book, is mostly based on users' engagement with the pervasive centuries-old legacy of colonial thinking that has been responsible not only to naturalise racism in contemporary society, but also to reinforce, perpetuate and conceal it in a variety of ways (e.g., cultural manifestations such as popular songs and race joking, in advertisements, in textbooks, political discourses, soap operas, and movie productions).

Currently, it is possible to notice that the symbolical meaning of the ancient *quilombo* communities as distinctive spaces of resistance are mirrored in the establishment of several online communities led by black Brazilian women aiming to challenge Brazil's ingrained racism. Moreover, in this book, Trindade brings to light the many practical and symbolical achievements reached by black Brazilians as a result of demands raised by the organised black movement, the strong political significance of female Afro hairstyle and the social transformations fostered by these initiatives.

Language is capable of constructing, solidifying or challenging political and social designs not only through texts but, in the current digital society, also through 'memes' and pictorial images that allow us both to understand the ever-changing dynamics of contemporary society and search for ways to promote social and behavioural change. And it is also true that in today's social media platforms, human interaction is performed by an immense number of nodes of interconnected users and mediated (or controlled) by powerful corporations. This aspect represents just a simple reminder of the relevance of understanding the mechanisms and motivation behind the construction and dissemination of racist hate speech in the online environment and challenging this practice, as revealed by the present work.

The upward social mobility of a new generation of black Brazilian women, despite their overall challenging lived experiences of racism and historical disadvantaged racial hierarchy position, contributes to transforming the fabric of Brazilian racial relations. Even facing the challenging intersectionality dimensions of race, class, gender, place of origin, religious affiliation, amongst others, the resistance movement against Brazilian ingrained racism brought forward by black women, and evidenced in this book, plays a decisive role in paving the way towards an improved future ruled by more egalitarian racial and gender relations in Brazil and beyond.

Tarcízio Silva

Master in Contemporary Communication and Culture (*UFBA – Universidade Federal da Bahia*)

PhD in Human and Social Sciences (*UFABC – Universidade Federal do ABC*)

Co-founder of IBPAD (*Instituto Brasileiro de Pesquisa e Análise de Dados*)

To Martha. The strongest black woman I have ever known.

Acknowledgements

To pay tribute to people who have proved important in supporting me over a long academic journey is quite challenging because there is always the risk to, inadvertently and unconsciously, leave some names behind. Thus, to avoid this undesirable mistake, and also to avoid writing a prolonged exposition with a long list of names, I have instead decided to keep it simple, but still meaningful.

I would like to express my sincere gratitude to all my friends both in Brazil and abroad with whom I have had the privilege to share ideas, thoughts and moments. I also thank my academic mentors and supervisors, who have been demanding to extract the best of me and also extremely inspiring, and my peers both during my masters' in Brazil and doctoral studies in England. Within that, I also express my gratitude to my interviewees in Brazil for their time, availability and for sharing their invaluable reflections during my fieldwork trip for data collection. Moreover, I thank the anonymous reviewer for dedicating precious time in critically assessing the manuscript and providing insightful comments and suggestions for its improvements, and for Tarcízio Silva for writing a tremendous preface. My gratitude also goes to Vernon Press for believing in this project when I submitted the proposal and for its staff who have always been very professional and courteous to my contacts. And, finally, my gratitude to my family in Brazil and in Italy, including the invaluable support of my wife Giulia. Please, feel all genuinely embraced.

Introduction

For a long time in the international arena, Brazil has been known as a singular example of a harmonious post-racial society, or the so-called 'racial democracy'. This ideology implies the existence of racial equality, egalitarian opportunities to all individuals, independently of the race, and that any instability in the system is due solely to class inequalities. Nevertheless, far from depicting the real lived experiences of inequality faced by black Brazilians, the belief in this ideology also results in other negative impacts.

First, the belief in the 'racial democracy' blurs people's perceptions concerning the unequal upward social mobility opportunities experienced by black people and fuelled by racial prejudice. Second, it prevents society from raising constructive debates about racism and overshadows efforts towards the implementation of social policies aiming to tackle this phenomenon. The inner logic is 'since racism is not a pressing issue, there is no need to discuss it'. Third, 'racial democracy' foments the fallacious idea of meritocracy regarding successful upward social mobility. Nevertheless, the proponents of this ideology completely disregard that, oftentimes, the starting point for most black Brazilians is from a very disadvantaged position in comparison to whites. Consequently, the upward social mobility achieved by the two racial groups tends to be considerably different.

In combination with the belief in the 'racial democracy', since the beginning of the twentieth century, the whitening ideology has become an ingrained element in Brazilian racial relations. This ideology is based on a contrasting dualistic dynamic. On the one hand, it praises and promotes whiteness as the ultimate symbol of a Eurocentric beauty standard, modernity, social development and material and intellectual progress. On the other hand, blackness has constantly been associated with many negative attributes such as backwardness, ugliness, and lack of moral traits and cleverness, among others.

Hence, over time, the combination of 'racial democracy' and the whitening ideology has been shaping Brazilian racial relations and influencing people's discourses regarding race. However, whilst social conventions tend to 'regulate' and restrain the enactment of racist discourses in everyday social circumstances, race joking offers a convenient escape route. Given the fact that it represents a socially acceptable form of communication, it also allows people to freely convey racist ideologies without sounding blatantly racist. After all, it is 'just a joke'. This scenario coalesces with the paradoxical circumstance known as 'racism without racists', meaning that the act and its negative impacts are capable of being identified and acknowledged by society, but the agent is absent.

With the emergence of major social media platforms in the early 2000s and its exponential growth rate and popularity in Brazil, a different social phenomenon has also emerged. This disruptive digital technology has enabled the proponents of racist ideologies to disregard any social convention and unleash their discriminatory discourses in the online environment without any *crise de conscience*.

Two major drivers are fuelling such attitudes. First, a false belief that online anonymity bestows users with implied permission to mock and/or offend anyone in the online environment. Second, an illusory perception that the online environment is detached from the offline environment and, consequently, that users cannot be held accountable for their attitudes. Moreover, there is evidence revealing that once their racist discourses become subject of news articles, the users take at least one of the following four actions: 1) delete the original post, 2) shift their profile status from public to private, 3) delete the account, and 4) claim that it was 'just' a harmless jest.

Within this context, from the mid-2000s onwards, major social media platforms such as Facebook, Instagram, Twitter, WhatsApp and YouTube have become a breeding ground for the construction and wide dissemination of racist discourses against black people. Such discourses are oftentimes conveyed through race joking and the preferred target are upwardly mobile black women. Furthermore, due to its networking capabilities, social media platforms enable these individuals to accomplish three things: 1) disseminate their discriminatory ideologies towards a wide audience, 2) disregard any conventional social distance[1] that might exist between themselves and the victims, and 3) engage an increasing number of like-minded users which, consequently, amplifies the reach and reverberation of their hateful voices in ways not seen in the offline context in Brazil.

Having said that, the new generation of upwardly mobile black women seems to be upsetting certain pre-established perceptions and limited social roles. As they achieve social progress through better tertiary education, engagement in professions requiring specialised skills (e.g. journalism, medicine, law, engineering, etc.), they become the target of racial discourses. Their achievements undermine the ingrained belief that their 'legitimate' social

---

[1] It is important to explain that, in this book, 'social distance' stands for the degree of proximity or distance between people but regarding previous relationships either in the online environment or the offline. In other words, it refers to the idea of strong or weak bonds which, respectively, implies short social distance and big social distance.

space is restricted only to subservient positions, and they threaten the achievement of the desired 'whitened' Eurocentric national identity.

The interplay of the belief in the existence of a 'racial democracy' and the aspirational fully whitening of Brazil fuels racist discourses. Once embedded in humour statements, they become socially acceptable and grant the 'it was only a joke' excuse for the proponents of white supremacy. As they are enacted and disseminated on major social media platforms, the technology becomes a sort of modern-day pillory for inflicting public virtual 'whipping' on 'trespassers' of social spaces associated with white privilege and, consequently, racism is perpetuated and reinforced in Brazil through this disruptive digital technology.

Nonetheless, despite this picture, it can also be observed that social media is becoming an important arena for resistance manifestations, especially led by black women. Indeed, black women have had a highlighted role (although historically not always appropriately recognised or acknowledged) in resisting racism and enslavement since colonial times. The same has happened in the abolitionist movement in the late years of the nineteenth century, and it continued this way throughout the twentieth century both in organised groups and through emerging influential agents of social change.

Yet, what can be observed is that in the current scenario, social media platforms have allowed the agglutination of initiatives. Moreover, given the fact that this technology enables the amplification of black women's voices, this aspect composes a significant difference in comparison to previous organised black movements. It means that social media is enabling ordinary black women to have their voices heard and convey their specific anti-racist narratives. Within that, these women speak the same 'language' of other equally oppressed black women that might experience similar circumstances of racism both on social media and in the offline environment. Consequently, this emerging leadership empowered by social media is contributing to inspiring other black women to deconstruct their whitened minds, 'becoming' blacks just like them, and ultimately, challenging Brazil's enduring ingrained racism, sexism and social inequalities.

Data and Methodology

Facebook is currently the world's leading social media platform with over 2.1 billion monthly users; Brazil represents its third-largest market with 130 million monthly active users, and the second largest in terms of the time users spend on the platform daily (Kemp, 2019). Consequently, given the considerable reach and popularity of Facebook in Brazil, it represents a suitable source of primary data. Moreover, the emergence of a social media platform with this reach and exponential growth rate encourages us to reflect on "the ways in which race and ethnicity connect to, are affected by and are enacted" in this environment (boyd and Ellison, 2007, p. 222). The online search for gathering spontaneously generated textual data was conducted in Brazil during the summer of 2016, driven by a set of 131 keywords in Portuguese related to racial insults and racist jokes selected from previous studies addressing both topics (Fonseca, 1994; Guimarães, 2003; Dahia, 2008; 2010; Machado and Muniz, 2013). This process led to the identification of a series of 217 publicly available Facebook pages and 224 news articles addressing 42 cases of racism on Facebook within the timeframe 2012-2016. In complement to that, I have also interviewed eight social actors in São Paulo and Rio de Janeiro, including policymakers, leaders of non-governmental organisations, and individual social activists. It is relevant to highlight that, although the data is publicly available, the study safeguards users' privacy and no personal identification is disclosed, what conforms with best research practices suggested in previous studies (Zimmer, 2010; Salmons and Woodfield, 2013; Kosinski *et al.*, 2015).

The study adopts a qualitative approach in the investigation of the embedded meaning of race joking, and the data was explored in an iterative process to allow the emergence of key concepts (Potter, 1996; Jorgensen and Phillips, 2002; Lichtman, 2010). The data were analysed applying critical discourse analysis because it contributes towards unveiling a system of social and racial relations that evolves, and it is shaped by the context where they are created and reproduced (Arango, 2013). Moreover, language and discourse are not just descriptive but, in fact, a form of social action and, as such, are capable of being systematically interpreted and explained (Fairclough, 1989). Finally, critical discourse analysis allows the social researcher to examine how shared meanings, beliefs and ideologies are created and reproduced through people's discourses (Starks and Trinidad, 2007).

Organisation of the book

As the title of this book suggests, my study develops a critical sociological analysis of race joking (also called derogatory or disparagement humour in the literature) as a convenient vehicle to convey racist ideologies against vulnerable social groups on social media. Indeed, it takes into consideration that race joking is no laughing matter since it can bring a series of negative impacts in people's lives. However, the book also brings to the surface the resistance initiatives fomented by black Brazilians (especially women) in the very same arena where they have been belittled and subjected to new types of lived experiences of racism. In other words, the present work aims to bring a balanced and innovative view about the enduring phenomenon of racism in Brazil, in the sense that, on the one hand, it reveals contemporary forms of bigotry whereas, on the other hand, how the phenomenon is being challenged as well. For this purpose, the present book (which is derived from my PhD thesis in Sociology[2] at the University of Southampton) has been organised into six major chapters.

The **Introduction** brings an overview of the subsequent six chapters; and moreover, it summarises the key findings and the main arguments developed throughout the book, it explains the methodology applied in the research, and also presents the major conclusions.

As for **Chapter 1**, there is an old Brazilian adage, whose authorship is attributed to the musician Tom Jobim in the early 1960s, stating that 'Brazil is not for beginners' (Castro, 2008; Holanda, 2012). Certainly that, *strictu sensu*, no country is for 'beginners' as such, and each one holds its specificities and unique characteristics that make them what they are. In fact, putting it simple, Tom Jobim's adage conveys the need to revisit a country's key historical milestones in order to make sense of how and why society operates in particular ways. Without this review, chances are that to understand its *modus operandi*, one might miss important elements needed to unpack their embedded meaning.

With that in mind, more than a historical account of key aspects concerning the formation of Brazilian society, the chapter develops a profound critical analysis of the core ideologies that have guided the country's social and racial relations to date. For this purpose, Chapter 1 develops a robust and necessary contextualisation of the social condition of black Brazilians, including bringing to the surface the negative legacies inherited from the colonial society and three-and-a-half centuries of slavery history which, to date, still influence their current lived experiences of racism and discrimination.

The subsequent **Chapter 2** brings to light the evolution of black resistance to racism and discrimination. It develops a thoroughly historical journey spanning over four centuries of history, however, with a dedicated focus on four major aspects: a) the enduring legacy of *Quilombo dos Palmares* as the ultimate symbol of resistance to racism and enslavement, b) the emerging voice of black Brazilians, c) the political significance of Afro hairstyle as a tool to challenge hegemonic Eurocentric beauty standards and also to establish a clear political position, and d) a discussion addressing the contemporary achievements and challenges faced by black Brazilians and the organised black movement. Furthermore, this chapter also addresses the major historical milestones regarding the organised anti-racism movement in Brazil and discusses how the

---

[2] Title: It is not that funny. Critical analysis of racial ideologies embedded in racialized humour discourses on social media in Brazil

current online initiatives are empowering many black women and enabling them to have their voice heard among a wide audience.

Chapter 3 addresses three intertwined topics that, combined, also contribute towards the better understanding of the Brazilian social and institutional context surrounding racism on social media platforms. It starts with an important discussion regarding the key disparagement humour theoretical concepts, what makes race joking 'funny', and the major characteristics of Brazilian racist humour. The second section introduces the major aspects that have contributed to turning social media platforms into a convenient breeding ground for people to distil varied forms of bigotry and racist discourses in Brazil. And, finally, the third section brings an overview of the Brazilian anti-racism legal landscape. It aims at addressing the paradoxical context that, despite the existence of several legal anti-racism mechanisms, the practice is still very active and, data reveal that the trend has been on the rise, rather than decreasing.

As for **Chapter 4**, it aims to discuss the four major elements that compose the anatomy of racism on social media, which are: a) the target of the discourses, b) the proponents of racist discourses, c) the long life span of racist discourses on social media that can reach around three years, and d) what the title of certain online communities reveals to us regarding their nature and scope. The detailed critical analysis of these topics is important because it reveals a clearer and more robust picture concerning the dynamic of racist discourses on social media platforms. Moreover, the chapter also explores the dynamics of sexism, in combination with race and class, affecting the lived experiences of racism faced by black Brazilian women, which contribute to turning them into the predominant target of racist discourses on social media.

The following **Chapter 5** focuses on unveiling the embedded meaning of several race joking posts circulating on social media in Brazil. The critical analysis resorts to the key theoretical framework extensively discussed in Chapter 1. Hence, the analysis establishes a clear dialogue with those key theoretical concepts and reveals the strong manifestation of colonial legacies shaping Brazilian contemporary racial relations, and how society constructs legitimate national identities and perceives blackness. Furthermore, the chapter also explores the decisive role played by social media in enabling the proponents of white supremacist ideologies to disseminate their beliefs, engage like-minded people, and reverberate their voices in ways not seen in the offline social context.

Having said that, the analysis of the data has revealed five salient derogatory discourses against black women. Briefly, they encompass the following set of themes: a) challenging the legitimacy of social improvements achieved by upwardly mobile black women, b) the reinforcement of a series of negative stereotypes, especially associating blackness with delinquency, c) disregarding blacks' educational level, d) black Brazilians are treated as laughable subjects, and e) delegitimising demands for greater racial equality.

Conversely, in **Chapter 6**, the aim is to investigate the anti-racist narrative being enacted also on social media. Whilst data reveal the increasing trend of enactment of racist discourses in the online environment, it is important to understand which resistance initiatives are being fomented by black Brazilians. The development of this analysis has revealed the emergence of four major discursive strategies employed by black Brazilians aimed both at deconstructing ingrained racist ideologies and, simultaneously, empowering black women in particular. They comprise: a) Afro hairstyle as an important symbol of resistance and empowerment, b) the role played by discourses praising black beauty, c) sharing lived experiences of racism to empower black women, and d) encouraging blacks to take effective legal actions against their offenders.

Finally, the **Conclusions** weaver together the historic milestones and theoretical framework discussed in Chapters 1 to 3, with the critical analysis developed in the subsequent Chapters 4 to 6.

Chapter 1

Blackness in Brazil:
past legacies still reflected today

Introduction

Race is a complex and sensitive subject matter in Brazil (likewise in many other societies), and one of its most intriguing aspects concerns the existence of a large array of self-declared race denominations. It is certainly not the sole aspect comprising Brazilian racism as this book addresses, but it reveals a great deal about people's perceptions of race. In effect, there is a vast body of literature discussing the origins and conceptualisation of racial terminologies (e.g. van den Berghe, 1967; Bulmer and Solomos, 1999; Back and Solomos, 2000; Bulmer and Solomos, 2004) and, amongst them, van den Berghe (1967) brings a clear definition. This author explains race as a relational social construct that can encompass not only physical features but also behavioural. The author says that race is a "human group that defines itself, and/or is defined by other groups, as different from other groups by virtue of innate immutable physical characteristics" (van den Berghe, 1967, p. 9). Furthermore, the same author adds, "these physical characteristics are in turn believed to be intrinsically related to moral, intellectual, and other non-physical attributes or abilities" (van den Berghe, 1967, p. 9).

Brazilians' perception of racial identification became more evident in a survey conducted by the official statistical bureau IBGE in 1976 which revealed 135 racial denominations based on self-declared skin tones (Rodrigues, 1995; Maier, 2006). This particular finding has led IBGE to drop the use of self-declared racial denominations, and since the 1991 Census IBGE adopts only five categories: 1) *amarelo* (yellow or Asian-descent), 2) *branco* (white), 3) *indígena* (indigenous), 4) *pardo* (brown or miscegenated), and 5) *preto* (black). Within that, another distinct peculiarity comprises the fact that the actual Brazilian black population (*negros*)[1] encompasses the combination of *pretos* and *pardos* (i.e. blacks and browns altogether). This combined categorization

---

[1] Given the fact that the spelling both in English and in Portuguese is the same, it has been chosen to adopt italic to indicate the use of the terminology in Portuguese whenever necessary throughout the book.

has been adopted not only by IBGE, but also by the major organised black movements, social activists and scholars (Sansone, 1996; Guimarães, 2003; Osorio, 2003; Domingues, 2007; IBGE, 2010).

Years later after the aforementioned 1976 IBGE survey, Sansone (1996) conducted a study in two working-class cities in the Northern state of Bahia to identify and understand individuals' self-images regarding racial identifiers and the development of their racial identity. The study revealed that the interviewees had employed 36 different racial identifiers to classify themselves. This finding has led the author to argue that this myriad of terminologies reflects the difficulty that part of the population feels in self-declaring themselves *pretos* (blacks) whilst aiming at being recognised as light-skin and, consequently, closer to *branco* (white).

Whilst in English-speaking countries the use of the terminology negro sounds archaic and black is the terminology commonly employed, in the Brazilian social context it is slightly different. In Portuguese, the terminology black is equivalent to *preto*, but many authors consider that this terminology carries a series of pejorative and negative attributes (although it is still in use). By contrast, different scholars and leaders of the black movement consider that *negro* conveys more positive attributes than *preto* (Moura, 1988; Skidmore, 1992; Sansone, 1996; Goldstein, 2003). Having said that, Figure 1.1 and Table 1.1 reveal that, currently, Brazil is a country whose population is composed mainly of black people (Gillam, 2017; IBGE, 2017; Silveira, 2017; 2019).

Figure 1.1: Evolution of Brazil's racial composition

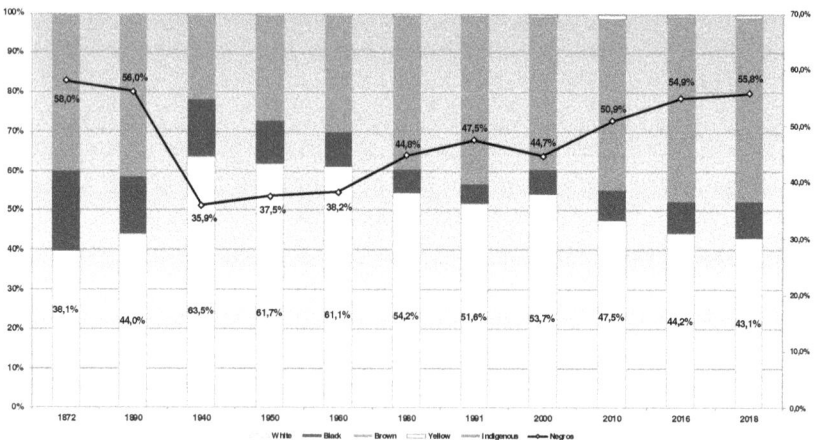

Table 1.1: Evolution of Brazil's census data

Year	1872	1890	1940	1950	1960	1980	1991	2000	2010	2016	2018
White	38.1%	44%	63.5%	61.7%	61.1%	54.2%	51.6%	53.7%	47.5%	44.2%	43.1%
Black	19.7%	14.6%	14.6%	11.0%	8.7%	5.9%	5.0%	6.2%	7.5%	8.2%	9.3%
Brown	38.3%	41.4%	21.2%	26.5%	29.4%	38.9%	42.5%	38.5%	43.4%	46.7%	46.5%
Yellow	---	---	0.6%	0.6%	0.7%	0.6%	0.4%	0.5%	1.1%	0.5%	0.7%
Indigenous	---	---	---	---	---	---	0.2%	0.4%	0.4%	0.4%	0.4%
Negros	58.0%	56.0%	35.9%	37.5%	38.2%	44.8%	47.50%	44.7%	50.9%	57.9%	55.8%
Country's Population	9,930,478	14,333,915	41,236,315	51,944,397	70,191,370	119,011,052	146,521,661	173,448,346	195,497,797	205,500,000	207,606,525

Hence, whilst currently, black Brazilians comprise 55.8% of the country's population (as indicated in Figure 1.1), historically, it has been the social group most subjected to social inequalities. Different authors reveal a worrisome picture. Oftentimes, they have reduced access to higher education in comparison to white people. Proportionally speaking, they are more prone to live in precarious housing conditions. They are more likely to be the victims of violent crimes, especially young male adults. Moreover, they usually have fewer opportunities in the job market, earn less than their white counterparts for equivalent occupations and, consequently, they experience fewer chances for upward social mobility (Hasenbalg, 1979; Henriques, 2001; Jaccoud *et al.*, 2008; Charão, 2011; Nascimento and Alves, 2011).

Nevertheless, despite this overall negative picture, there is also evidence revealing that, within the past four decades, black Brazilians have experienced a series of social improvements and important symbolic achievements. Examples include: a) an increasing number of black young people attending tertiary education, b) the enactment of the Federal Law number 7,716 in 1989 establishing racism as a punishable crime, c) the mandatory teaching of African history in public primary and secondary schools, d) the constitutional freedom to profess any religion of African origin, and e) the implementation of social policies aimed at promoting greater racial equality in the job market and social representation on means of mass communication (Moehlecke, 2002; Martins *et al.*, 2004; IBGE, 2012; Tokarnia, 2015).

However, what is simultaneously intriguing and revealing about Brazilian racism, is the fact that such achievements have not only been ignored and disqualified by the dominant elite. Actually, their symbolic value has been reduced, challenged and neglected either explicitly and/or, covertly, through race joking.

Consequently, this picture raises intriguing reflections. If for a long time Brazil has been promoting itself as a so-called post-racial society, what explains its enduring racism? What major elements constitute the fundamental pillars sustaining the perpetuation of Brazilian racism? Furthermore, how black agency and resistance has evolved in Brazil over the years? The subsequent sections of this chapter aim to address these important and pertinent questions.

Race and racism: a brief discussion

As previously addressed in the Introduction of the present chapter, there are two major common elements regarding the theoretical definition of race: a) difference among people, and b) group classification. In effect, these two elements are important not only in the theoretical definition of race as a social construct, but also first in the understanding of racial hierarchy, and second to racism as an ideology. In other words, racism is fostered by intricate systems of social differentiation among people and group classification according to rankings. Their combination attribute differentiated social positions (hierarchies) to people according to the racial group to which they belong. In complement to this argument, symbols of racial difference become apparent to people's senses and, consequently, lead towards differentiated perceptions (i.e. positive or negative) concerning racial groups (Gilroy, 1998).

Evolving from this point, rather than a state-of-mind, "racism is first and foremost a social practice, which means that it is an action and a rationale for action, or both at once" (Fields and Fields, 2012, p. 17). Moreover, racism is also understood as a unidirectional system of domination, where blacks are stigmatised as a racial group; while whiteness becomes the norm and not racialised (Cobb, 2018). However, the important question that must be raised is, what triggers racism? In essence, the answer to this relevant question is the belief in the superiority of one racial group over others. Nevertheless, looking at this subject matter through Frantz Fanon critical lenses, it is possible to examine the issue from a different perspective. The author analyses both sides of the equation ('superior' and 'inferior') arguing, "the Negro enslaved by his inferiority, the white man enslaved by his superiority alike behave in accordance with a neurotic orientation" (Fanon, 1986, p. 42). Moreover, the author adds, the acceptance of one's inferiority leads him/her to aspire to win admittance into the white world, what it is also known as internalised racism. Namely, on the one hand, racism oppresses the 'dominated' group by enforcing upon them the values and beliefs of the 'dominant' group. On the other hand, as the 'dominated' group embraces and internalises such values and beliefs, it indirectly validates the practice and consequently reinforces the 'dominant' group's privileged position.

The roots of racism as an ideology are found in the so-called theories of scientific racism fostered in the early years of the nineteenth-century-Europe (Mikulak, 2011; Fields and Fields, 2012; Santos and Barbosa e Silva, 2018). Additionally, they have also influenced many leading Brazilian authors of that same period. Briefly, the main postulate of such ideologies was the idea of the racial superiority of white Europeans in comparison to other racial groups, especially black African peoples. Regarding the operation of racism in contemporary societies, systemic racism includes a diverse assortment of racist practices. They include, for example, "the unjustly gain of economic and political power of whites; the continuing resource inequalities; the rationalizing white-racist frame; and the major institutions created to preserve white advantage and power" (Wimmer, 2015, p. 2189). Furthermore, despite the deconstruction of the postulates of the scientific racism from the mid-1950s onwards (Mikulak, 2011; Santos and Barbosa e Silva, 2018), the ideology is still vivid in the collective mind-set in Brazil. In fact, since the early twentieth century, "racism has included a discourse of power, through which an asymmetrical relationship is established between racial groups" in Brazilian society (Santos and Barbosa e Silva, 2018, p. 266).

Consequently, racism as an ideology plays an important role in the context of undermining the social improvements achieved by Black Brazilians, since it is rooted in the strong belief in the duality superiority-inferiority, the establishment of rankings (or racial hierarchies) and boundaries of belonging or 'invisible colour lines' as advocated by Du Bois (1903).

Brazilian society in the colonial period

Colonialism in Brazil comprised the period 1530-1822 (Bethel, 1984; Schwartz, 1985; Andrews, 1997), and although the country was 'discovered' in 1500, only three decades later did Portugal effectively started to occupy the territory (Hébrard, 2013). Evolving from that, historians argue that the slave trade of African peoples to Brazil encompassed around 4.7 million people between 1560 to 1850 (Duchet *et al.*, 1979; Database, 2009; Hébrard, 2013). Within this context, two important questions arise. First, how Brazilian society was structured during that historical period and, second, how racial relations operated during that time.

It is also clear that the country's current social structure and racial relations have evolved and improved considerably since then. Nevertheless, there is a strong legacy inherited from that historical period on the formation of the Brazilian society over time, and the review of their fundamental pillars and characteristic elements greatly contribute to shedding some light towards the understanding of current racial relations and racial hierarchy dynamic. Furthermore, the historian Stuart B. Schwartz rightly argues that "it [is] impossible to pen a page of Brazilian history without the question of slavery forcing its way into the discussion" (Hébrard, 2013, p. 49).

Seminal accounts and reports of distinctive aspects of Brazilian social organisation during the colonial period were made mainly by foreign visitors. A sample of such works includes 'Voyage to Guinea, Brazil and the West Indies' (Atkins, 1735), 'Travels in Brazil' (Koster, 1816), 'Travels in Brazil, in the years 1817-1820' (von Spix *et al.*, 1824), 'Life in Brazil, or a journal of a visit to the land of cocoa and the palm' (Ewbank, 1856), and 'A Journey in Brazil' (Agassiz, 1868). In addition to these studies, a sample of other authors who have investigated this historical period includes Willems (1970), Conrad (1983), Bethel (1984), Schwartz (1974; 1985), Andrews (1997), Metcalf (2005) and Hébrard (2013).

These studies allow us to identify three important characteristics of the prevailing social organisation: 1) the Portuguese settlers were predominantly young single men who established the fundamental roots of a patriarchal society, where they had both symbolic and ideological power over women, children and slaves, 2) the labour force was comprised predominantly of black slaves who were mostly male. Although they were socially downgraded by the slave owners, they also developed intricate horizontal racial hierarchy among themselves, and 3) the social stratification system naturally favoured the white ruling landowners, but even so there were some limited opportunities for upward social mobility, mostly for freed mulatto people, but not towards the upper positions.

A patriarchal society

Regarding the first Portuguese settlers, it is interesting to observe that authors describe them as a cohort of young men that were considered second class citizens in their homeland and, to a certain extent, unwanted there. Moreover, they are characterised in the literature as ambitious enough to leave their families behind to explore the newly discovered land, with the expectation to make their fortune and/or becoming nobles. Since Portugal had a very small population in comparison to the huge land just discovered, they could not spare their best men (and nor did such people wish to go) to the endeavour of colonising the new territory (Koster, 1816; Bethel, 1984).

Consequently, oftentimes they were "degraded, or exiles, who could be anyone from a political offender to a common criminal. With a few exceptions, they were on the whole undesirable [in Portugal]" (Bethel, 1984, p. 16). This cohort of settlers established the roots of a patriarchal society, where they had not only control of the power mechanisms in place, but also strong authority over women, the existing indigenous community, and the African slaves. In fact, the white settlers "reigned unchallenged above everyone and everything, as the very core of the power structure whence all relevant decisions emanated" (Tavolaro, 2008, p. 112).

Evolving from this picture, once settled in the new territory, occupying a variety of leadership positions and with a multitude of African slaves at their disposal, it is interesting to observe, for example, their approach towards work. The Portuguese settlers used to boast that they had not been born to labour but, rather, to lead. Hence, when inquired why they did not learn a trade and live more independently, the questioning could be interpreted as outrageous and, in reply, they would say: "Work! Work! Screamed one; we have blacks to do that" (Ewbank, 1856, p. 184). Based on this account, the derived question could be, why the Portuguese settlers had the perception that work was meant for blacks rather than for whites. First, it is necessary to put into context that colonial society was essentially rural, and consequently, most of the jobs available were manual rather than intellectual or more sophisticated. Thus, performing such type of activities could be associated with belonging to the lower social classes and being subject to somebody else's command. Second, the white Portuguese settlers aspired for upper social class positions and their associated privileges. Within that, "nobility was, in a sense, defined by what a person did not do. Working with one's own hands, shopkeeping, artisan crafting, and other 'mean' occupations were the domain of the commoners. Nobles were expected to live without recourse of such activities" (Schwartz, 1985, p. 247).

In corroboration with this argumentation, many foreign artists depicting scenes of Brazilian colonial society in painting, lithography and drawings[2] have

---

[2] A sample of such iconic everyday images include the following paintings: a) *Um mascate e seu escravo* (A peddler and his slave) painted by Henry Chamberlain in 1822, b) *Uma família brasileira* (A Brazilian family) also painted by Henry Chamberlain in 1822, c) *Un employé du gouvern servant de chez lui avec familie* (A government employee walking with his family) painted by Jean Baptiste Debret, and d) *Retour, a la ville, d'un propriétaire de chakra* (The return of a slave owner) also painted by Jean Baptiste Debret. To visualize the reproduction of the mentioned images, please, refer to:
http://enciclopedia.itaucultural.org.br and http://pinacoteca.org/acervo/obras/

portrayed everyday situations where African slaves carry the slave masters, and/or members of their immediate family, and/or their belongings (hat, umbrella, coat, pets, luggage, etc.). Moreover, even the excrement produced by the white households had to be transported by the slaves (usually on buckets or bowls on top of their heads) early in the morning to be thrown in the nearest rivers (Santos, M. 2009).

Thus, submitting their slaves to visible circumstances of servitude contributed to legitimise and reinforce the master's leadership position before the eyes of the wider colonial society, and not only within the domains of their private life. Furthermore, it is also emblematic to notice the distinction between what occupation was worthy of a noble, or upper-class people, and what was worthy only to the commoners in general and the slaves in particular. This dynamic also reveals the dominant understanding that leadership positions were meant for white men, whilst white women should take care of the house and children, and the slaves should perform menial occupations of servitude. Over time, this ideology or perception has undergone significant transformations in Brazilian society, but even nowadays, there is evidence demonstrating that traces of this dynamic are still in place. Hence, this patriarchal model centred on personal authority in combination with social hierarchies based on race, have set the parameters of Brazilian social life over time.

A horizontal racial hierarchy

The first blacks in Brazil were shipped by Portugal after being captured in the African continent (mainly from the West Coast). Over time, many black people were born in the colony, but the arrival of Africans remained practically uninterrupted from 1560 to 1850 (Database, 2009). However, a peculiar characteristic of this social group lays in the fact that, contrary to what might look like at first sight, the slaves did not form a homogenous group; although they were sharing the same experience of exploitation. In the first place, the people were captured in different regions of Africa and mixed up to avoid solidarity and uprisings (Eltis, 2007). Given the fact that the labour-intensive work in the plantations demanded strong physical capabilities, the Portuguese 'imported' a greater number of male Africans than females (Klein, 1986; Hawthorne, 2010). Moreover, the price paid for male Africans was higher than that of females and children, which indicates their higher commercial value (Willems, 1970; Santos, 2004; Gomes, 2019).

On top of that, over time, the blacks also developed differentiation among themselves or a type of an embryonic caste system. Thus, the Brazilian-born blacks were called *crioulo* (creole) to differentiate themselves from the Africans given that they had lighter skin tone in comparison to the newcomers. This approach was so peculiar that the *crioulos* have even created a subdivision to classify the Africans. Those newly arrived from Africa were called *boçal* and the ones who were already acculturated in the colony were called *ladino* (Bethel, 1984; Schwartz, 1985; Moura, 2004).

Most of the young Portuguese settlers were single men and soon after arriving got married or engaged either with Indian or African women, since there were considerably few white women around. The offspring of those relationships were called *mameluco* in the case of miscegenation between white and Indian, and mulatto regarding white and African (Metcalf, 2005). However, two major aspects call our attention in this context. First, *mamelucos* were granted an almost white-like social status, although many indigenous people had also been treated as slaves for a period. In effect, the Portuguese "commonly considered *mamelucos* to be 'white', which may reflect the early meaning of '*mameluk*' as a Caucasian slave" (Metcalf, 2005, p. 95). Second, Brazilian-born blacks (*crioulos*) and mulattoes were preferred as house slaves, whilst oftentimes mulattoes performed artisan tasks which, in that context, were considered improved duties in comparison to the work in the plantations (Bethel, 1984).

This picture reveals that differentiated occupational distribution among the racial groups has led to a type of task-based racial hierarchy operating in that social setting. Within that, the Portuguese considered the *mamelucos* almost white; the mulattoes were granted reasonable occupations, either in the white men's Big House[3] or in other activities that required some skills such as in the sugar mills. Brazilian-born blacks (*crioulos*) were given equivalent opportunities, and the majority of the Africans (*boçal* and *ladino*) were considered slaves of sickle and hoe, what implies that they were perceived useful solely for rustic manual and unskilled labour that required nothing but physical strength (Bethel, 1984).

An important aspect in this dynamic is the fact that whilst "mulattoes and, to a lesser extent, *crioulos* were favoured as house slaves, artisans and sugar specialists, [...] Africans, on the other hand, were strangers, pagans, thought to be untrustworthy or dangerous" (Schwartz, 1985, p. 330). Moreover, "Africans were portrayed as inherently brutish, stupid, uncivilized, barbarians" (Andrews, 1997, p. 9). Thereafter, this set of negative perceptions directly

---

[3] The Big House (*Casa Grande* in Portuguese) stands for the residence of the landowner and also the social space and symbol of the white settler's power. Inside it lived all the members of the immediate family of the slave master and he was also the supreme authority in that setting. It oftentimes had a separate place in the backyard where the household slaves in charge to provide the family with basic services such as cooking and cleaning, were allowed to sleep overnight (Moura, 2004).

associated with blackness contribute to our understanding of the onset of many derogatory stereotypes still currently circulating in Brazilian society. In contrast, "whiteness was equated with intelligence, rationality, civilization, virtue" (Andrews, 1997, p. 9), and such positive perceptions have persisted over time in Brazilian society and the collective mindset.

Then, the development of hierarchies based on skin colour and occupations was made possible because the slave owners had the power to assign whatever occupation or duty they wished to the slaves since they were their property. Nevertheless, the slaves themselves also played an active relevant role in the reinforcement and operation of such a system. Since the colonial society was essentially rural, the working conditions in the plantations and sugar mills were highly precarious and harsh, any opportunity to perform a slightly fewer degrading or excruciating task could be considered as an advantage. In effect, foreigner observers who visited Brazil during that period oftentimes reported the brutality the slaves were subjected to in the plantations and sugar mills, and that they "were poorly fed, housed and clothed" (Schwartz, 1985, p. 132). Actually, it used to be advocated that only "three P's were required for [managing the] slaves, that were: *pão*, *páo*[4] and *pano* (bread, a stick for punishment, and a piece of cloth)" (Conrad, 1983, p. 58).

In contrast to this picture, the 'house slaves' (also called 'household slaves') were granted slightly better working conditions than the slaves of sickle and hoe (predominantly *boçal* and *ladino* Africans). However, it is important to stress that those slightly 'better' working conditions should not be interpreted as a synonym of humane treatment (especially regarding the female house slaves, who oftentimes were sexually abused, as revealed by many authors). The consideration and reflection made here are that those differentiated conditions might have contributed or played a distinct role, towards the development of hierarchies amongst the blacks themselves.

In conclusion, this dynamic brings to the surface the reflection that racial hierarchy in colonial Brazil operated not only vertically downwards (white settlers towards blacks), but also horizontally (i.e. amongst blacks themselves). In this context, the social relations built amongst slaves were not hierarchical in terms of social position but rather based on differences in everyday living conditions. Since the slaves were considered and treated as merchandise by their masters and the wider society (rather than persons or citizens), it makes sense that in-group social hierarchy per se was not that feasible or common practice. Thus, hierarchy derived from their different occupations, duties and

---

[4] The original spelling adopted by Conrad (1983) has been reproduced, but the current accurate one in Portuguese is *pau*.

place of belonging (e.g. in the Big House, the plantations or the *senzala*[5]) could contribute to the development of the reported division among *crioulo, boçal* and *ladino* although, in essence, they were all slaves before the eyes of the patriarchal society ruled by white male settlers.

Social stratification and limited upward social mobility possibilities

Another key point in colonial society is to understand the broader picture regarding the prevailing social stratification and the existing possibilities for upward social mobility for black people. Willems (1970) advocates that there was a type of heterogeneous middle-class in colonial society, composed not only of whites (although they were the majority) but also of freed mulatto slaves. Besides, in 1816, a French cotton buyer reported his view of the broad social stratification in rural Pernambuco. According to his account, the society was composed of three classes of people: 1) the owners of sugar mills (*senhores de engenho*) or great landowners; 2) the *lavradores*, a type of tenant farmer; and 3) the *moradores*, squatters or small cultivators. Regarding the slaves, they were considered "nothing but cattle" (Conrad, 1983, p. 63). His particular perception of slaves comparable to 'cattle' illustrates the prevailing ideas considering this social group not as people but as mere commodities devoid of humanity.

Nevertheless, the social stratification in the colonial period was all but that simple and, although as a general rule, slaves were positioned at the lowest social strata possible (or not even that if we consider the standpoint of the aforementioned Frenchmen), there was some degree of upward social mobility possibilities for black people. Over the course of several manumission in the seventeenth century, a new class of freedmen started to emerge, composed of former slaves filling a series of low and intermediary social roles in Brazilian economic life. Indeed, considering that to some mulattoes and *crioulos* were allowed to learn or develop some skills in the Big House and the sugar mill, the emergence of this new class seems viable.

However, it is imperative to consider these arguments carefully because they can potentially blur people's perception. First, the upward social mobility experienced by some former slaves was not evenly distributed among *crioulo, boçal* and *ladino* but very much concentrated on light-skinned people (mulattoes in particular). Evidence of this is found in the differentiated occupations performed by them. Second, their social improvement did not

---

[5] *Senzala* stands for the accommodation for the slaves. It was usually located in the back of the farm property and away from the Big House. It had no comfort at all, no artificial lighting, no windows and very poor ventilation (if any) and the slaves were left to sleep straight on the floor (Moura, 2004).

necessarily represent a flawless rule. Finally, oftentimes the intersectionality of dimensions such as birthplace (Brazil or Africa) and skin tone (the lighter, the better) performed a considerable influence on the tasks assigned to them within that social context.

Moreover, manumission did not necessarily mean the immediate end of a condition of servitude. There were many cases and situations where the former masters demanded that the freedmen/women continued working without being paid for an unspecified period, and/or passed on their skills to another slave before fully enjoying their freedom (Schwartz, 1974; Truz, 2013). In other words, even after gaining freedom, former slaves did not enjoy a social or legal status comparable to those of white people. Within that, even as freedmen, they were not allowed to vote or become a candidate for an elective post (Andrews, 1997; Moura, 2004). Moreover, the imperial legislation in place divided colonial society into a racial hierarchy in which the full rights of freedom were reserved for whites only. The prevailing and dominant perception established a relationship where African was practically synonymous with an enslaved person, and dark skin represented a strong barrier against upward social mobility.

This picture leads us to infer, first, that there were some opportunities for upward social mobility for black people, although this does not mean to say that they were widely available and exempt from several barriers and challenges. Second, the social stratification was not as rigid as the aforementioned French cotton buyer had suggested in 1816. Actually, "caste systems were loose enough to provide mobility between the groups directly above and below one, but functioned to keep most dark-skinned Africans from entering middling or elite society" (Johnson, 2004, p. 62). Thus, it indicates the existence of an intersection of racial hierarchy and social stratification in colonial society. In other words, a person's position in the racial hierarchy scale could have a strong influence on their social class positioning, and hence their social mobility possibilities, or their restrictions and limitations.

Another distinct aspect to take into consideration in this intricate web of influential factors consists of different castes of people, based not only on their skin tone but also on their civilian condition. During the colonial period black people, in particular, could be classified not only as *crioulo*, *boçal* or *ladino*, but also as freedmen/women, manumitted, or slave (Schwartz, 1974; Johnson, 2004; Machado, 2006). The intersection and overlap of all those elements, combined with a person's position in the racial hierarchy based on skin colour, contributed towards the complexity of the dynamic of social stratification. Hence, racial labels and categories did have considerable importance and role in that social context in creating distinctions among the social groups and defining who was at the top, at the centre or the margin. Consequently, one question that can be raised is: how non-white people managed to navigate in that social setting. On this regard, there is historical evidence indicating that non-white people (and mulattoes more often) tried to circumvent the barriers imposed by the legislation by passing as white, and hiding any trace of African origin in their documents (Koster, 1816; Conrad, 1983).

Nevertheless, passing as white was not the only strategy employed by this social group. There is also historical evidence revealing that a considerable number of former slaves had also purchased slaves themselves (Schwartz, 1985; Castro, 1998). Besides, there were also instances of captive slaves who had other slaves at their service. Within that, in contrast to the majority of the slaves who worked solely in the plantations and sugar mills, some of those working in the urban areas also had opportunities to earn a salary and save some resources (Andrews, 1997). Consequently, taking into consideration that "ownership of slaves may be assumed to be a yardstick of the relative socio-economic position of the proprietor", that contributes to understanding their inner motivation to purchase slaves and ascend socially (Willems, 1970, p. 37). The ascension was not completely economic, given that their savings were modest, but at least symbolic, in an attempt not be perceived as a slave anymore by the society. Moreover, since slaves were affordable merchandise, their possession by former dark-skinned slaves had the purpose not only to demonstrate their new social condition but mainly to deny the previous one. In complement to this reflection, "as for the social condition of the free coloured class, it appears that well before the end of slavery they had achieved an important style of life intermediate between the white master and coloured slave classes" (Klein, 1969, p. 42).

Still, regarding this group of freedmen/women before the emancipation of slavery in 1888, an intriguing question that arises is; who were they after all? They were predominantly the offspring of white fathers and slave mothers, and consequently, the class of freed black people was dominated by mulattoes, whilst African-born blacks were less represented in this group. Therefore, in summary, within that colonial social context, white people occupied predominantly the middle and upper social positions. The mulattoes, especially the manumitted group, enjoyed a slightly less negatively stigmatised position in the racial hierarchy and, as a rule, they had a slightly greater chance to ascend socially to intermediate positions. Besides, those with some minimal level of savings ventured to pass as white by purchasing slaves or concealing their African ancestry. Finally, the remaining group of blacks (*crioulos* and Africans alike) were positioned at the lowest social strata possible and, on top of that, they were associated with many negative and derogatory perceptions and depreciated symbolic markers associated with slavery, servitude and backwardness.

The key phases of racial relations in Brazil

Evolving from the previous discussion addressing Brazilian colonial society, and to achieve a clearer and well-structured understanding of racial relations in Brazil, a critical analysis of its three key historical phases is required. However, although distinctive markers separate these phases they are, actually, intertwined and over time, they have developed important roles in shaping Brazil's current racial relation landscape. *The first phase* comprises the early years after the emancipation of slaves in 1888 and the Proclamation of Republic in 1889. At that time, given the fact that, altogether, black and miscegenated people outnumbered whites (see Figure 1.1), the prevailing belief was that *mestizaje* represented a social problem that needed to be tackled. Whitening (also known as positive eugenics) was the strategy adopted through official public policy sponsoring white European immigration, under the assumption that their mixing with the miscegenated Brazilians would lead towards a white-only population within three generations (Lacerda, 1911; Schwarcz, 2011).

The second phase comes with the publication of Gilberto Freyre's book 'The Masters and the Slaves' in 1933 that, contrary to the leading voices of the previous phase, praised miscegenation as the country's distinctive positive feature rather than its 'Achilles heel'. The study contributed decisively to the rise of the concept of 'racial democracy' that is still manifested in today's racial relations and institutional discourses. Finally, *the third phase* was inaugurated with the studies of the sociologist Florestan Fernandes in 1965 challenging the discourses praising Brazil as a post-racial society, as well as the studies that came afterwards revealing that, rather than a 'racial democracy', Brazilian racism is skilfully denied, disguised, and concealed in many attitudes through a range of mechanisms. Additionally, the studies of this phase also reveal a tension regarding the improved social roles and symbolic social places occupied by black people in contrast with those expected and/or 'reserved' for them by the dominant elite.

Phase I: Fostering whitening soon after the emancipation of slaves

According to available census data (see Figure 1.1), by the time the Proclamation of Republic took place in 1889 the country's population was composed of 44% *branco*, 14.6% *preto* and 41.4% *pardo* people. In other words, non-white people outnumbered white people considerably (56% *vs* 44%). The government and the dominant elite of the newly established republic viewed this picture as an undesirable situation and considered it as a form of social problem that needed to be tackled (Mikulak, 2011; Pinto and Ferreira, 2014). Moreover, the majority of the freedmen/women were mulattoes. Hence, for the ruling elite, this social group could represent a threat to their leadership, taking into consideration that the mulattoes had aspirations of upward social mobility themselves, and some of them already occupied intermediary social class positions.

The new republican regime aimed to shape the country's national identity as a modern and developed nation (mirrored in Western European societies), and therefore race discussions played an important role in this process (Andrews, 1991; Schwarcz, 1994; Guimarães, 2004). The dominant Western racial beliefs at that time were based on the so-called 'theories of human biology'. Such theories argued that 'scientific' evidence supported the claim that black and indigenous peoples were inferior in comparison to whites in many aspects (e.g. intelligence, behaviour, social interaction, moral traits, and beauty). Moreover, they also advocated that miscegenated people were degenerated individuals (Skidmore, 1993; Schwarcz, 1994; Wade, 2010). The most influential international voices advocating for these ideas were the Swedish Carl von Linné (1707-1778), the German Johann Friedrich Blumenbach (1752-1840) and the French Arthur de Gobineau (1816-1882). The echoes of their ideas are also found in the studies of influential Brazilian authors, such as Lacerda (1911), Kehl (1920; 1931), Melo (1922) and Rodrigues (1932).

Thus, the aforementioned 'undesirable' social context led the government to pursue a specific strategy that encouraged the immigration of white European people (mainly from Germany, Italy, Portugal and Spain)[6]. This immigration policy was supported by influential opinion-makers. In 1914, the journalist Caio de Menezes published a pamphlet praising the benefits of German immigration in Brazil. The document claimed that "the Brazilian people, more than any other, needs the influence of advanced peoples in building a race. The ethnic preponderance of the foreigner can only bring marvellous results for the formation of our race" (Skidmore, 1993, p. 130; Lorenz, 2008, p. 32). Consequently, the goal was that "mixture would supposedly bring about the elimination of blacks and indigenous people and the creation of a mixed society that was at the distinctly whiter end of the spectrum" (Wade, 2010, p. 31).

Within this context, there is an emblematic letter written by Arthur de Gobineau in 1869 (then serving as a French Minister to Brazil) depicting his view of Brazil's social problems. The letter stated that Brazilians were "a

---

[6] For detailed information and documentation regarding European immigration to Brazil, please refer to the following sources:
   1) Museu da Imigração, São Paulo: http://museudaimigracao.org.br/en/collection-and-research/acervo
   2) Brazil: Five centuries of change: https://library.brown.edu/create/fivecenturiesof change/chapters/chapter-4/immigration/

population totally mulatto, vitiated in its blood and spirit, and fearfully ugly. Not a single Brazilian has pure blood because of the pattern of marriages among whites, Indians and Negroes are so widespread that the nuances of color are infinite, causing a degeneration of the most depressing type" (Skidmore, 1993, p. 30). Besides, Arthur de Gobineau suggested that the best solution for this social problem was for Brazil to "fortify itself through joining with the higher value of European race" (Skidmore, 1993, p. 30). Thus, the aforementioned group of four influential Brazilian authors (Kehl, Lacerda, Melo, and Rodrigues) shared three analogous arguments: 1) miscegenation was equivalent to moral degeneration, 2) miscegenation represented simply an intermediary step towards the complete whitening of the Brazilian population, and 3) in a matter of few decades there would no longer be *pretos* and *pardos* in the country.

At the 'First Universal Race Congress' in London in 1911, Lacerda (1911) advocated that in no more than 100 years or three generations, the whitening process would be completed, and Brazil would become a whites-only nation. Similarly, Melo (1922) wrote an influential article arguing that it would not take too long for the disappearance of mulattoes as a 'natural' whitening consequence of miscegenation. Besides, Rodrigues (1932) published the book 'The Africans in Brazil' expressing his ideas regarding the inferiority of black Brazilians, which coalesces with claims previously made by Arthur de Gobineau. Amongst the beliefs advocated in the book, the author claims, "the Negro's organic constitution, shaped by the physical and moral habitat where he has been raised, does not equip him to adapt to the civilization of superior races that derive from diverse physical and cultural environment" (Rodrigues, 1932, p. 289). Moreover, the author also raises concerns regarding the capacity of the country in achieving higher levels of social development due to its black population. The author says, "what matters most to Brazil is to determine to what extent its inferiority is resulting from the Negroes' civilisation difficulties or if it can be compensated by the natural miscegenation process" (Rodrigues, 1932, p. 291). The pharmacist Kehl (1931) was an open and strong advocate of eugenic practices to tackle the miscegenation and the social 'problems' associated with it, publishing several articles expressing his ideas and even in 1918 establishing Latin America's first eugenic association; the 'São Paulo Eugenics Society'. One of the strongest ideas advocated by him consisted in the mass sterilisation of mestizo and black people as a mean to avoid mixed offspring and to reach the complete whitening of the society in a matter of a few decades (Kehl, 1920).

In summary, the period is marked with a perception that *mestizaje* (represented by the greater proportion of non-whites in the population, being many of them former slaves) was an obstacle towards achieving the desired level of social development and modern national identity that was supposed to be all white. The dominant theories of human biology contributed to fostering the idea of the inferiority and social/moral degeneration of non-whites and, ultimately, that miscegenation was simply an intermediary step towards the 'inevitable and natural' complete whitening of the population within a few decades.

In complement to this argumentation, there is a famous and iconic painting of Brazilian art made by the Spanish artist Modesto Brocos in 1895 called *A Redenção de Cam* (Ham's redemption)[7]. The painting has even been used by Lacerda (1911) to illustrate his arguments in the 'First Universal Race Congress' in London in 1911 because it skilfully summarizes the whitening concept. The painting portrays a rural family composed of a black elderly woman, that has been interpreted by different authors as the mother of the mulatto woman holding a white new-born baby on her lap, and the white father (interpreted as a European immigrant) looking proudly at the baby (Bilac, 1895; Bosi, 1992; Silva, 2011). Moreover, what is strongly symbolic in the painting is the gesture of the old woman raising her hands towards the sky in prayer position, giving thanks for the birth of the white grandson, who would be free from the stigmas associated with blackness and slavery. Actually, "this orientation toward whitening ones' children reproduces a symbolic order that links whiteness to material privilege while linking blackness to impoverishment and inferiority" (Twine, 1998, p. 108).

Phase II: The emergence of 'racial democracy'

As discussed in the previous section, the group of four influential Brazilian authors of *Phase I* (Kehl, Lacerda, Melo, and Rodrigues) advocated the existence of biological inferiority and degeneration of non-whites, and also that the gradual whitening of the population would eradicate this 'social problem'. However, not many years later, the publication of 'The Masters and the Slaves'[8] in 1933 by Gilberto Freyre would promote a considerable shift in the

---

[7] To visualize the reproduction of this image, refer to: http://enciclopedia.itaucultural. org.br/obra3281/a-redencao-de-cam

[8] It is pertinent to explain that the original title in Portuguese *Casa Grande & Senzala* carries a stronger symbolic meaning than the title in English. In fact, the original title introduces us to an oppositional duality concealed in these two social spaces. On the one hand, *Casa Grande* (Big House) represents a metaphor of a social space associated with privilege, power and freedom, in direct oppositional contrast to the backwardness and servitude represented by the *Senzala* (Slave House). Additionally, since the *Senzala* used to be located in the backyard of the *Casa Grande*, it also conveys a subtle dualistic symbology of differentiated class positions (i.e. superior vs inferior).

understanding of Brazil's racial relations. Different from his predecessors, Freyre (1987) considered that miscegenation was, actually, Brazil's main positive defining feature rather than its weakness or a social problem as Rodrigues (1932) used to argue so vehemently. Although there is some historical evidence indicating that two other authors (Castro, 1889; and Moraes, 1924) had explored the idea of 'racial democracy' before Freyre, over time he became widely known as the scholar responsible for its development. Most probably, this might have happened due to the influence and high impact reached by his work quite immediately after its publication[9].

There is a vast body of literature addressing the subject matter of 'racial democracy' and, indeed, the subject matter represents "one of the most exhaustively studied issues in modern Brazilian scholarship" (Owensby, 2005, p. 324). Within this vast scholarship, Dzidzienyo (1971, p. 5) brings an interesting contribution arguing that 'racial democracy' represents the idea of a place "where people of different races live together in harmony and where opportunities are open to all irrespective of racial background". In line with this argumentation, Andrews (1996, p. 483) says that 'racial democracy' refers to a context "in which blacks, mulattoes, and whites live under conditions of juridical and, to a large degree, social equality". Finally, Joseph (2013, p. 1524) explains that in Brazil's 'racial democracy', "racial classification was fluid, interracial relationships were socially accepted and racism was considered non-existent relative to the US".

Therefore, these definitions demonstrate that denial of the existence of racism and its damaging effects upon discriminated people is at the core of 'racial democracy' belief. In complement to that, two distinctive historical events contribute to reinforce this argument. First, the distinguished Brazilian policymaker Rui Barbosa (1849-1923) issued an executive order on 14 December 1890 demanding that all documents and records related to slavery ownership available in the archives of Finance Ministry under his administration should be burned (Lacombe, 1986; Jacomino, 2010). The supporting argument for issuing such an order was that it had been taken "in honour of our fraternity and solidarity duties with a large number of citizens who, through the abolition of enslavement, had just joined the Brazilian

---

[9] The analysis of several leading newspapers published in the 1930s allows us to identify dozens of strong positive comments made by prominent figures, opinion makers and scholars about the book such as, for example: "A book that has already been released as a masterpiece" (Roquete Pinto), "Vigorous work of science and art" (Agripino Grieco), "Genesis of current Brazil" (Azevedo Amaral), "The Bible of Brazilian sociologists" (Ovidio da Cunha), and "A watershed in Brazil's history" (Murilo Marroquim).

communion" (Lacombe, 1986, p. 338). However, this claim was already an indirect discourse praising the country's harmonious racial relation soon after the slave emancipation. Moreover, it also conveys a perception that the freed slaves were full citizens such as the white people but does not acknowledge the absence of social policies to support their integration into the emerging class society (Dzidzienyo, 1971; Barros *et al.*, 2000). Actually, slavery was (and remains) an inconvenient event in Brazil's history. It is inconvenient because it represents an undesirable hallmark in the country's history that upsets the dominant elite, proud of their whitening modernisation ideals and that, for a long time, has attempted to neglect it.

The second distinct historical event consists of the release of 'Hymn to the Proclamation of Republic' in 1890. It brings the following verses: 'We do not even believe that slaves once / There have been in such a noble country... / Today the flash of dawn / Find brothers, not hostile tyrants. / We are all the same!' (Albuquerque and Miguez, 1890). The hymn (sung to date in primary and secondary schools across the country and official celebrations) represents an interesting piece of evidence of the prevailing ideologies of that time. The lyric was composed and registered only two years after the emancipation of slaves and it already conveyed a discourse denying the slave heritage. Moreover, it also claims an egalitarian discourse ('we are all the same'), which is analogous to the so-called 'Brazilian communion' advocated by Rui Barbosa in the same year 1890, and within the context of the shaping of a 'modern' Brazil.

Thus, within this social context, it is possible to observe that Freyre depicted and interpreted colonial society as built on top of a harmonic social relation between masters and slaves. Clear supporting evidence for this argument is found on the preface to the first English-language edition of *The Masters and the Slaves* signed by Gilberto Freyre in 1945. According to the author, the majority of the Brazilian population is "the near descendants either of masters or slaves, and many of them have sprung from the union of slave-owners with slave women" (Freyre, 1987, p. xi). Certainly, that 'union' has got different meanings and connotations but in that social circumstance, as the author himself explores later in the book, was resulting mostly of abuse rather than consensual relationships.

Moreover, Freyre adds, the foreign visitor would not have completely seen Brazil unless he had visited or seen a Big House and all its surrounding structure (i.e., the sugar mills, the *senzala*, the sugar or coffee plantations, the chapel, the fine house porcelains, etc.). Still, according to Freyre, the visitor would have noticed that the combination of all those elements contributed to evidence that "they have grown up together fraternally, and that, rather than being mutually hostile by reason of their antagonisms, they complemented one another with their difference" (Freyre, 1987, p. xii). Furthermore, the author complements, the combination of all those elements contributed "to form one of the most harmonious unions of culture with nature and of one culture with another that the lands of this hemisphere have ever known" (Freyre, 1987, p. xii). Indeed, in a later study, (Freyre, 1977, p. 13) advocates that "the black African has been integrated not only biologically, but also sociologically".

On top of that, there is another emblematic passage where the author recognises that slaves were subjected to abuses and strain by their masters. However, to maximize the slaves' production capacity, "it was to the master's interest to preserve that efficiency, for the Negro was his capital, his work-machine" (Freyre, 1987, p. 65). Furthermore, the author also explains that black women were often victims of abuse by their masters, whose onset of such behaviour was due to "sadism of the conqueror toward the conquered" (Freyre, 1987, p. 76). However, the author explains that they were indeed nothing more than natural consequences of that patriarchal society. In other words, this passage implies that the slaves were subjected to abuses by their masters but, probably, not beyond the point to jeopardise their production capacity. Moreover, such abuses were a natural component of that social context.

Finally, another controversial aspect in this study is the assertion that one of the conditions allowing the masters abusing their power, was the "servile conformity on the part of the Negro" (Freyre, 1987, p. 329), which implies that black people passively accepted the inhuman conditions they were subjected. Furthermore, it also denies their agency capacity to escape that condition and their struggles to achieve freedom. Thus, despite the undeniable historical values of *The Masters and the Slaves*, it is also possible to understand why it has become subject to many criticisms over time by numerous scholars (e.g. van den Berghe, 1967; Twine, 1998; Winant, 1999; Vargas, 2004; Wade, 2010).

The legacy of 'racial democracy'

The development of Freyre's studies, as well as that of the social psychologist Ramos (1940; 1942; 1946), who was another strong advocate of 'racial democracy', led to a widespread belief, both in Brazil and internationally, in the existence of a unique racial harmony (or a post-racial society). Moreover, they also led towards a misleading understanding that "there is no racism but only a benign, relatively insignificant form of prejudice" in Brazil that did not represent obstacles for blacks' social advancements (Nascimento, 1980, p. 200). In fact, the proponents of 'racial democracy' advocated that "centuries of miscegenation between populations of European, African, and indigenous descent have blurred the colour line between discrete racial categories, such as black and white" (Gillam, 2017, p. 613). Consequently, this narrative has led towards a belief that class stratification was Brazil's core social problem, whilst racial inequalities were secondary or irrelevant.

In the international arena, for example, two works call our attention. First, the influential Austrian writer Stefan Zweig published in 1941 a book called 'Brazil: Land of the Future'. One of the ideas advocated in this book stated that:

> "Whereas our world is more than ever ruled by the insane attempt to breed people racially pure, like race-horses and dogs, the Brazilian nation for centuries has been built upon the principle of free and unsuppressed miscegenation, the complete equalization of black and white, brown and yellow" (Zweig, 1941, p. 8).

The second work comprises the publication of an emblematic two-part special report in the influential Afro-American magazine 'Ebony' in 1965. The journalist spent two months in Brazil in order "to see if amalgamation, as practised there, is working and if so, why" (Thompson, 1965b, p. 34). The conclusion reached by the author was that amalgamation encompassed Brazil's 'innovative solution' to racial problems, and that "it may not be a definitive answer but so far is the best [in comparison to the US]" (Thompson, 1965b, p. 42). Thus, these examples reveal the effectiveness of the prevailing discourse praising 'racial democracy', the inexistence of racial inequalities and, (in)directly supporting white superiority. On this regard, Thompson (1965a, p. 28) reports, first, that "if discrimination do occur, they are economic, not racial; committed by foreigners, not Brazilians". Second, "a white nation is considered ideal for both countries. In this respect, they differ only in methods used to maintain in the United States and to obtain it for Brazil" (Thompson, 1965b, p. 33).

In effect, the belief in a 'softer kind of racism' was to be explored as a powerful and convenient instrument by politicians in different moments throughout Brazil's history, but especially during what is known as the 'Vargas's Era' (1930-1945), and during the military regime some decades later (from 1964 to 1985). The core discourse behind the 'softer and kinder' racism was that black people in Brazil did not experience the same segregational practices found in other countries with a history of slavery and that, consequently, they did not face obstacles towards their social integration and upward social mobility possibilities (Skidmore, 1993; Owensby, 2005; Pacheco, 2011; Cicalo, 2018).

However, it can be observed that the political use of 'racial democracy' discourse is not restricted solely to a distant past. Not many years ago, the federal government sponsored a set of public policies and debates aimed at promoting greater racial equality that was officially named 'Building Racial Democracy' (Cardoso, 1998). More recently in 2018, the Brazilian president Jair

Bolsonaro fostered during his electoral campaign the motto 'Brazil is my colour', clearly aiming at conveying an idea that racial inequalities are inexistent and that blacks experience full social integration (Trindade, 2018a). This argument coalesces with what Da Costa (2014, p. 503) calls the "we are all mixed" fallacy statement. The core idea embedded in this type of discourse is that, since we are all mixed, we are not racist. Additionally, the president, who is already notoriously known for a series of controversial statements about ethnic minority communities (Bertoni, 2018; Leaver and Costa, 2018; Philips and Kaiser, 2019), has also claimed that racism is a rare phenomenon in Brazil and that this subject matter does not represent a relevant social issue (Alfonso, 2019; Tavae, 2019). Thus, these initiatives demonstrate that the 'racial democracy' idea remains vivid in the minds of current policymakers, and denial of Brazil's ingrained racism (and its pervasive effects) is openly and strongly advocated.

It is also relevant to bring to the surface that the concept of 'racial democracy' replacing the previous belief in a 'natural' and 'irreversible' inferiority of non-white people also benefited from the international context of the 1940s. Soon after the end of World War II in 1945, increasing international debates were challenging the 'scientific' arguments of the inferiority of non-white people. Evidence of this fact can be found in an article supported by UNESCO published in 1950 and undersigned by 18 international scholars, including one Brazilian (the sociologist Luis Aguiar Costa Pinto), called 'The fallacies of racism exposed' (Beaglehole *et al.*, 1950). In the article, the authors developed arguments refuting the validity of the previous 'scientific' beliefs. In the subsequent years, UNESCO supported the publication of several other similar articles and statements reinforcing the challenge to 'scientific' ideas about race and inferiority of non-white people (Klineberg, 1954; Rose, 1958; Debetz, 1965; Koffler, 1968; Glezerman, 1973). Consequently, this international context contributed to putting an end to the official eugenic discourses that miscegenation would whiten Brazil within three generations. Moreover, at the end of the 1920s and early 1930s, the government's programme of subsidies fostering European immigration had come to an end. Actually, "the effort to transform Brazil into a white, European society in the tropics had failed" because the country was not becoming whiter, as it was expected and previously advocated (Andrews, 1996, p. 487).

As the belief in the 'racial democracy' ideology flourished through the 1930s and 1940s, both in Brazil and internationally, in 1950 UNESCO commissioned a research team led by the American anthropologist Charles Wagley to carry out a one-year ethnographic study of Brazil's racial relations (Métraux, 1951; 1952; Wade, 2010). In search of means to avoid a repetition of the horrors of Nazism and trying to combat racist practices worldwide, UNESCO had decided to turn its eyes towards Brazil's world-famous 'racial democracy'. The aim was to clearly understand how it operated and possibly emulate it in other parts of the world (Andrews, 1996; Maio, 1997). The study revealed that, contrary to what Brazil claimed, there were, indeed, racial relations issues in the country, but the scholars attributed them to be of social class origin rather than racial-based due to the huge gap between rich (predominantly white) and poor (predominantly black) (Maio, 1997; Silva, 2000). Nevertheless, on the second edition of the original report, released 11 years later, there is clear support of racial democracy arguing, "racial origin has not become a serious point of conflict in Brazilian society. Brazilians can still call their society a racial democracy. [...] Brazil remains a lesson in racial democracy for the rest of the world" (Wagley, 1963, p. 2).

The origins of the whitening ideology

Whilst the international debates influenced the end of the official eugenic policy and discourse, it did not eliminate the widespread belief in Brazilian society that whitening could bring both tangible and intangible symbolic benefits to the offspring. Over the years, the belief that miscegenation would give birth to lighter-skinned children, and consequently grant them better life prospects, as depicted in the painting *A Redenção de Cam* (Ham's redemption), has become an integral part of Brazil's racial relation. Thus, whilst the supporting pillars of scientific racism were being challenged and abandoned, the dominant elite maintained vivid its belief in the whitening process through miscegenation. They defended the argument that whitening was a process of 'ethnic integration' which, in the long-run, would sort out Brazil's racial problems.

Furthermore, while white European immigrants benefited from social policies that supported their settlement and consequent upward social mobility in Brazil, the newly emancipated blacks were predominantly experiencing unemployment and deprived living conditions in the emerging *favelas*[10] (Maringoni, 2011). The outcome of this contrasting picture has also contributed to reinforcing the general perception that whiteness was associated with better life prospects, whereas blackness meant backwardness (Silva, 2000). Actually, even part of the black community also embraced and endorsed this belief considering that they had aspirations to become part of the mainstream medium class. Some leading black figures used to verbalise, "let us not seek to perpetuate our race, but, yes, to infiltrate ourselves into the bosom of the privileged race, the white race, because, we repeat, we are not

---

[10] *Favela* is a Portuguese word meaning slum, or a low-income deprived community in urban areas.

Africans but rather purely Brazilian" (Andrews, 1991, p. 136). Over the years, the whitening ideology has been maintained, reinforced, and disseminated through a range of tools of power manifestation. They include means of mass communication (notably television and advertising), cultural products (movies, sitcoms and soap operas), literature, and textbooks. Overall, they convey the idea of a prevailing social group capable of representing all people in the social setting and consequently that the others should aspire to look like or get as close as possible to them (Trindade, 2008; Acevedo and Trindade, 2010; Gillam, 2017).

This reflection leads us to an interesting point. If since the colonial period whitening has been fostered as the summit of social evolution, and blackness represents the opposite idea, what would be the 'escape route' left for the black community? To tackle this issue, the dominant elite developed the discourse that "Brazilians of color could escape degeneracy by whitening through social ascension" (Dávila, 2003, p. 7). In other words, it conveys the belief that 'money whitens', meaning that upward social mobility would shield black people from racism. According to its proponents, "once a person of dark colour earns money, he can literally buy himself out of the black category and into the white category, because along with money comes all the social benefits which are commonly associated with whiteness and success in Brazil" (Dzidzienyo, 1971, p. 8).

However, even ascending socially, the person's whitening "is not completely fulfilled [because] he/she can achieve a white's social status, but not all the associated benefits are granted to the black. There are restrictions" (Silva, 2000, p. 105). Hence, the 'whitening' through upward social mobility is not complete because, before the eyes of society, the person remains black and all the common negative associated attributes remain immutable. It means that upward social mobility does not eliminate experiences of racism for black people because, in reality, they become a strange body in predominantly white spaces. In line with this reflection, an interesting illustrative example of this contrasting scenario is an old Brazilian anecdote depicting a rich black man that soon after moving to a well-off white neighbourhood found an inscription painted on the external wall of his mansion saying, 'here lives a black man'. He then added on the following day, 'but I have money'; what was complemented in the subsequent day with 'but you're still black' (Lima, 2010). The picture displayed is an anecdote whose origin is unknown, but it is considered relevant. After all, it summarizes quite well the contrasting picture just analysed and, moreover, because its circulation contributes to disseminating and reinforcing the embedded message that no matter how successful a black person becomes, their attributed social place remains unchanged. In line with this picture, in the post-Civil Rights Movement in the US, Afro-Americans have gained access to many social spaces associated with whiteness and privilege. However, rather than acceptance, they have instead experienced prejudice, marginalisation and active reminder of their outsider status as a means to put them into 'their place' (Anderson, 2015).

Hence, whilst the belief in the 'racial democracy' replaced the official eugenic policies, it did not change society's view regarding the symbolic benefits granted by whitening, considering that such ideology was (and still is) widely disseminated in Brazil. In line with this reflection, in the book 'Becoming *Negro*', Souza (1990) argues that Brazilian racism hides its true face either behind blatant obstacles to the social advancement of black people, or oftentimes behind subtle barriers such as the whitening ideology. The author continues explaining that in Brazil the colour continuum (i.e. a large array of racial terminologies employed by miscegenated people), in combination with both the 'racial democracy' and the whitening ideology have been the determinant elements shaping blacks' upward social mobility prospects. In effect, over the years, Brazilian society has managed to assimilate both ideologies and they play a fundamental role in shaping current racial relations. On the one hand, 'racial democracy' fosters the idea of a society with almost non-existent racism. A land that offers egalitarian opportunities for upward social mobility to all its citizens regardless of racial background, and a place of harmonious racial relations in contrast to many other nations. On the other hand, the whitening ideology disseminates, praises and reinforces whiteness as the aspirational social condition to the non-whites and the summit of social evolution, modernity and beauty standard. In other words, Brazil's racial relations are shaped by an intricate game that uses 'racial democracy' to politely disguise, conceal, and subtly legitimise racism whilst praising whitening as its only proud visible face. Rather than opposing forces within this intricate game, they are indeed complementary.

Phase III: Contemporary racial relations

In the study called 'The Negro in Brazilian Society', Fernandes (1965, p. 312) argues that the myth of 'racial democracy' "contributed to disseminate and generalise a false understanding of Brazil's racial reality", blurring the perception around the core of the racial problems and avoiding tackling them. It is interesting to observe that the author has coined 'racial democracy' as a myth, rather than a concept or ideology, for instance. The choice was not by chance, because "myth is not an ordinary discourse. It is a discourse aimed at disguising reality; deny history and making it all acceptable" (Souza, 1990, p. 25). Moreover, myths "can have a powerful impact on people because they communicate and reinforce a particular worldview" whilst discrediting opposing ideas (Bailey, 2004, p. 729).

Thus, Fernandes (1965) indicates that five main ethnocentric convictions have been developed in Brazil derived from the belief in the 'racial democracy': 1) black people do not have any issues or concerns in Brazil, 2) given the Brazilian friendly temper, there are no racial distinctions among its people, 3) the opportunities for upward social mobility and symbolic power are evenly distributed, 4) blacks are satisfied with their social condition, and 5) there is not, there was never, and there will never be other issues of social justice regarding black people. Additionally, "it was possible to observe a wicked dilemma repeatedly faced both by the emancipated and born-free blacks. Integrating into social life meant, for the black and mulatto alike, to passively accept the rules of the game, established by and for the white" (Fernandes, 1965, p. 346). The acceptance to these 'rules of the game' involves the internalisation by the black people of the negative social representations associated with blackness and the belief that denying their blackness would qualify them to pass as white (Souza, 1990).

The major studies conducted by Fernandes (1965; 1972), in combination with others conducted by his disciples Cardoso (1962) and Ianni (1962), revealed that Brazil did not experience a 'racial democracy', as previously advocated and disseminated by Freyre (1977; 1987), Zweig (1941), Ramos (1942; 1946) and other followers. In fact, the emancipation of slaves, devoid of implementation of any supporting social policy, had created unequal and challenging conditions for the integration of black people in the emerging class society. Consequently, the majority of them were, in fact, at the margin of society regarding access to education and professional qualifications, housing conditions, employment prospects and opportunities for upward social mobility (Skidmore, 1993; Wade, 2010). In contrast to this picture, as previously addressed, the white European immigrants benefited from governmental subsidies to settle in Brazilian society, which illustrates the different treatment provided for the two social groups. In effect, "the economic handicap borne by Afro-Brazilians and the distinct advantages enjoyed by immigrants and Brazilian whites were reinforced by prevalent cultural ideologies" (Butler, 1998, p. 46). In other words, the unequal treatment received by black people, in combination with the dominant whitening ideology, played a strong role in the marginalisation process of this social group over time. Ultimately, "together, these economic and cultural obstacles made bridging the gap of inequality in the twentieth century a Herculean task" (Butler, 1998, p. 50).

Nevertheless, more important than challenging and contesting 'racial democracy' per se, the studies and reflections that emerged during this phase bring to the surface the core issue of Brazil's racial relation: the social place of black people in Brazilian class society. As the country's economic and social conditions have improved over time, there has been a constant tension between the emerging improved social roles and symbolic social spaces occupied by a growing number of black people and the ones that historically have been attributed and/or 'reserved' for them by the dominant elite. There is a prevalent and deep-rooted idea in Brazil that associates skin colour with one's social class position, which invariably considers black people positioned at the lowest social strata, whilst whites are located in the highest positions (Gonzalez and Hasenbalg, 1982). In Brazilian society, "racial categorization enables allocating people in different positions within the social class structure according to their proximity [or distance] to the standard dominant white racial group" (Souza, 1990, p. 20). Returning to the patriarchal colonial society, it is possible to observe the existence of a discourse advocating that white settlers were born to lead, whereas unskilled occupations were meant for blacks. Based on that, it can be asked: has the essence of this discourse been eliminated from the Brazilian society, or has it been transformed and assumed renewed packaging?

It is noticeable that the Brazilian society has improved considerably over time in comparison to the colonial rural society and, consequently, the current types of occupations people engage with are certainly different. Nevertheless, there is evidence demonstrating that the core colonial idea regarding work has remained unchanged. The perception that has been fostered over time is that the most prestigious and leading occupations in society are expected to be performed by white people, whereas the non-whites might perform mostly menial and subservient roles. Except in football and entertainment, black Brazilians are oftentimes at the marginal positions in society and underrepresented in many decision-making positions such as in policymaking, business, higher education and public administration (Dzidzienyo, 1971). Moreover, recent studies reveal that, to date, this picture has not changed significantly in Brazil (Trindade, 2008; Acevedo and Trindade, 2011; Vasques, 2014; Johnson, 2018). In fact, breaking the barriers towards achieving more prestigious leading occupations in Brazilian society is challenging for blacks because "the person who ascends socially is considered the exception and not the rule", what does not contribute towards the valorisation of blacks as a social group (Silva, 2000, p. 105).

In conclusion, whilst black people struggle to achieve upward social mobility, there are opposing forces that prevent, postpone or challenge collective successes. The fact is that the Brazilian elite has adopted "'an ideology of compromise', allowing social mobility for some blacks and repressing the majority" (Wade, 2010, p. 70). Single and isolated success stories, although they are not exempt from challenges, are praised by the dominant elite as evidence of 'racial democracy', egalitarian opportunities to all, and the rule of meritocracy. In other words, the black person who works hard enough will achieve success on their own merits, regardless of racial background, and achieve upward social mobility. Consequently, praising single success stories contributes to reinforcing the argument of almost non-existing racial barriers and besides "do not threaten to upset the fixed nature of existing unequal relationships" (Dzidzienyo, 1971).

Racial hierarchy in Brazil

Retrospectively analysing several studies depicting racial relations in Brazil, it is possible to identify that racial hierarchy discourse is permeated throughout the three phases. Hence, it can be observed that for long, both racial relations and racial hierarchy encompass two intertwined social constructs. The official social policy fostering European immigration soon after the emancipation of slaves, for example, aimed at creating "a mixed society that was at the distinctively whiter end of the spectrum" represents a clear indication of this bond (Wade, 2010, p. 31). Moreover, the ingrained collective belief in the whitening ideology as a national value has been contributing to reproduce "a symbolic order that links whiteness to material privilege while linking blackness to impoverishment and inferiority" (Twine, 1998, p. 108). Therefore, it is imperative to analyse the main aspects regarding the development and operation of Brazil's racial hierarchy system, which is characterised by two strong contrasting oppositional poles: black & white. Furthermore, it is also important to address their expected differentiated social spaces and roles, and an intricate (practically fluid) intermediary array of racial self-identifiers which enable people to swing back and forth between the two poles in accordance with the circumstance and context.

The opposing poles of the racial hierarchy system

The first phase of Brazil's racial relations has been responsible for the establishment of the country's fundamental pillars of a racial hierarchy system that prevails to date. The review of the studies reveals what Crenshaw (2000, p. 551) has coined as the "historical oppositional dualities", or the contrasting positive-negative poles of the racial scale associated, respectively, with whiteness and blackness. Over time in Brazil, whiteness has been associated with many positive attributes such as, for instance: a) model of modernity, b) synonym of development, c) better educational level, d) ultimate symbol of beauty standard, and e) aspirational progress. By contrast, for a long time, blackness has been carrying on its shoulders all the negative legacies of over 350 years of enslavement, backwardness and underdevelopment. In between both poles, mulatto (or miscegenated) has represented an idea of an intermediary step towards whiteness, considering that this racial group aspires to achieve social progress; meaning getting as close as possible to whiteness status (Silva, 2000; Mikulak, 2011)

To a certain extent, this picture unveils how Brazilian society sees and perceives skin colour and has developed its understanding of social distance amongst racial groups. This particular 'way of seeing' skin colour in Brazil is also linked to what is called 'mark prejudice' in contrast to 'origin prejudice' (Nascimento, 1980; Nogueira, 2007). It means that externally visible features (or phenotypes) such as, for example, complexion, hairstyle, nose shape, lips size, buttocks, etc. represent a person's 'mark' and based on them people are racially categorised positively or negatively by the dominant group (Nogueira, 2007). On the other hand, 'origin prejudice' takes into consideration solely the person's ancestry to categorise them. The best example of this being the so-called 'one-drop-rule' applied in the US social context (Nascimento, 1980; Nogueira, 2007).

Taking into consideration that before the emancipation of slaves in Brazil black people were seen as devoid of humanity (Camargo, 1988; Fonseca, 1994; 2012), soon afterwards the emergent ideologies of racial differences repositioned them into their 'original place' of inferiority. It can be considered that this stage comprises the root of the oppositional dualities between black & white racial categories in the Brazilian social context. Besides, the unequal treatment given by the government to the newly emancipated black people, in contrast with the supporting social policies offered to the white European immigrants, represented an institutional legitimization of differences between the two social groups (Butler, 1998). Over time, the repetition and/or amplification of "such mechanisms of production of racial inequalities have been fostered in such a way that they have granted to the white people the privilege to predominantly occupy the highest social class positions" (Schucman, 2012, p. 14). On the other hand, the remaining depreciated social places have been left to the others and, not only that but also the burden of associated negative attributes.

In effect, "social hierarchies appeal to a natural order that is meant to justify and legitimise itself" (Guimarães, 1995, p. 31). In other words, social hierarchy systems (class, status, gender and racial) are built on top of simultaneous dualities of inclusion and exclusion. On the one hand, they naturalise a set of attributes as the most valued ones within a given social setting, whilst the lack of such attributes represents the oppositional depreciated pole. Thus, this intricate duality of inclusion and exclusion coexisting in the same social setting represents one of the main features of Brazilian racism (Telles, 2003).

Simultaneously, considering that the oppositional dualities oftentimes cast predominantly negative 'marks' upon black people, it can also be asked how the opposite pole experience its relational privileges within this racial hierarchy system. What can be observed is that, oftentimes, white Brazilians occupy 'power positions' that bestow material and symbolic advantages to them, and such condition is frequently taken for granted or seen as natural by this social group (Schucman, 2012). Moreover, there are three intertwined elements in Brazilian whiteness: 1) *silence*, meaning the absence of debates around this topic since it is taken for granted and naturalised, 2) *neglect* or the omission of its effects towards the non-whites, and 3) *distortion*, meaning the disproportional representations of white people as the only visible face in Brazil. Altogether, they play the role to safeguard the whites' privileged social positioning (Trindade, 2008; Bento, 2014).

Consequently, it becomes clearer that the racial hierarchy system in Brazil has intermingling aspects of both the whitening ideology and 'racial democracy'. Over time, the oppositional dualities between the black & white poles have been supported and maintained by strong and deep-seated beliefs and the naturalisation of symbolic privileges and better life prospects attached to whiteness; whilst attributing oppositional negative features to blackness. Concurrent, 'racial democracy' contributes to the naturalisation of expected and/or 'legitimate' social roles to people within the racial scale in accordance to their visible 'marks' (or phenotypes) and their proximity or distance in relation to the white pole. Finally, it is also interesting to notice that the mechanisms, or the internal logic of the racial hierarchy system, is capable of even transcending class hierarchies and manifest itself in conditions of social destitution. On this regard, Goldstein (2003) reveals that even among people living in *favelas* in Rio de Janeiro, many residents believe that lighter skin colour can work for their benefit in comparison to darker skin people. They believe that having lighter skin can provide them with "a better chance of succeeding in life, including greater job opportunities and even greater possibilities for leaving the poorest shantytowns and moving into neighbourhoods that qualify as poor but respectable" (Goldstein, 2003, p. 108).

The fluid intermediary racial identifiers

As in many other countries, the racial classification system in Brazil is self-declared by the person (Allan, 2001), and over time, this aspect has contributed to people making up an immense array of creative racial identifiers. As previously addressed in the Introduction, a large survey conducted by IBGE in 1976, for example, has revealed a myriad of 135 different racial identifiers (Rodrigues, 1995; Maier, 2006). Moreover, two decades later, the study conducted by Sansone (1996) in two working-class cities in the Northern state of Bahia revealed 36 different self-declared racial identifiers. The embedded symbolic meaning in this immense variety of racial terminologies is the fact that people are expressing their inner desire to keep a distance from one

depreciated pole of the racial hierarchy scale (black) and get closer to the
opposite one (white). In other words, it reveals three major aspects: 1) the
denial of one's depreciated ethnic identity in favour of another one that they
believe will bring them improved symbolic benefits, 2) protect them from
stigmatisation and stereotyped portrayals, 3) provide intangible privileges or a
better symbolic social positioning.

Thus, in essence, the picture depicted both in the 1976 IBGE survey and the
study conducted by Sansone (1996) is summarised in Figure 1.2.

Figure 1.2: Brazilian Racial Hierarchy Dynamic

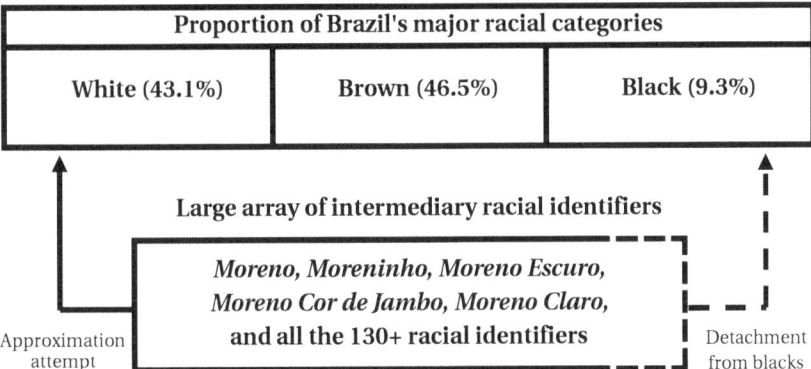

Figure 1.2 displays first the current proportion of the three major racial
groups in Brazilian population, as for the most recently available census data
(Campos, 2017; IBGE, 2017; Silveira, 2017; 2019). However, as in everyday life
Brazilians employ a multitude of intermediary racial identifiers between white
and black, this attitude carries a twofold unspoken objective. It aims, first, to
detach themselves from the lower end of the racial hierarchy, and to break links
with blackness (represented by the dashed line in Figure 1.2). Second, to
establish a closer bond with the upper end of the racial hierarchy, and as much
as possible pass as white. In other words, there is a subtle (and undeclared)
move from the lower end of the racial hierarchy, towards the upper end (in this
case, represented by the continuous line in Figure 1.2). However, since people
may not feel completely at ease to openly self-declare their white status (after
all, their visible marks might not support such a claim), the intermediary racial
terminologies contribute to shortening this distance and, at the same time,
they move away from blackness. The embedded discourse in the adoption of
this myriad of intermediary racial terminologies is that the miscegenated
person might not be 'genuinely' white but, at least, might not be perceived by
society as black either.

Amongst the multitude of intermediary racial identifiers, *moreno* (and its numerous variations) stands out, and its social meaning has been investigated by several authors (e.g. Moura, 1988; Maier, 2006; Telles, 2006; Daflon, 2014). Over time, this racial identifier has achieved a considerable degree of overlapping and fluidity that enables its use in a multitude of circumstances, making it difficult to be accurately interpreted without other supporting elements or a broader context. Actually, there are many 'contingency factors' influencing people's perception of race in Brazil, and hence impacting the adoption of different racial identifiers. Such factors can encompass time, affective bonds, income level or social class position, age and place of origin (Rosa, 2014). Practical examples of everyday situations where such factors can be employed include, for instance, the fact that strong affective bonds may lead to the adoption of *moreno* rather than *preto*; whilst weaker bonds may lead people to employ *escuro* or *escurinho*, also to avoid *preto* or *negro*. Moreover, people in higher social class positions are considered either white or *moreno* in contrast with people at lower social strata that are prone to be called *pretinho* or *negro* (Daflon, 2014; Rosa, 2014).

Furthermore, "*moreno* is a 'neutral' term that refers to almost any combination of phenotypical features or a continuum of skin colour with physical features that do not represent African phenotypes" (Mikulak, 2011, p. 83). Nevertheless, more importantly, is the fact that this fluid extra-official racial category enables people to navigate smoothly along the colour continuum according to the circumstance, the context and the convenience (i.e. it is not fixed, but rather highly contextualised). In effect, *moreno* represents a particular element of Brazil's racial hierarchy system, in combination with the frequent use of diminutives, and in many circumstances, they equip people to talk about race without sounding racist. Examples of this reflection include common expressions in Brazil such as: a) but you are not that black but *moreno*, b) you are not one of those black guys. You are *moreno(a)*, c) wow, what a gorgeous *morena*. You must know how to dance *samba* very well, d) you are not black, but rather sunburnt, e) you have got an exotic *morena* beauty, f) you are *moreninho(a)*, not black, and g) I would rather call you *moreno(a)* because black could sound disrespectful (Isis, 2015). These verbal expressions are meant to be received as a compliment but, in reality, they conceal the belief that being addressed *moreno* is better or more polite than *negro*, *preto* or *pardo* because it implies that the recipient is being positioned closer to the upper white end of the racial scale, rather than the lower black end.

Additionally, over the years, this racial identifier has contributed to the development of misconceptions that acknowledging a person's blackness could be offensive and should be avoided. On this aspect, Osorio (2003, p. 17), for example, claims that "the use of the racial identifier *moreno* as a euphemism to avoid addressing someone as *negro*, *preto* or *pardo*, represents the perfect expression of social etiquette of racial relations". Besides, the author continues, "this attitude is a type of polite concession in order not to depreciate the person" (Osorio, 2003, p. 17). Nonetheless, this sort of attitude can be understood as a subtle manoeuvre to conceal the unspoken and unwritten rules of Brazil's racial boundaries or the expression of the silent racism in Brazil.

In conclusion, the racial hierarchy phenomenon matters because it can be a determinant element towards triggering and perpetuating racism in a given social setting. Hence, this system of classification according to social attributes (ranging from positive to negative, in combination with a nebulous grey area in-between) associated with one's racial group, shapes social relations and influences the life prospects of black Brazilians.

Intersectional hierarchies of race, gender and class

The analysis of the Brazilian racial hierarchy system also leads us towards another salient aspect of racial relations in the country: the intersecting hierarchies of race, gender and class. The intersectionality concept indicates that different dimensions of inequalities can overlap and bring more challenging circumstances to certain social groups in comparison to hegemonic ones (Brah and Phoenix, 2004; Harnois and Ifatunji, 2011; Anthias, 2012). In this context, the traditional perspectives of social inequalities consider, first, that gender discrimination applies to women in general (indistinctively of the race); second, racial discrimination is circumscribed to a single racial group and, finally, social discrimination applies solely to poor people. In other words, this approach fragments people into specific and disconnected boxes, whilst intersectionality proposes that such boxes are not isolated stand-alone entities. They are rather dynamic and constantly overlapping (Crenshaw, 2012; Purkayastha, 2012). This leads us to understand that men and women can experience situations of racism specifically related to their gender, which evidence that the impacts of racism are not evenly distributed between the two genders in different social contexts. Thus, the interplay of these three dimensions can have a variety of impacts on black men and women.

Furthermore, it is also important to highlight that not only the impact may be different between the two genders, but also within the gender itself, revealing the relational facet of intersectionality. That is to say that "in a society organised by the intersecting of race and gender, it is not possible to capture the full range of black women's mistreatment without comparing their experiences to those of racially privileged women" (Harnois and Ifatunji, 2011, p. 1010). Although this argumentation is based on the US social context, it is possible to find a considerable degree of alignment with the Brazilian social context. The analysis of the living conditions of black Brazilian women reveals many relational disadvantages experienced by them in comparison to their white female counterparts. They include, for instance, lower salaries, reduced access to higher education, reduced access to the judiciary system, greater exposition to violence, and worse treatment in the public healthcare system (Olinto and Olinto, 2000; Marcondes *et al.*, 2013).

Concerning healthcare, for instance, studies reveal that whilst 5.1% of white women in normal labour procedure do not receive anaesthesia, the figure reaches 11.1% for black women (Marinho *et al.*, 2011). These figures reflect an ingrained colonial belief that black women feel less pain than their white female counterparts and, consequently, they would not need as much anaesthesia in several medical procedures (Castro, 2016; Júnia, 2016). As with exposure to violence, recent figures reveal that whilst the mortality rate of white women dropped by 7.4% between 2005 and 2015, for black women the rate increased by 22% in the same period, and this rate is even higher than the overall national average (Cerqueira *et al.*, 2017).

Consequently, what other distinctive aspects do these pictures reveal about racial relations in Brazil? In the first place, they contribute to the evidence that black women encompass a vulnerable social group exposed to many relational inequalities. Second, the overlapping of dimensions such as gender, race, and class compose a picture that turns their living conditions considerably challenging in comparison to men and even within their gender. Finally, they also reinforce the predominance of a strong patriarchal social structure in Brazil, because men (mostly white) occupy the majority of the instances of symbolic power, enforcing their views upon 'the others'. Moreover, it is possible to observe that racialized black women are oftentimes victimised by their male partners in over 30% of the reported cases of domestic violence (Cerqueira *et al.*, 2017)

It is also relevant to highlight that although the intersectionality analysis developed in this book is centred on three dimensions (gender, race, and class), this does not mean that, in reality, they are the only ones at play. Indeed, "the focus on gender, ethnicity/race and class, does not imply that sexuality, age, disability, faith and so on" could not be added to the debate (Anthias, 2012, p. 4). Thus, a broader analysis of intersectionality within the Brazilian social context could also ponder, for example, the person's place of origin and religious affiliation.

Regarding the place of origin, studies reveal that black women from the North-eastern region of Brazil experience many circumstances of racism in the Southern and South-eastern regions amplified by their place of origin (Carneiro, 2003; Miranda, 2016). One of the reasons suggested by the authors is due to an enduring contrasting duality of negative and positive attributes. Whilst the North-eastern region has constantly been associated with poverty, underdevelopment, precarious housing conditions and lower levels of formal education, the Southern and South-eastern regions have been associated with modernity, the cradle of European immigration in the early twentieth century, higher development rate, wealth, and many other positive attributes.

As for the engagement with African-derived religions such as *Candomblé*[11] and *Umbanda*[12], they can also lead towards diverse forms of bigotry, mockery and racial discrimination. This is because they are commonly associated with a myriad of negative attributes such as primitive, backwardness, evil and witchcraft (Selka, 2007; Silva, 2014). Hence, these two additional dimensions contribute to demonstrating the range of complexity of the challenges black women can potentially be exposed to when all of them simultaneously intersect in ordinary social circumstances.

Thus, resuming the focus on the three predominant dimensions of intersectionality (gender, race and class), there are some important reflections to be made concerning class. The intertwined dimensions of being black, female, and belonging to underprivileged classes are strongly connected; and they overlap in such a way that make their lived experiences of racism particularly challenging (Marcondes *et al.*, 2013; Hirata, 2014; White, 2014). In other words, lower social class positioning represents a very important variable in the intersectionality equation. Nevertheless, despite the relevant intrinsic connection revealed in previous studies, there is something else to take into consideration. The approach adopted by these authors can lead us towards an understanding that gendered discrimination in Brazil is restricted solely to people belonging to the lower social strata. It is noticeable that the underprivileged class position adds a considerable challenge for the person, but this does not mean that people positioned in upper classes are not exposed to circumstances of racism.

Indeed, as previously addressed, the proponents of 'racial democracy' in Brazil in the early years of the twentieth century used to argue that, rather than a racial problem, there was only a class problem in the country. In other words, tackling the big social class gap would be enough to end Brazil's enduring

---

[11] The name stands for 'Dance in honour of the Gods". The religion, inspired by traditions brought by enslaved Africans, has also incorporated some aspects of the Catholic faith over time. Music and choreographed dances are important elements of their ceremonies. Source: http://www.bbc.co.uk/religion/religions/candomble/ataglance/glance.shtml and Bastide, R. (1958) *Le candomblé de Bahia*. Mounton: Paris.

[12] In addition to the African traditions, this religion incorporates indigenous influences, Catholicism and Spiritism. Source: http://www.religionfacts.com/umbanda

inequalities. Consequently, in line with this argumentation, successful upward social mobility of black Brazilians would potentially remove them from the racist realm. Nonetheless, black people' successful upward social mobility does not exempt them from experiencing circumstances of racism in Brazil (Dávila, 2003; Figueiredo, 2004). The lived experiences of racism for black men and women may differ based on the social settings, the circumstances in which racism is manifested, other people's attitudes towards them, the vocabulary employed and the level of subtleness or explicitly in racist attitudes or discourses. However, "contrary to what many believe, racism in Brazil does not vanish once you become wealthier" (Colonna, 2016, p. 2). In other words, money does not 'whiten' black people and grant them better life prospects free of racism.

Hence, in conclusion, the racial relations in Brazil embody an intersection picture where black women represent the most vulnerable racial group. They are subjected to a variety of dimensions of exclusions and discrimination that can be amplified by the country's patriarchal social structure. Moreover, even within their gender, black women oftentimes experience a series of relational disadvantages in comparison to their white female counterparts. Finally, even black women belonging to privileged social classes may also experience situations of racism, since successful upward social mobility does not represent a flawless guarantee that such experiences will cease to happen. The latter group may have greater access to institutional mechanisms to have their voice heard, but that does not mean that they are free of being racialized just like black women belonging to lower social strata (Trindade, 2018b).

The construction of Brazilian national identity

The key events contributing to shaping the construction of Brazilian national identity took place mostly during the late years of the nineteenth century and throughout the first half of the twentieth century. Although it is possible to go back in time to as far as the proclamation of independence in 1822, as previously done by Fiorin (2009) and Barbato (2014), in the present book it has been adopted a different approach and to prioritise the events post-emancipation of the slaves in 1888. For this purpose, Figure 1.3 displays a selection of key events from the late years of the nineteenth century onwards with the objective to provide some contextual signposting to the subsequent discussions.

Having said that, to understand Brazilian national identity, it is necessary to examine four major intertwined elements that compose its fundamental pillars. I start by examining the role played by football and its legacy in shaping the belief in the blacks' 'natural' ability to play this game, and one of their few possibilities to achieve upward social mobility. The following discussion addresses the development of Brazilian female beauty standards and some of their impacts on black women. As for the third topic addressing the modernist movement of the 1920s, it helps us to understand the social transformations embedded in the context of the 'racial democracy' and the institutional project to foster a 'modern' and distinct vision of Brazil. Finally, discussing carnival not only present elements intertwined with the previous ones but also allows us to understand how this popular celebration became one of the strongest pillars in Brazilian national identity.

Figure 1.3: Brazilian national identity timeline of major influential events

1888	Emancipation of the slaves	
1889	Proclamation of the Republic	
1890	Hymn of the Proclamation of the Republic	Ruy Barbosa demands the burning of slavery documents
1895	Introduction of football in Brazil by Charles Miller	
1922	100th Anniversary of the Independence	Modern Art Week Exhibition (February, São Paulo)
1923	Vasco da Gama wins the football championship in Rio de Janeiro with a predominantly non-white team	
1933	Publication of Gilberto Freyre's *The Masters and the Slaves*	
1947	Publication of Mário Filho's *O Negro no Futebol Brasileiro*	
1964-1985	Military ruling in Brazil	

Brazil: land of football

Although Brazil is internationally renowned by its numerous talented black and miscegenated football players over many decades (e.g. Pelé, Garrincha, Romário, Ronaldo, Ronaldinho, Neymar Jr., and many others), at the beginning of the twentieth century, non-white players were not welcomed in many professional clubs and even less in the national team (or *seleção*, in Portuguese).

According to sport historians, football was introduced in Brazil by Charles Miller (1874-1953) who, besides his Anglo-Saxon name, was born in Brazil but his father was a Scottish immigrant while the mother was Brazilian. After spending ten years attending primary and secondary education in England, in 1894 he went back to Brazil, however, determined to keep practising the emerging sport, football, that he had been introduced to while living abroad. Around a year after his return, on 14 April 1895, he managed to organise what is considered as the first official football match in Brazil (Máximo, 1999; Mills, 2005). However, let us also consider some other important contextual aspects. First, this event took place only seven years after the emancipation of the slaves. Second, as previously addressed, in 1890, there were already institutional efforts to eliminate from Brazilian history its three-centuries-long slavery legacy. Finally, also by the end of the nineteenth century, Brazil was trying to shape its national identity as close as possible to the US and Europe, as already discussed. Consequently, within this context, and considering the fact that the emerging sport had been introduced by a second-generation middle-class white man, it has contributed to turning football elitist from the very beginning, and off-limits for blacks and mulattoes. Actually, as highlighted by Máximo (1999), the Brazilian elite of the late nineteenth-century-São Paulo and Rio de Janeiro encompassed either European immigrants and/or their descendants, notably from Italy, Germany, Portugal, Switzerland, and Britain. Thus, it becomes evident that non-whites would not be easily welcomed to join such an elitist group.

As football started to grow in popularity in Brazil, there was the establishment of the first clubs such as, for example, *São Paulo Athletic Club* (1896), *Sport Club Germania* (1889), *Mackenzie Athletic Association* (1898), *Fluminense Foot-ball Club* (1902), *Rio Foot-ball Club* (1902), *Bangu Athletic Club* (1904), among others, as explained by Máximo (1999). It is noteworthy to mention that most of these football clubs were established employing English language terminologies to name them, rather than Portuguese. According to Filho (1947), this was due to the strong influence of the elite British immigrant community in the introduction of the sport in Brazil. Besides, the author complements, even to name the players' positions in the field they used to employ English terminologies rather than Portuguese[13]. Within this scenario, soon it was possible to identify a clear distinction between the elite clubs (formed predominantly by white middle-class players) and second-tier clubs who admitted some black and mulatto players (mostly working-class people). These second-tier clubs were often established either as teams formed by employees of industries or based in the suburbs.

---

[13] Such positions were: goalkeeper, fullback-right, fullback-left, halfback-right, center-half, halfback-left, winger-right, inside-right, center-forward, inside-left, and winger-left (Filho, 1947, p. 31)

Having said that, three emblematic events call our attention to the emergence of football in Brazil and the insertion of black and mulatto players in this game which, ultimately, helps us to understand how racial relations operated in that social context. First, Arthur Friedenreich (1892-1969) was one of the few exceptions amongst non-white players allowed to play in elite clubs such as *Sport Club Germania* in 1909. First, because he was extremely talented and, second, because he was considered "half mulatto" due to his green eyes (Filho, 1947, p. 58). However, still according to the author, besides the mentioned aspects, he had to spend a great amount of time before each game straightening his naturally curled hair to reduce traces of black ancestry since his father was a German immigrant and the mother a black woman. The other distinct aspect encompasses a controversial makeup strategy that would have been adopted by another talented mulatto player named Carlos Alberto playing for *Fluminense Foot-ball Club* in Rio de Janeiro. According to Filho (1947, p. 58), the player would have applied the makeup once "to disguise his black ancestry applying a thick layer of white face powder". But apparently, the result was not what he would have expected, and this would have led the supporters to nickname first him and later on the football club as *pó-de-arroz* (face powder). The event is indeed controversial because to date, voices claim that this account is not accurate enough (Esporte, 2019), however, even so, this story has become consolidated in the Brazilian football chronicle. Finally, it also calls the attention the fact that in 1921, the Brazilian president Epitácio Pessoa (1865-1942) recommended that the national team, that was about to participate in the South American Football Championship in Argentina, should not have either black or mulatto among its players. The reason for such recommendation was that Brazil should portray its best image possible abroad (Filho, 1947; Máximo, 1999; Santos, J. 2019).

In line with the predominant whitening ideology of the late nineteenth-century-Brazil, the low presence of black and mulatto players in the emerging elite football clubs contributed to reinforce the racial inequality picture. The first signs of significative change in this scenario would come only in 1923 when *Vasco da Gama*, a predominantly working-class football team with black and mulatto players, won the Rio de Janeiro championship leaving behind several whites-only clubs. And three years later, another working-class football team, *São Cristóvão* also with black and mulatto players, managed to repeat this achievement (Filho, 1947; Máximo, 1999; Santos, J. 2019).

However, what is interesting to observe is the fact that some years later, these two iconic victories in Brazilian football history, were emphatically praised by Filho (1947) as evidence of the prevalence of meritocracy and 'racial democracy' over white supremacist ideologies. Indeed, not by chance, the author resonates ideas of Gilberto Freyre in his influential book. According to

Haag (2014), Filho and Freyre were introduced to each other in a dinner in 1946 when Filho handed over to Freyre the manuscript of his book for critical appraisal and invited him to write the book's preface. The book was published in the following year and in the preface, Freyre reiterates the contribution of black football players in incorporating a unique Brazilian touch to an originally-British sport, and the possibility of upward social mobility that football provided for blacks. With this in mind, it is also relevant to explain that in the early 1900s the football teams were part of private clubs and as such, the players should also be members of the clubs what, in the elite's mind, it would be unthinkable having black and mulatto players as their peers in such a privileged social space. Nevertheless, the participation of non-white players was increasing considerably in most teams due to their skilful performance. Thus, this context led to the professionalisation of football in the 1930s because as an employee, the black and mulatto players would not necessarily become members of the clubs and the distinction between the elite and the commoners would remain intact.

Over the years, football became an important component of Brazilianess, or 'the country of football boots' as coined by Rodrigues (1994) to represent the strong symbiosis between national identity and football, especially during the World Cup tournaments every four years. Besides that, football alongside samba and carnival, became strongly associated with the idea that they represent one of the few alternatives for upward social mobility for blacks and mulattoes. The idea is that, first, these activities (football and entertainment) do not demand university education and, second, because black and mulatto can rely on their 'natural' abilities to play football and dance (Vasques, 2014). However, although numerous black and mulatto players have indeed achieved successful upward social mobility through this sport, it is also true that they are not in leadership positions (e.g. coach, manager, or executive director). According to the most recent data available, the participation of black and mulatto in leadership positions amongst elite clubs (in Brazil they are called *Série A*), is fewer than 3% (Madureira, 2019). Thus, in conclusion, the introduction of football in Brazil in the late nineteenth century has contributed to reproduce and reinforce the white supremacist ideologies and widening and maintaining social and racial inequalities. Furthermore, although currently, the picture has improved significantly on this aspect, it is still possible to observe the echoes of a colonial mentality where leadership positions are 'reserved' for whites whilst blacks and mulattoes are 'destined' to follow orders.

Female beauty standards

Another important aspect contributing to shaping Brazilian national identity in the early twentieth century was the first beauty contests. They happened in the 1920s and played the important role of projecting "an idealised image of an inclusive, democratic culture, thus obscuring the reality of racial, class and gender exclusions and promoting identification with the nation-state" (Besse, 2005, p. 96). In the collective mindset, the beauty contests contributed to conveying the image of what it meant to be Brazilian and, at the same time, a modern country, in alignment with the aspirations of the dominant elite. Furthermore, the beauty contests also served the purpose to projecting Brazil's image internationally, meaning that it aimed that its visible face would "demonstrate the 'progress' of Brazil and its capacity for achieving the highest level of civilization" (Besse, 2005, p. 98).

In effect, the whitening ideology was openly advocated by the organisers of the 1920s beauty contests. Clear evidence is found in the statement made by the organisers in a leading newspaper of that time arguing, "the beauty contest is no longer a mere exercise of vanity or an ordinary entertainment show for shallow gossip magazine readers, but it has achieved a meaning of eugenic value certifying the physical attributes of a race" (Semana, 1921, p. 12). Although the beauty contests were meant to be (or at least advertised as such) representative of Brazilian racial diversity and embrace "the great variety of regional types" (Semana, 1921, p. 12), white women were always the runners-up and winners chosen by the white male jury (Besse, 2005). Moreover, in another international beauty contest that took place in Rio de Janeiro in 1930[14], also calls our attention the official statement made by the organisers after the winner had been announced (a 19 years old white woman named Yolanda Pereira). It was argued that "she was Brazilian in her most high personification. Her complexion conveys what every woman should look like to be called Brazilian. She is the symbol of our race" (Lever, 1930, p. 3; Souza, 1930, front cover).

Thus, the intersection of gender and race is revealing of the dominant thinking that has contributed to shaping the construction of Brazilianness, likewise football and carnival. It reveals an intricate and subtle game of inclusion and exclusion. On the one hand, it is possible to notice a clear adoption of white beauty as the ultimate representation of the 'national type' whilst, on the other hand, excluding the other racial groups without even mentioning them. Hence, for the dominant elite, female beauty could be an

---

[14] The organisers of this beauty contest claimed that the winner would be crowned Miss Universe. However, this title has never been officially recognised by the Miss Universe Organization, given that the first award was granted only in 1952 (source: https://missuniverse.com/past-winners). Besides, accounts suggest that, in reality, the contest was organised as a type of revenge to the one held in Galveston (US) in 1929 where the Brazilian representative, Olga Bergamini de Sá, was not shortlisted amongst the top ten (source: "Brazil: Revenge", Time Magazine, edition 22/09/1930).

important element to represent the Brazilianness both at home and internationally. However, since the aspirational progress and modernity was strongly influenced by eugenic ideologies, only white women would be the legitimate symbol of the national identity in the making. As for the remaining racial groups, they were left with the possibility of emulating the dominant beauty standard, but not effectively being levelled with it.

However, this overall picture also raises an intriguing question. On the one hand, whitening has been praised and continuously reinforced as a synonym of Brazilian beauty and one of the fundamental pillars of the national identity. On the other hand, blackness embodies its direct contrasting opposition. Then, what happened to the distinctive and celebrated Brazilian *mestizaje* emerged from Gilberto Freyre's *The Masters and the Slaves* that supported the 'racial democracy' discourse? It can be observed that the female beauty associated with *mestizaje* in Brazil has not been praised or valued with an equivalent level of importance to white beauty. Actually, the mestizo beauty has been developed predominantly associated with sensual attributes and overexposure of their body, as it will be further discussed in the topic addressing carnival.

On this regard, at the beginning of the twentieth century, coexisted a dualistic discourse praising Brazilian beauty and national identity internationally, however, with distinct objectives. The white female beauty had the aim of promoting the Brazilian 'progress' and 'modernity' to the world. On the other hand, there was also an institutional effort to 'selling' Brazil as an attractive touristic destination (Caetano, 2004; Gomes, 2010). Nevertheless, for this purpose, the core message was that Brazil would be a type of tropical paradise and, within this context, the sensual figure of mulatto women played a central role in this discourse, conveying an image of sexual permissiveness (Caetano, 2004; Gomes, 2010). Thus, this context reinforces the depictions of white Brazilian women predominantly associated with positive attributes, whilst black women would be subservient, and the mixed-race women sexual objects.

In the 1960s, mulatto women were on the rise in Brazil. However, not because they were being praised in equal standing with white women, but rather because their sensuality was being over-explored. An emblematic example in support to this analysis comprises the establishment of a successful variety show in Rio de Janeiro named *As Mulatas do Sargentelli*[15] (Araújo, 1999; Gomes,

---

[15] The Sargentielli's Mulatas. Its creator, Osvaldo Sargentelli (1924-2002), was a samba singer, radio broadcaster, TV host, businessman and self-declared '*mulatólogo*' (or a *mulata* expert). The entertainment show lasted from 1969 until the mid-1980s (Araújo, 1999; Lima and Lessa, 2017). However, after he passed away, the show was taken over by his niece Sandra Sargentelli and might still be in operation nowadays (source: http://www.sargentelli.com.br).

2010; Lima and Lessa, 2017). In line with that, a well-known vocational school also in Rio de Janeiro settled a '*mulata* training' targeted at women who aimed to become samba dancers (Giacomini, 2006; Gomes, 2010). However, the offering of this training represents an intriguing paradox because if *mulata* is essentially an intermediary racial identifier, similar to *moreno* and many others as previously discussed (see Figure 1.2), how is it possible that it became 'a profession' that could be systematically taught in a school? Interviewing several of the women who attended the training, Giacomini (2006) discovered some revealing statements such as: a) *mulata* meant to know how to dance samba, b) *mulata* is related to your skin tone, c) *mulata* is something that it is in the blood-stream (it is innate), and d) *mulata* must have a gorgeous well-shaped body, attractive and firm buttocks, and slim waist.

Accordingly, such statements reveal that the female participants have reported a series of attributes predominantly of physical and sensual nature to describe what *mulata* meant for them. They contribute to revealing the naturalised dominant ideas in Brazil associating mixed-race women (*mulata*, *morena*, and all the myriad of intermediary racial terminologies) with sensuality, desire and lust. Ultimately, over time, this type of ideology depicting *mulata* as a sexual object, has been embedded, disseminated, and reinforced, for example, in many TV programmes such as *Da cor do Pecado* and *Sexo & as Negas* (Barbosa, 2004; Souza, 2015; Soares, K. 2016), and in influential fictional novels that became classical in the country's literature such as *O Cortiço* and *Gabriela, Cravo e Canela*[16].

The Brazilian modernist movement

Whilst in the early twentieth century Brazil was experiencing the process of shaping its national identity, aiming to emulate a Eurocentric society as already explained, this process brought impacts beyond everyday racial relations. Brazilian art, literature, music, and architecture have also been strongly influenced by European school (Philippou, 2005; Witoslawski, 2005). As an example of this influence, Goldstein (2003, p. 78) explains that during the early years of the republic, "Rio's elite travelled to Paris, read French, and admired Paris as an example of what a 'civilized' city should look like". Moreover, as previously discussed, the major football clubs in Rio de Janeiro and São Paulo in the early 1900s were strongly influenced by British culture, and even

---

[16] *O Cortiço* (The Slum) was published in 1890 by Aluisio Azevedo. It is considered one of the classic novels in Brazilian literature, and mandatory reading for the admission exams for Brazil's most prestigious and competitive universities. As for *Gabriela, Cravo e Canela* (Gabriela, Clove and Cinnamon), it was published in 1958 by Jorge Amado and it has been translated to over 40 languages.

employing English-language terminologies on their names and the players' position in the field.

However, the Brazilian context of post-World War I brought to the surface nationalistic values and also the beginning of the industrialization in replacement to rural activities, especially in São Paulo (Ajzenberg, 2012; Cardoso, 2012). Within this scenario, some young middle-class artists and intellectuals were engaging in challenging the dominant Eurocentric cultural pattern and proposing innovative perspectives (Witoslawski, 2005; Ajzenberg, 2012; Chan, 2015). Their approach was mostly to deconstruct the prevailing Eurocentric aesthetic pattern in Brazilian art and introducing a genuinely national school that would value its traditions, its people, its national values, and also allowing the emergence of cultural emancipation from Europe. In effect, both Philippou (2005) and Ajzenberg (2012) advocate that in this atmosphere, the modernist movement represented a sort of 'second discovery' of Brazil. Nonetheless, despite its nationalistic roots, the modernist movement was not xenophobic. It rather aimed at transforming Brazilian art, influenced by the European school, from inside out, what was coined by one of its leaders, Oswald de Andrade, as an 'anthropophagic movement' (Andrade, 1928; Witoslawski, 2005; Chan, 2015). The summit of this movement was the Modern Art Week in São Paulo in February 1922 (also the year that celebrated the 100th anniversary of the independence), which encompassed exhibitions of artwork, literature, and musical performances (Witoslawski, 2005; Ajzenberg, 2012; Cardoso, 2012). Whilst the event aimed at combining political independence with cultural emancipation, Cardoso (2012, p. 22) explains that the Modern Art Week had "relatively little impact at the time". But despite this fact, its relevance in Brazilian cultural history is undeniable to this date.

Having said that, and in line with the scope of the present book, what is particularly relevant in the modernist movement and its reverberation along the subsequent years, is their portrayal of Brazilianness. In the case of paintings, for instance, it becomes clear a shift in the representation form of the 'typical' Brazilian. Different from the colonial pictorial images emphasising the big power asymmetry between masters and slaves, the modernist paintings depicted miscegenation more positively (Witoslawski, 2005). On this regard, there are many emblematic paintings[17], such as, for instance, *A Negra* (by

---

[17] The reproduction of mentioned paintings and many others produced during the modernist movement, is available from the following sources:

1) About the Modern Art Week http://enciclopedia.itaucultural.org.br/evento84382/semana-de-arte-moderna

2) Candido Portinari biography and major works: http://enciclopedia.itaucultural.org.br/pessoa10686/candido-portinari

Tarsila do Amaral, 1923), *O Morro da Favela* (by Tarsila do Amaral, 1924), *Samba* (by Di Cavalcanti, 1925), *Meninas Cariocas* (by Di Cavalcanti, 1926), *Mulatas* (by Di Cavalcanti, 1927), *Operários* (by Tarsila do Amaral, 1933), *O Lavrador de Café* (by Candido Portinari, 1934), *Mestiço* (by Candido Portinari, 1934), and *Negro de Chapéu e Perfil* (by Candido Portinari, 1935). Such paintings explore the images of miscegenated working-class men, mulatto women, shantytown scenario, coffee plantation black worker, among other motifs. Not by chance, most of these artworks were produced in the context of the emerging 'racial democracy' and influenced by the ideas advocated in the 1933 Gilberto Freyre's *The Masters and the Slaves*. That is to say that the artists were portraying the image of a country that no longer considered miscegenation as a social problem that needed to be tackled but rather its distinctive and proud national feature (Philippou, 2005).

Actually, from the 1930s onwards, cultural manifestations embodied with African and/or *mestizaje* heritage have gained a more positive status. On this aspect, Philippou (2005) explains that in the 1930s carnival became firmly established as a national icon, in 1937 the government proclaimed *capoeira*[18] as a national sport, and in the following year *candomblé* was decriminalised. Nevertheless, whilst the modernist movement was exposing the 'true nature' of the Brazilianness, there were incongruencies. First, the elite did not identify themselves with that depiction since their modernity reference was still centred on a Eurocentric model. Second, the ordinary working-class Brazilian did not have access to that level of cultural manifestation and, consequently, they also could not identify themselves with that representation. Furthermore, it is also possible to notice that whilst *mestizaje* was becoming an important element of Brazilian national identity, blackness remained practically absent. It means that while the Brazilian mainstream culture embraces miscegenation as a discourse, the Brazilian elite still aspired to reach Eurocentric modernity and, in this process, *mestizaje* represented an acceptable intermediary step, whereas blackness embodied the oppositional pole, in line with what has been previously addressed.

---

3) Di Cavalcanti biography and major works: http://enciclopedia.itaucultural.org.br/pessoa971/di-cavalcanti
4) Tarsila do Amaral biography and major works: http://enciclopedia.itaucultural.org.br/pessoa824/tarsila-do-amaral
[18] It is a sort of self-defence martial art whose origin is subjected to some controversy. While some authors argue that it was developed in Angola, others claim that it was created in Brazil by the African slaves. In colonial times, it used to be performed as a type of dance to fool the masters and avoiding that they forbid its practice by the slaves (Moura, 2004).

Carnival, blackness and sensuality in Brazil

Carnival is considered an ancient festivity and it is said that it was introduced in Brazil by the Portuguese settlers (Arantes, 2013), and over time it has received many influences from the black people that transformed it in a particular celebration in Brazil. In effect, music and dancing were a common practice among the captive black people in colonial society, which used to gather on Sundays on the streets and public square "to play, to perform capoeira dancing, and to play the drums" (Gomes, 2007, p. 231).

Within that, it is also interesting to observe that, in colonial times, the singing and dancing performed by black people was considered "inferior, primitive and lustful" form of popular manifestation (Azevedo, 2018, p. 49). A relevant clue to understanding the origin of this negative perception is found in the travel book written by von Spix *et al.* (1824). The authors describe their visit to a farmhouse named *Estiva* where they are saluted with singing and dancing. At a certain point, the authors say that "notwithstanding its indecency, this dance is common throughout Brazil, and the property of the lower classes, [...] introduced into Brazil by negro slaves" (von Spix *et al.*, 1824, p. 496). In reality, this sort of depiction not only contributed to the development of a primitive perception concerning music and dance of African roots in Brazil but also its forbidden sensuality, with black women representing lust (Soihet, 2003).

However, despite this negative portrayal, dancing and singing also represented an incipient form of resistance to racism and captivity, in such a way that "in 1835, any *batuque*[19] was largely interpreted as an attempt against slavery" (Reis, 2005, p. 208). Moreover, by performing their dance, singing, and especially playing the drums, "they communicated that the Africans and their descendants had not accepted being mentally enslaved" (Reis, 2005, p. 210). As for the *batuque* aforementioned, it is relevant to add that it is considered the root of a series of musical styles which later evolved until it turned into samba which, on its turn, would become a well-defined music genre only in the early decades of the twentieth century, and intrinsically connected with carnival to the present day (Chasteen, 1996).

It is also interesting to notice that despite the black (or Afro) influence in shaping and transforming carnival in Brazil, blacks did not play central roles in the celebrations in the early years of the republic. Supporting evidence for this reflection lays in the allegories developed for the 1890 carnival in Rio de Janeiro that associated the white female figure representing the republic (Neponucemo, 2013). In effect, this approach was in alignment with the

---

[19] It stands for black percussion music usually accompanied by dance (Reis, 2005).

prevailing whitening ideology in Brazil, as already discussed, and explains the absence (or low relevance) of black figures in the celebrations.

Significant changes though would take place mostly in the 1930s during the ruling of president Getúlio Vargas. Different from the previous decades where the whitening ideology was dominant, the Vargas era witnessed the emergence of the 'racial democracy' and the echoes of the modernist movement. Within this context, carnival becomes an effective symbol of Brazilianess (translated in race mixing) and an important pillar of the national identity under construction, just like football. Besides, in the late 1930s, Getúlio Vargas also implemented pioneering advertising campaigns abroad to promote Rio de Janeiro as a touristic destination and using carnival as one of the major attractions (Filho, 2007; Almeida, 2017). This communication strategy had the twofold objective to give an impulse to the incipient tourist industry and also to 'sell' Brazil in the international arena as the land of 'racial democracy'. Thus, following this policy, Rio de Janeiro becomes Brazil's most important touristic destination. In this scenario, it is emblematic to observe the production of a short video by the American moviemaker James A. Fitzpatrick praising Rio's beauties and targeted to the American audience. At a certain point in the movie, the narrator says that "the colour of one's skin does not determine one's social standing, and [...] the colour line seems to be so thinly drawn that it has become a heaven of tolerance for all races" (Fitzpatrick, 1932, 2:07 - 2:13). Hence, in the 1930s, carnival becomes one of the pillars of Brazilian national identity by contributing to reinforcing the image of a successful post-racial society.

Moving forward to the 1960s and 1970s, when Brazil was during military ruling (see Figure 1.3), it is possible to notice other significant transformations. Alongside carnival and football as elements of the national identity, there was the incorporation of the sensual mulatto woman composing the scenario of a post-racial tropical paradise (Almeida, 2017). On the one hand, Pelé (already a well-known and successful football player) was the visible face of this racially democratic Brazil. On the other hand, indistinct sensual mulatto women, either wearing tiny bikinis or carnival costumes, 'invited' foreigners to visit Brazil (Kajihara, 2010). In effect, analysing the presence of black women in São Paulo's carnival during the timeframe 1921 to 1967, Z. Silva (2018) identifies the increasing trend of exploration of mulatto and black women's sensuality in the carnival parades. Within that, not by chance, in the subsequent decades, it is possible to observe the consolidation of this phenomenon, in such a way that sensual *mulata* becomes synonymous of Brazilian carnival. Furthermore, the objectification of their body becomes naturalized in mainstream means of mass communication. Thus, not by chance, in this overall scenario emerges the successful variety shown named *As Mulatas do Sargentelli*, as previously addressed in this chapter, whose slogan was '*mulata* export type' (Gomes, 2010). This slogan embedded, first, the idea that their body was a distinct world-class asset and, second, it turned them into merchandise just like their African ancestors in the colonial society.

Finally, as from the 1990s, we notice the consolidation of the objectification of the mulatto women's sensual body reaching Brazil's most important and influential TV channel with the figure of the so-called *Mulata Globeleza*. This figure is equivalent to a carnival queen, dancing samba usually wearing tiny carnival costumes or simply body painting to promote the carnival parades on short TV spots throughout the carnival season several times a day (Santos, 2018). However, although carnival is strongly associated with black culture, it is expected that this particular carnival queen would be rather light-skin than dark since in the collective mindset mix-racing is what represents Brazilianness, and not blackness (Anthony, 2016; Lankaster-Owen *et al.*, 2016).

The attributed social space of black Brazilians

There is an adage in Brazil asserting that there is no racism in the country because black people are aware of 'their place' in class society (Dzidzienyo, 1971; Sales Jr., 2006). However, more than a popular adage, this quote embodies deeper beliefs circulating in Brazilian society concerning boundaries of belonging to differentiated social spaces. In fact, it implies that black people's 'right' place is associated with inferiority and that as long as they remain at the bottom of the social hierarchy, racial tensions would be absent. Thus, this notion of one's naturalized and proper place within the Brazilian social structure is constantly outlined, reinforced and internalized (Goldstein, 2003).

These unwritten and unspoken 'rules' of one's proper social place derive from an ingrained racial hierarchy system based on skin colour, and strongly influenced by the whitening ideology emerged in the context of the construction of Brazilian national identity, as previously discussed. The whitening ideology, alongside the process of construction of national identity, has created the conditions to the establishment of an internalized "symbolic order that links whiteness to material privilege while linking blackness to impoverishment and inferiority" (Twine, 1998, p. 108). Actually, studies reveal that by fostering whitening ideology in the early twentieth century did not integrate black people into the emerging class society; rather it marginalised them and pushed them away from the city centre (associated with modernity and whiteness) towards deprived areas that would subsequently become the *favelas* (Fernandes, 1965; Goldstein, 2003; Maringoni, 2011).

In line with this picture, Anderson (2015) explains that in the post-civil rights movement in the US, Afro-Americans have gained access to many social spaces associated with whiteness and privilege. However, rather than acceptance, they have experienced prejudice, marginalisation and active reminders of their outsider status, all designed to position them into 'their place'. Similarly, the moment that black Brazilians ascend socially, the dominant elite challenges them; reinforcing the notion that black Brazilians cannot expect to occupy arenas associated with privilege and whiteness (Trindade, 2018b). An interesting illustrative example of this ingrained ideology is epitomized by the joke: 'When does a black person ascend socially? When his *favela* shack explodes'. The embedded message is that black people are liable to live in a *favela* and, consequently, belong to the lowest social stratum, given that the *favela* represents a clear negative social marker in Brazil (Goldstein, 2003). Additionally, the joke deftly integrates the assumption that this racial group's upward social mobility is unlikely or resulting only from an extraordinary event such as a figurative 'explosion' propelling the person upwards. All of which is to say, whenever a black person ascends socially, it is considered the exception rather than the rule.

Furthermore, to deny the damaging impacts of racism in Brazilian society, the proponents of the whitening ideology have developed a discourse asserting that 'money whitens', which propagates the notion that "Brazilians of colour could escape degeneracy by whitening through social ascension" (Dávila, 2003, p. 7). However, as previously addressed, successful upward social mobility does not exempt black people from experiences of racism because, before the eyes of the elite, they remain black and all the common negative attributes associated with blackness remain equally immutable (Trindade, 2018b). Consequently, whilst the attributed social space of black Brazilians is oftentimes associated with positions of inferiority and subservience, crossing these boundaries is challenging. First, because, on an individual level, this logic has created both external and internalized notions of where one's natural place in the world is, and where one properly belongs (Goldstein, 2003). Second, because whilst in everyday social interactions such 'rules' of belonging might not be explicitly verbalized, in the context of social media they are openly (and sometimes aggressively) displayed, disseminated, and reinforced.

White supremacy within the Brazilian context

It is relevant to introduce a contextualised explanation concerning the use of the expression 'white supremacy' in this book, since several international studies employ this same expression under the context of political and civil rights movements (e.g. Hage, 1998; Bonilla-Silva, 2001; Daniels, 2009). However, the question is how pertinent is the adoption of this expression within the Brazilian social context to analyse racial relations? Three previous studies have employed this expression within the Brazilian context to convey the notion of the superiority of the white racial group in relation to others and granting them symbolic privileges (Twine, 1998; Vargas, 2004; Nogueira, 2013). In the study analysing whitening ideology and 'racial democracy' in Brazil, Twine (1998, p. 66) uses white supremacy to convey the idea that "the predominance of Euro-Brazilians among the economic, political, religious, and social elite is taken for granted and thus not visible". In other words, the symbolic predominance of whites in positions of power, leadership and privilege is naturalised in the collective mindset and considered as the inevitable norm. Furthermore, Twine (1998, p. 136) adds that "joking is a socially acceptable way to articulate beliefs publicly and reproduce white supremacy and black inferiority". Again, the author employs white supremacy to express the oppositional dualistic aspect of Brazilian racism that praises whitening as a symbol of modernity and progress, in contrast to the backwardness attributed to black people. Vargas (2004), on his turn, advocates that white supremacy in Brazil embodies a system of beliefs that maintains white people's symbolic privileges unchallenged through neglecting racism's damaging effects on black people. As with Nogueira (2013, p. 24), the author explains that white supremacy is an "ideology stating that European descents and white skin people are superior to others, such as African and native indigenous".

Therefore, the use of white supremacy in this book has the aim to convey the idea of how racial hierarchies and privileges have been socially constructed in Brazil over time. It reflects the deep-seated colonial ideology of white people occupying the upper positions in the social and racial hierarchy. By contrast, any attempt from other racial groups aspiring to achieve such privileged positions is understood as a threat to the *status quo*. Such attempts, as this book addresses, are challenged and discredited by the dominant elite in such a way that the privileged positions remain immutable. Ultimately, in Brazil "the ideology of white racial supremacy blends with the threefold ideology: the myth of 'racial democracy', whitening ideology and prejudice of colour" (Nogueira, 2013, p. 25).

Chapter 2

Evolution of black Brazilian
resistance to racism

Introduction

Resistance to racism, or anti-racism efforts, is considered a form of political reaction fostered by oppressed people or social groups and is shaped and influenced by different social contexts where it is enacted (Solomos and Back, 1996). With that in mind, this chapter explores the evolution of the major forms of resistance fostered by black Brazilians in general but with magnifier lenses to highlight the role played by black women in this process. For this purpose, the reader is conducted through a historical journey spanning over 400 years but, to make it smoother, the chapter focuses on five major topics.

It starts with a debate about the ancient *Quilombo dos Palmares* in colonial Brazil and its male and female black leaders. Although these events belong to a distant past, the topic is very important to support the discussion of black resistance in Brazil. First, because up to the present day, it remains the strongest and utmost symbol of black resistance to racism and enslavement (both physical and ideological). Second, because without revisiting the history of *Quilombo dos Palmares*, and its iconic male leader Zumbi, it is not possible to fully understand, for instance, the symbolic meaning of 20 November as the Black Consciousness Day.

Subsequent to this topic, the chapter addresses the abolitionist movement in the late nineteenth century, which preceded the emancipation of the slaves two decades later. Still, in this same topic, the reader is introduced to the relevant debate addressing the female participation in the growing resistance against racism and captivity.

Evolving from this point, but also intertwined with the previous discussion, the third topic covers the important phenomenon of the emerging black press that contributed to give a voice for the oppressed black Brazilians. Besides, the topic also addresses the significant emergence of black women to the central stage of the initiatives to resisting to Brazilian ingrained racism. This foreground participation is evidenced by the growing number of NGOs (non-governmental organisations) established and led by black women since the 1950s but more strongly from the 1980s onwards.

In line with this reflection, the fourth topic aims to discuss the political significance of Afro hairstyle for the empowerment of black women and also as a symbolic tool to challenge hegemonic whitened beauty standards.

Finally, the fifth topic raises some of the most pressing challenges faced by the organised black movement in contemporary Brazil. It is certainly not an exhaustive and definitive discussion, but even so, it raises important reflections.

In complement to the aforementioned five topics, Figure 2.1 has the objective to provide the reader with a concise, yet useful, perspective of the major events discussed in the chapter and their relative position in a timeline. The expectation is that in combination with previous Figure 1.1 and Figure 1.3 it might help the reader to have a more comprehensive view of many important milestones in Brazil's history.

Figure 2.1: Timeline of important milestones in the black resistance

1600-1700	1700-1950	1950-1990	1990-2020
>1605: Establishment of *Quilombo dos Palmares*.	> 1871: Enactment of the Law Number 2,040 (Free-Womb Law).	> 1953-1963: Establishment of 09 black publications.	> 1990-1999: Establishment of 17 NGOs led by black women.
> 1605-1694: First black female warriors (Aqualtune and Dandara).	> 1885: Enactment of the Law Number 3,270 (Sexagenarian Law).	> 1964-1985: Military ruling in Brazil.	> 1991: IBGE adopts only five racial categories.
> 1694: Destruction of *Quilombo dos Palmares*.	> 1888: Emancipation of the slaves on 13 May.	> 1976: IBGE's survey identifies 135 self-declared racial terminologies.	> 2001: United Nations World Racial Congress (Durban, South Africa).
> 1695: Death of Zumbi dos Palmares on 20 November.	> 1889: Proclamation of the Republic on 15 November.	> 1978: Establishment of the second NGO led by black women.	> 2001-2005: Establishment of 09 NGOs led by black women.

	> 1890: Hymn of the Republic.	> 1980-1989: Establishment of 14 NGOs led by black women.	> 2003: Enactment of the law establishing the Crime of Racial Injury.
	> 1911: First Universal Race Congress (London, UK).	> 1988: Enactment of Brazil's new constitution.	> 2003: Establishment of SEPPIR.
	> 1915-1950: Establishment of 25 black publications.	> 1988: 100th Anniversary of the emancipation of the slaves.	> 2004-2010: Establishment of major social media platforms.
	> 1922: Modern Art Week (São Paulo).	> 1989: Enactment of the Law Number 7,716 (Crime of Racism).	> 2005: President Luiz Inácio Lula da Silva apologises for the enslavement (Senegal).
	> 1933: Publication of Gilberto Freyre's The Masters and the Slaves.		> 2010: Enactment of the Law Number 12,965 (*Marco Civil da Internet*).
	> 1950: Establishment of the first NGO led by black women.		> 2018: Change of political forces (from progressive to extreme far-right).

Quilombo dos Palmares

To address the evolution of the black resistance to racism in Brazil, it is inevitable (and even imperative) to review the role and the legacy of *Quilombo dos Palmares* and its leaders over time. After all, this was the first successful organised resistance movement in Brazil whose symbolic representation remains vivid and relevant to the organised black movement up to the present day. As previously addressed in Chapter 1, the working conditions in the cotton plantations and sugar mills were extremely harsh and abusive for the slaves.

With the aim to escaping the inhuman captivity and enslavement condition, at the beginning of the seventeenth century in the Northeast of Brazil, runaway slaves settled in a hilly forest area called *Palmares*, whose access was very difficult and, consequently, providing them with a natural defence against invaders (Chapman, 1918; Funari, 2003; Mello e Souza, 2006).

Quilombo[1] communities were scattered all across Brazil but, oftentimes, they did not last longer than two years. They represented a threat to the Portuguese ruling of the colony by encouraging and inspiring mass escape of slaves. Thus, among "the ten major *quilombos* in colonial Brazil, seven were destroyed within two years after being formed" (Kent, 1965, p. 162). Nevertheless, within this scenario, *Quilombo dos Palmares* was one of a kind, because it became the most well-known, the most successful in terms of resistance to the enslavement of black and indigenous peoples, and the long-lasting. On this aspect, the literature reveals that it might have lasted for almost a century, from 1605 to 1694 (Chapman, 1918; Lockhart and Schwartz, 1983; Funari, 2003). Besides, both Chapman (1918) and Funari (2003) reveal that between 10,000 and 20,000 people might have lived in the community. Regarding its structure, *Quilombo dos Palmares* might have been formed by nine small villages; each one having a local leader who elected the *quilombo* king (Chapman, 1918; Kent, 1965; Mello e Souza, 2006). And this leader "ruled with absolute authority during the term of his life" (Chapman, 1918, p. 30). Indeed, as explained by Mello e Souza (2006), this political structure in *Quilombo dos Palmares* emulated the organisation already present in tribal communities in Western Africa, and it was relatively analogous to the European concept of kingdoms.

Due to the lack of robust documented historical data, it is not possible to accurately list all the leaders who have ruled *Quilombo dos Palmers* over its almost century-long history. However, it is possible to identify that, surprisingly enough, one of them might have been a woman named Aqualtune, originally from Congo (Schwarz-Bart and Schwarz-Bart, 2001; Costa, 2016). It is also unknown for how long she ruled the community, but the literature reveals that her son, Ganga Zumba (meaning 'great lord') became her successor and he ruled up to his death in 1678. Since *quilombo* warriors used to invade farms to free slaves, in 1678 Ganga Zumba would have negotiated a peace treaty with the Portuguese governor of Pernambuco. But since not everyone in *Quilombo dos Palmares* supported such a deal, he might have been killed by poisoning by

---

[1] The word quilombo (or *ki-lombo* for some authors) is derived from *quimbundo*, as it was spoken in one of the dialects in Angola, whose meaning was camp, village, community, or shack (Gomes, 2019).

one of his political adversaries. He was then replaced by his nephew Zumbi (1655-1695), who was the son of Ganga Zona (Kent, 1965; Gomes, 2019).

Whilst *Quilombo dos Palmares* lasted for almost a century, for the Portuguese ruling, this was an undesirable alien community of rebels and runaway slaves that needed to be terminated (Kent, 1965). As a consequence, there were many expeditions during the seventeenth century against *Quilombo dos Palmares* until the successful one in 1694, which not only put an end in this community but also finished the tenure of Zumbi as the most iconic leader in its history (Kent, 1965; Lockhart and Schwartz, 1983; Funari, 2003; Mello e Souza, 2006). After the destruction of *Quilombo dos Palmares*, Zumbi managed to escape, and he was captured and killed on 20 November 1695 due to the betrayal of one of his followers. Moreover, since legends claimed that Zumbi was immortal, he was decapitated and had his head publicly exposed in Recife, first to put an end in this legend, and second, to intimidate other slaves from establishing new *quilombo* communities (Kent, 1965; Gomes, 2019). Nevertheless, what history books do not address is the account that Zumbi's wife, Dandara, likewise Aqualtune before her, might also have played a central role in *Quilombo dos Palmares* as a warrior (Santos, A. 2019). Actually, history books do not address Dandara due to a lack of concrete factual data about her, in such a way that Lopes (2014) classifies her as a 'legendary figure' and Araujo (2019) claims that she might have never existed. Thus, given the lack of documented evidence, her role as, possibly a pioneer black Brazilian woman resisting racism has rather been passed on through oral traditions, as explained by A. Santos (2019) which, still according to the author, deserves to be respected and seriously considered as a valid historical reference.

However, it cannot also be disregarded that the lack or scarcity of robust documented evidence about these pioneering black leaders (Aqualtune, Ganga Zumba, Zumbi and Dandara) should not be that surprising. First, *Quilombo dos Palmares* was destroyed by mercenaries and bush-captains[2] hired by the white settlers to terminate an alien state in the colony (Kent, 1965). Thus, it is expected that the winners would not have any interest in glorifying and/or portraying the defeated in light of their possible achievements and leadership roles. Second, even the battles to destroy *Quilombo dos Palmares* might not have happened exactly as depicted in history books because archaeological research conducted in the 1990s did not find remains of carbonized wood, weaponry or remains of human skeletons but rather a considerable array of pottery and other objects (Orser, 1992; Funari, 2003). Finally, it cannot also be

---

[2] Bush-captain (*capitão-do-mato*, in Portuguese) stands for the man in charge of capturing runaway slaves and bring them back to the slave owners, and oftentimes, they used sadistic and cruel technics to punish the rebel slaves (Moura, 2004).

forgotten that, as discussed in Chapter 1, in 1890 (just two years after the emancipation of the slaves) Ruy Barbosa demanded that many documents related to slave ownership be burned. Hence, whilst it might be possible that Dandara was rather a legendary figure, the lack of documented evidence might also be a consequence of this overall context.

But despite these mentioned aspects, on 20 November 1997 Zumbi dos Palmares had his name officially added to the 'Book of Heroes and Heroines of the Nation[3]', and on 24 April 2019, it was added Dandara dos Palmares in recognition for their historical role in fighting for justice, equality and freedom (Cardoso, 1996; Bolsonaro, 2019). Furthermore, although history has reserved a more prominent role to Zumbi dos Palmares as the ultimate symbol of black Brazilian resistance to racism, it is also important to rescue the memory of the legendary figures of Aqualtune and Dandara. The scarcity of more robust documented evidence about them might indeed be very difficult to overcome. Nonetheless, this does not offset their symbolical historical relevance and the inspiration that they might bring for the present and future generations of black women resisting Brazilian ingrained racism.

The abolitionist movement

Just like it is inevitable to revisit *Quilombo dos Palmares* to address resistance to racism in Brazil, the same logic applies to the abolitionist movement of the late nineteenth century. Whilst in Europe abolitionist ideals and debates had emerged from the eighteenth century, in Brazil, such discussions echoed much later; only in the 1870s (Telles, 1989). In effect, in a society that had lived on top of an institutionalised slavery regime for over three centuries, proposing emancipation debates were very challenging. The perspective of full, or even progressive, emancipation of slaves represented a considerable threat to the *status quo* and the established social order (Ferrari, 2016).

The literature also reveals that the major agents of social change in the abolitionist movement were five men: a) André Rebouças (engineer, 1838-1898), b) Joaquim Nabuco (politician, 1849-1910), c) José do Patrocínio (writer and journalist, 1853-1905), d) Luiz Gama (lawyer, 1830-1882), and e) Machado de Assis (writer, 1839-1908). Amongst these idealists, Joaquim Nabuco is usually considered one of the most important figures in the movement with immense contributions to the cause (Souza, 2018). However, as Alonso (2014, p. 117) advocates, Joaquim Nabuco might have received greater highlight in

---

[3] This book registers the names of historical figures honoured as national heroes/heroines and it is housed in the building *Panteão da Pátria e Liberdade 'Tancredo Neves'* in Brasília.

history literature probably due to "his parliamentary performance, and the wealthy of his personal archive". Although the abolitionist movement is considered to have started only from the 1870s onwards, this does not mean to say that other movements did not happen before this period. Indeed, Alonso (2014) has conducted extensive research in 35 newspapers of the nineteenth century and managed to discover a total of 1,446 anti-slavery demonstration events starting in 1868 up to 1888.

Having said that, in the abolitionist movement post the 1870s three particular events call our attention. First, in September 1871, the Law Number 2,040 was enacted. Known as 'Free-Womb Law' (*Lei do Ventre Livre*, in Portuguese), it established that the new-borns of enslaved women would be free from captivity (Baronov, 2000; Costa, 2013; Alonso, 2014). However, the trick aspect of this law is the fact that it allowed the slave-owners to retain the child's custody up to the age of eight. From that point, the slave-owners could either claim compensation from the government or use their 'services' up to the age of 21 (Souza, 2018). The second distinct event comprises the establishment of the Brazilian Society Against Slavery, in September 1880, by Joaquim Nabuco and André Rebouças. According to its manifesto, the objective was to strive for a country where "no one should be the property of somebody else, and that no nation should benefit from the tears and sufferings of the race who contributed to building it" (Nabuco *et al.*, 1880, p. 17). Finally, the third distinct event comprises the enactment of the Law Number 3,270 in September 1885, known as the 'Sexagenarian Law' (*Lei do Sexagenário*, in Portuguese); establishing that slaves over the age of 65 would be released (Baronov, 2000). However, once again, the law had been made to benefit the slave-owners, rather than to protect the oppressed blacks. The explanation for this argument is very simple. Due to the harsh working conditions that the slaves were subjected to, their life expectancy was oftentimes much lower than 40 years (Nogueira, 2011).

Although not all the aforementioned events were beneficial to the black slaves, combined they contribute to revealing the overall political scenario of the late eighteenth century in Brazil. On the one hand, the abolitionist movement was gaining ground with their demands for change in the centenary slavery regime. On the other hand, the elite pretended to give concessions to alleviate the burden of slavery but, in reality, they were implementing mechanisms to perpetuate their privileges. Therefore, the definitive emancipation of all slaves would take place only on 13 May 1888 with the enactment of the Imperial Law Number 3,353 known as 'Golden Law' (*Lei Áurea*, in Portuguese) signed by Princess Isabel (Baronov, 2000; Souza, 2018).

Female participation in the abolitionist movement

Having addressed some of the distinctive milestones in the abolitionist movement, it is interesting to observe that, once more, history has dedicated prominent roles mostly to male figures. However, Costa (2013) for example, is one of the few authors acknowledging the female presence in the abolitionist movement. The author explains that women "formed emancipationist and abolitionist associations, promoted charity sales of donated articles, and [...] organised conferences favouring the end of slavery" (Costa, 2013, p. 35). As for Telles (1989), two women deserve the appropriate attention and credit; the writers Maria Firmina dos Reis (1822-1917) and Narcisa Amália (1856-1924), due to their pioneering literary production challenging ingrained racist ideologies.

More controversial though is the role played by Princess Isabel as a female figure challenging racism. Although Souza (2018) defends that she represents an important social agent in the emancipation process, this standpoint is not shared within the organised black movement. In effect, since the 1970s the organised black movement disregards the 13 May (associated with Princess Isabel) as a symbolic date to represent resistance to racism. Instead of that, it has been adopted 20 November as the most meaningful date because it is the day that Zumbi dos Palmares was assassinated (Domingues, 2007; Alonso, 2014; Souza, 2018). Thus, since 2003, 20 November has been officially recognised as the Black Consciousness Day because, according to the organised black movement, Zumbi dos Palmares is alive, since the fight against racism is not over yet (Domingues, 2007; Gonzaga, 2019).

The emerging voice of black Brazilians

Despite the social marginalisation experienced by black Brazilians during the early years of the republic, many blacks established dozens of institutions (e.g. clubs and associations) to defend their rights, resist racism and challenge the pervasive impacts of the institutional discrimination (Domingues, 2007). They were scattered all across Brazil but according to a study conducted by E. Pinto (1993), the majority of them (123 in total) were based in São Paulo. Probably, this concentration was due to the industrialisation process experienced by São Paulo at the beginning of the twentieth century, as previously addressed in the topic about the Modern Art Week in Chapter 1. Within this scenario, what calls our attention, in particular, is the concomitant emergence of a black press; that is publications such as newspapers and magazines produced by and for black Brazilians (see Table 2.1). This phenomenon is important because it reveals that blacks were trying to make their voice heard, and also creating the means to provide a voice for the oppressed people. The topics covered in such publications encompassed, for example, advertisement of products targeted to black people such as cosmetics and hair treatment, demands for fairer opportunities in the job market, better educational opportunities, among others (Domingues, 2007; Trindade, 2008).

Table 2.1: List of black publications in the first half of the twentieth century

#	Publication name	City	Lifespan		
			Start	Finish	Months
1	Menelik	São Paulo	October 1915	January 1916	3
2	A Rua	São Paulo	February 1916	n.a.	---
3	O Xauter	São Paulo	May 1916	n.a.	---
4	O Bandeirante	São Paulo	September 1918	April 1919	7
5	O Alfinete	São Paulo	September 1918	November 1921	39
6	A Liberdade	São Paulo	July 1919	October 1920	15
7	A Sentinela	São Paulo	October 1920	n.a.	---
8	O Kosmos	São Paulo	August 1922	January 1925	29
9	Getulino	Campinas	August 1923	May 1926	33
10	Elite	São Paulo	January 1924	March 1924	2
11	O Clarim	São Paulo	January 1924	September 1940	203
12	Auriverde	São Paulo	April 1928	May 1928	1
13	O Patrocínio	Piracicaba	June 1928	November 1931	42
14	Progresso	São Paulo	June 1928	November 1931	42
15	Chibata	São Paulo	February 1932	March 1932	1
16	A Voz da Raça	São Paulo	March 1933	November 1937	56
17	Evolução	São Paulo	May 1933	n.a.	---
18	O Clarim	São Paulo	March 1935	n.a.	---
19	O Estímulo	São Paulo	May 1935	n.a.	---
20	Tribuna Negra	São Paulo	September 1935	n.a.	---

21	A Raça	Uberlândia	November 1935	December 1935	1
22	A Alvorada	Pelotas	April 1936	n.a.	---
23	Senzala	São Paulo	January 1946	February 1946	1
24	Quilombo	Rio de Janeiro	January 1950	n.a.	---
25	Mundo Novo	São Paulo	September 1950	n.a.	---
26	A Voz da Negritude	Niterói	October 1953	n.a.	---
27	Novo Horizonte	São Paulo	May 1946	n.a.	---
28	Notícias do Ébano	Santos	October 1957	n.a.	---
29	O Mutirão	São Paulo	May 1958	n.a.	---
30	Hifen	Campinas	February 1960	n.a.	---
31	Niger	São Paulo	July 1960	September 1960	2
32	Nosso Jornal	Piracicaba	Mays 1961	n.a.	---
33	O Baluarte	Campinas	June 1963	n.a.	---
34	Correio D'Ébano	Campinas	June 1963	n.a.	---

Source: Trindade (2008)

However, as Table 2.1 reveals, at the same time that many publications were established, many of them had a very short lifespan of just a couple of months. But others such as, for instance, *O Alfinete, Clarim, O Patrocínio, Progresso* e *A Voz da Raça* were in circulation for over three years each. Revisiting the literature that addresses this phenomenon of Brazilian black press, it was not possible to find solid evidence that could contribute to our understanding of why many publications had a short lifespan.

Notwithstanding this aspect, the emergence of the black press is an important phenomenon in the resistance movement against racism because, as aforementioned, these publications have contributed to give voice to the oppressed people who, otherwise in that social context, would not have other channels of mass communication. Furthermore, being able to articulate a discourse about oneself represents a relevant step towards the development and strengthening of one's self-esteem and ethnic identity. Actually, "one of the ways of exercising autonomy is having a discourse about oneself" (Souza, 1990, p. 17). In the subsequent decades of the twentieth century, the black press would continue in this movement of establishing new titles as reported by Domingues (2007). Again, some of them had a short lifespan whereas others lasted more. However, the important aspect to be highlighted is that these publications have left the legacy of proving voice for historically oppressed people.

The rise of black female resistance

Similar to what is observed in the abolitionist movement, in the organized black movement during the first half of the twentieth century, the literature has dedicated more prominent roles to male figures. But despite this dominance, Domingues (2007) reveals the establishment of two black women's associations in this period: *Sociedade de Socorros Mútuos Princesa do Sul* (1908) and *Sociedade Brinco das Princesas* (1925). Although they were the exception amongst the dozens of organisations established in that period, the same author also reveals that black women were also engaged in charity work, organising gala events and art festivals. In addition to that, R. Pinto (1993) brings to light the pioneering activism of Laudelina de Campos Melo (1904-1991), who established Brazil's first Association of Domestic Workers in 1936. Given the fact that, since colonial times up to the present day, domestic work is oftentimes performed by black women, her pioneering activism is highly representative.

Still, in the first half of the twentieth century, another important milestone encompasses the establishment of the National Black Women's Council in 1950 in Rio de Janeiro (Santos, S. 2009; Nova and Santos, 2013). Finally, another distinct black female social agent of this period comprises Carolina Maria de Jesus (1914-1977), due to the publication of the book Child of the Dark (*Quarto de Despejo*, in Portuguese) which has already been translated to 14 languages (Jesus, 1960). Although she was not exactly a social activist per se, her contribution is highly relevant because she describes in first person the difficult life of a socially marginalised black single-mother of three living in an urban shantytown in the mid-1950s.

Moving forward to the 1960s and 1970s, the context of Brazil under military ruling represented a significant challenge for the organised black movement. The strong military repression "demobilised the black leadership, throwing them into a type of semi-clandestinely political life" and, consequently, anti-racism public discussion was practically banned (Gonzalez and Hasenbalg, 1982, p. 30). The movement was repressed because the dominant ideology, influenced by the belief in the 'racial democracy', was that racism was not an issue in Brazil. Hence, according to this logic, the leaders of the organised black movement were raising a problem that Brazil did not have (Gonzalez and Hasenbalg, 1982; Trotta and Santos, 2012).

Consequently, only from the mid-1980s onwards it is possible to witness the re-emergence of the organised black movement in Brazil. This was due to the profound changes in the political scenario such as, for instance, the end of the military ruling in 1985 and the enactment of the new constitution in 1988 (Carneiro, 2003). Furthermore, also during this period, it is possible to observe a surge of NGOs established and led by black women. Whilst up to 1980 there were only two NGOs established by black women, from 1986 onwards there has been more than 40 (Santos, S. 2009). The determinant element in this process was the emergence of the feminist movement in Brazil that incorporated a racial dimension in its discourse and agenda. This approach gave origin to the expression 'blackening the feminism' (*enegrecendo o feminismo*, in Portuguese), which conveys black women's specific demands within the feminist movement (Carneiro, 2003).

Nonetheless, it is also important to bring to the surface the fact that despite the achievements reached by black women, this does not mean that they did not face big challenges as well, especially of misogynist nature. On this aspect, it is emblematic the statement made by male leadership of the black movement about the 1st National Encounter of Black Women in 1988. According to those men, the event was nothing more than a 'lesbians' encounter' (Santos, S. 2009). This sort of positioning not only reduces the relevance of their initiative but also reproduces a sexist discriminatory logic already present in Brazilian society that places black women in positions of inferiority. Thus, even within the organised black movement itself, sexism can get on the way and become an additional intersectional element amplifying the lived experiences of racism for black Brazilian women.

The political significance of Afro hairstyle

For many years, Afro hairstyle has been disqualified in Brazil (i.e. associated with a myriad of negative attributes) and, because of this process, many women did not easily accept their naturally curled hair. Instead of that, they usually desire to turn it straight and loose for a two-fold purpose: 1) escaping the negative attributes commonly associated with curly Afro hair and, 2) at the same time, getting closer or fitting within the hegemonic whitened beauty standard (Souza, 1990; Caldwell, 2003). Namely, in the Brazilian social context, not only skin colour and other physical features, such as lips and nose, can determine a person's position in the racial hierarchy, but also the hairstyle because it is an evident visible racial marker. Therefore, as an easily recognisable visible marker capable of assigning positive or negative belongings, men and women adopt different coping strategies to navigating within the racial hierarchy.

Non-white women try to straighten their hair to position themselves as close as possible within the dominant beauty standard. As with non-white men, it is not uncommon seeing them (especially prominent football players) passing as white by shaving their hair bald or dying the hair colour (Mendonça, 2009; Oliveira, 2018). This attitude represents an attempt to remove any visible trace of blackness to distance themselves from black heritage to become part of the dominant social group. To a certain extent, this move, resonates with the strategy adopted by many mulatto freedmen in colonial Brazil which, to avoid looking like the enslaved Africans before the scrutiny of society, they used to hide any trace of African origin in their documents (Conrad, 1983).

The prevailing Brazilian beauty standard imposes some intriguing challenges both for black and mixed-race women. First, the visible face of Brazilian national identity has been built on top of a whitening ideology that includes those who fit within the limited boundaries of the dominant characteristics, whilst subtly excluding the others. This process resembles what Ferreira (2002) coined as Brazilian silent racism, meaning that it is manifested in ways not easily noticed, given that many of its aspects are naturalised within the collective mindset. Moreover, the aesthetics norms represent another considerable challenge for non-white women split into two categories. On the one hand, "features such as skin colour, hair texture, and the shape and size of the nose and lips belong to the category of beauty" (Caldwell, 2003, p. 21). On the other hand, aspects such as "breasts, hips and buttocks are assigned to the sexual category" (Caldwell, 2003, p. 21). This scenario indicates that, in Brazil, the first category of attributes is positively depicted regarding white women, whilst for their black female counterparts, the same features are negatively portrayed. The origin of the negative associations is also found in the colonial society. It can be identified that Brazilian iconography used to depict black women in exaggerated proportions of certain aspects of their bodies (nose, lips and the buttocks), emphasising their ugliness in oppositional contrast to white female (Christo, 2009; Braga, 2011). As with the second category of sexual nature, over time it has been associated with mixed-race women, giving room to another type of national identity that praises the sensual permissiveness of a tropical carnival-like paradise, as previously discussed in Chapter 1 on the topic addressing national identity.

Nonetheless, despite this picture, there have also been many efforts and initiatives aimed at challenging this scenario and empowering black women. It can be observed, for instance, that prominent black female social activists, leaders of NGOs and opinion makers have taken ownership and assigned renewed meanings to *negro* as a meaningful and important racial terminology

(Oliveira, 2016; Tiraboschi et al., 2016). This move indicates that they are assuming a clear political positioning regarding their ethnic identity. As such, "one of the ways of exercising autonomy is having a discourse about oneself" (Souza, 1990, p. 17). Moreover, another important symbolic demonstration of how black Brazilian women have taken ownership of dominant perceptions of black beauty and transformed them into an empowering tool is through their hairstyle. For "black women and girls, identity is inextricably linked to their relationship to and presentation of their hair" (Johnson and Bankhead, 2014, p. 86); what contributes to bringing to the surface the importance of hairstyle not only as an element conveying femininity but also as a vehicle for expressing identity and belonging.

Thus, in conclusion, for black women, the Afro hairstyle has emerged as an important empowering element to escaping the challenging and complex intertwined web of variables composing Brazilian racism. Assuming their natural Afro hairstyle, in addition to attributing renewed meanings to *negro* as a distinct racial terminology, represents not only the assurance and self-recognition of the value of their beauty. It conveys their conscious political gesture and positioning. Indeed, "hair texture is regarded as one of the most important, visible signs of the socialaesthetic (sic) power of a woman and is related to culturally meaningful symbols of femininity" (Gordon, 2013, p. 212). Consequently, this political positioning contributes to challenging not only the hegemonic female beauty standard in Brazil, permeated by whitening ideology, but it also proposes a different national identity. It brings forward an Afro-Brazilian identity that rescues, or brings back to the surface, the ancient legacies of the African roots in the shaping of Brazilian society, however, renewed in meaning and symbology.

Contemporary achievements and challenges

The combination of the discussions developed in the previous four major topics of this chapter reveals the enduring resistance to Brazil's ingrained racism, alongside a selection of relevant agents of social change. Their ideals, perseverance, and struggles did not yet put an end to the phenomenon of racism, but they have played a decisive role in paving the way for many important achievements to black Brazilians as briefly mentioned in the Introduction. Within the array of achievements two, in particular, call our attention: a) the mandatory teaching of African history in public primary and secondary schools nationwide, and b) the establishment of affirmative actions in public universities.

Before addressing these two achievements, it is relevant to understand the overall social and political scenario where the debates about these subject matters has taken place. In April 2000 Brazil celebrated the 500th anniversary of its 'discovery' by Portugal, what also contributed to the emergence of debates and critical reflections about the legacies of colonialism in contemporary Brazil (Silva, K. 2003; Farias, 2018). In the international arena, in 2001 took place the UN World Conference on Racism in Durban, South Africa, whose reflections and discussions would inevitably reverberate in Brazil (UN, 2001; Htun, 2004; Martins *et al.*, 2004). In the early 2000s, Brazil was also experiencing a steady re-democratization process and a peaceful transition of power of elected presidents. Within that, in 2003, soon after his inauguration, Luiz Inácio Lula da Silva's administration implemented the social programme *Bolsa Família* to tackle hunger and extreme poverty (Fico, 2015). Moreover, in the same year, his administration established the Secretariat for Promotion of Racial Equality Policies (SEPPIR), whose aim is to tackle racial inequalities by proposing the implementation of several social policies and educational initiatives nationwide (Campos, 2003). Finally, in 2005, during an official visit to Senegal, president Luiz Inácio Lula da Silva apologised to the African peoples for their past forced enslavement. This symbolic gesture took place in front of the Door of no Return, where African people used to be shipped to the American continent in the sixteenth century (BBC, 2005; Cabral, 2005; Scolese, 2005; Gomes, 2019).

Far from aiming to bring a full and detailed chronology of Brazil's history in the 2000s, this sample of distinctive events contributes to our understanding that the overall scenario was more favourable to the organised black movement than, for example, during the military ruling. Thus, the debates that led to the implementation of the two aforementioned social policies found more fertile ground to flourish.

Mandatory teaching of African culture and history

The background regarding the research and teaching of African history in Brazil dates back to the early years of the twentieth century, however, the most important turning point in this field came only in the following century with the sanction of the law number 10,639 in January 2003 (Pereira, 2008). According to this regulation, the teaching of African history and culture, and their social evolution in Brazil over time became compulsory on primary and secondary education (Silva and Buarque, 2003; Pereira, 2008). The aim behind this regulation was to contribute towards tackling stigmas and negative stereotypes about black people and build a more inclusive ethnic identity that would not rely solely on their past slavery heritage.

With this in mind, according to the social anthropologist Pereira (2008), rather than a proactive benevolent governmental decision, the implementation of this law is resulting from the mobilization of the organised black movement, recent historical changes such as the new constitution proclaimed in 1988, and the democratization of the country in 1985. Nevertheless, this regulation has also imposed a big challenge to the country's primary and secondary educational system that Oliva (2003, p. 423) has skilfully addressed with an incisive questioning: "how is it possible to teach something we do not know?" What this author is addressing is the fact that Brazilians in general and teachers in particular, know very little about African history, culture, geography, traditions and so forth. Rosemberg *et al.* (2003) share a similar concern arguing that despite the important symbolic significance of the law number 10,639 it is possible to notice the lack of qualification of the teachers and also the low quality of the content of the textbooks. And on top of that, it is considered as being of greater concern identify that over a decade later that these authors raised these issues, the United Nations had still spotted the same inefficiencies as evidenced on its report released in September 2014 (Sheperd *et al.*, 2014).

The recurring flaws in the effective application of the regulation raise additional concern regarding the embedded discourses in textbooks and their implications towards the shaping of a more inclusive and diversified view of black people in these educational materials. In this context, Silva (1999) and Rosemberg *et al.* (2003) point out in their research that in social science and history textbooks the prevailing representation of black people is associated solely with slavery. In alignment with this argumentation, Oliva (2003) exemplifies that oftentimes history books build a simple equation where 'black = African = slave' and this idea, transmitted across different generations becomes internalized as a natural equation and influence people's perception and interpretations about black Brazilians. These aspects are relevant because textbooks represent a powerful vehicle for discourse dissemination, the building of ethnic and national identities and the recognition of people's value within a given social setting. Moreover, still regarding the flaws around the issue of greater egalitarian treatment of different ethnic groups in textbooks in Brazil, the United Nations has highlighted four distinctive gaps in this area: 1) lack of suitable training for teachers; 2) lack of relevant textbooks; 3) some evangelical sects contrary to the teaching of Afro-Brazilian cultural and religious traditions; and 4) resistance of some teachers in addressing Afro-Brazilian history and culture because they claim that it is irrelevant (Sheperd *et al.*, 2014). Hence, it becomes evident that textbooks keep conveying a discourse that not only reduces and fail to fully acknowledge the importance of black Brazilians in society, but they also contribute to perpetuating this limited portrayal in the collective mindset of current and future generations.

Affirmative actions

It has already been detailed addressed in Chapter 1 that in colonial Brazil, only the male sons of the Portuguese settlers were allowed to attend tertiary education (oftentimes in Portugal, since Brazil still did not have universities). Moreover, in the early years of the republic, whilst the government implemented a series of social policies to support the successful settling of European immigrants, black people did not receive any institutional support to integrate into better conditions in the emerging class society. Thus, this brief account contributes to providing an overall picture of the historical educational disadvantage that black people have been experiencing for a long time. Having said that, in the late 1990s started to take place the first debates towards the implementation of affirmative actions[4] to increase the participation of black people in higher education (especially in public institutions, since their educational quality is recognised as being better than the private ones). Then, from 2001 took place the first initiatives in a restricted number of public institutions before it could be expanded years later (Moehlecke, 2002; Martins *et al.*, 2004; Daflon *et al.*, 2013). However, this social policy has faced strong resistance from the very beginning in the early 2000s, first against its approval and implementation and, second, against its future expansion.

Within that, three manifestations call our attention. First, the publication of a book undersigned by many scholars and opinion-makers contrary to the implementation of this social policy (Fry *et al.*, 2007). Moreover, also in 2007, there was the publication of an emblematic news article in the influential weekly newsmagazine *Veja* where the authors openly challenged affirmative action policies. For this purpose, the authors criticise the admission process employed by the prestigious Universidade de Brasília, which relied on racial self-declaration as one of its admission criteria (Zakabi and Camargo, 2007). Finally, Brazil's best and most prestigious university, Universidade de São Paulo, has always opposed the idea of adopting affirmative actions on its courses, in such a way to become the last institution to adopt this policy just a few years ago (Lima, 2017; Ferreira, 2018). In general terms, the voices contrary to the adoption of this social policy advocated, for example, that rather than challenging racism, it would instead legally establish it (what is also considered as 'reverse racism' by some people). Moreover, there was also a belief that the adoption of this policy would affect the educational level since it would allow

---

[4] Although in Portuguese the equivalent terminology for affirmative action is *ação afirmativa*, it has become more popular the use of the word *cota* (quota). Thus, in the literature in Portuguese, both expressions are used to express the same concept.

the admittance of unprepared students. And finally, that this social policy is contrary to meritocracy values.

However, after almost a decade of the implementation of the first initiatives, the results are considerably positive. There has been an increase of black students in tertiary education, including, for instance, in medicine, whose standard student profile has always been strongly associated with white middle-class people (Santana, J. 2015). In line with that, between 2001 and 2011, the overall proportion of young black students (aged between 18 and 24 years) has increased from 10.2% to 35.8% (IBGE, 2012). Moreover, there is also data revealing that in the specific case of black girls, they have been improving their educational level considerably and engaging in a large array of qualified occupations (Artes and Ricoldi, 2015). Finally, concerning the educational quality (one of the biggest concerns raised by the opponents of affirmative actions), many studies reveal that the performance of *cotista*[5] students is not lower than that of the non-*cotista*, in some cases is even better and, overall, their successful graduation rate is usually higher (Bittencourt, 2017; Lagôa, 2018; Wainer and Melguizo, 2018; Cavalcanti *et al.*, 2019). In other words, the students admitted through affirmative action tend to give value to the opportunity, embracing it strongly, and making good use of it afterwards to improve their life prospects.

Current challenges

Moving forward towards more recent political scenario, it is possible to observe that despite all the relevant achievements reached by black Brazilians from the early 2000s, there are still considerable challenges ahead. Taking into consideration, for example, the shift of political forces from progressive towards the extreme far-right presidency, it can be noticed profound changes in discourses and approaches regarding Brazil's ingrained racism.

Starting from the 2018 presidential campaign, it calls our attention the promotion of the slogan 'Brazil is my colour' by the candidate Jair Bolsonaro. This sort of claim contributes towards the reinforcement of the irrelevance of debates about racism since it implies that 'we are all the same' and, consequently, racial inequalities might not be a relevant social issue (Trindade, 2018a). Indeed, before becoming a presidential candidate, Jair Bolsonaro was already well-known in Brazilian political scenario by a series of controversial statements about ethnic minorities, women, LBGT community, indigenous peoples, etc. (Child, 2018; Phillips, 2018).

---

[5] It stands for the beneficiary of affirmative actions.

But although the list of his controversial statements is immense, and most of the time he does not deny them, I think that in the context of the present book, is more relevant to analyse his discourses as elected president. First, because it brings more weight and greater repercussion given his symbolic position as an elected president and, second, because as the chief of the executive power, his discourses can indicate the direction the institutions under his command might follow. Having said that, calls our attention the statement that 'racism is a rare phenomenon in Brazil' (Alfonso, 2019; Tavae, 2019). Such claim clearly coalesces with the enduring denials of racism in Brazil fostered in the 1930s, the 'racial democracy' ideology, and the atmosphere during the military ruling that projected the image of a post-racial society, as previously addressed both in Chapter 1 and in the present chapter. By denying the existence of this social problem, the president indirectly delegitimises demands towards greater racial equality since, according to this standpoint, people would be raising an issue that does not exist (Trindade, 2018a).

However, to avoid the mistake of impersonating the critical analysis, lets us turn the lenses towards the institutions under Jair Bolsonaro's administration. Within that, two aspects, in particular, call our attention. First, different studies reveal that the violent death of the young black population (aged between 15 to 29 years) continues on the rise, what indicates that the Brazilian state is failing to protect this vulnerable social group (Brito, 2018; Silva, E. 2018). Moreover, this phenomenon also (in)directly offsets many other symbolic and practical achievements reached within the past decades by black Brazilians, since these youngsters are not living enough to experience them. On this aspect, recent data reveals that, on the one hand, over a ten-years' timeframe (2007-2017), the mortality rate of non-black young people have remained stable around 15 deaths per 100,000 inhabitants. On the other hand, for blacks, it has soared from 32 to 44 deaths per 100,000 inhabitants in the same period (Cerqueira *et al.*, 2019; Uneafro, 2019). What is more, according to other studies, this phenomenon is intertwined with the increase in police brutality over the past few years, taking into consideration that most of the victims of police shooting in poorer communities tend to be young black men (Souza, 2020). Not by chance, within this overall scenario, it has grown the movement *Vidas Negras Importam*, directly inspired by the US Black Lives Matter. Led by the organised black movement, and with the institutional support of organisations such as Amnesty International and the United Nations, the objective is to challenge the naturalisation of this enduring massive killing of black youngsters which has been coined as a sort of 'genocide of the black populace' (Anistia, 2017; UN, 2017).

Concerning the second major challenge, there are voices arguing that under this new administration, the Secretariat for the Promotion of Racial Equality Policies (SEPPIR) has experienced profound changes of qualified and experienced staff being made redundant, alongside changes in social policies that have affected the efficacy of prior initiatives to combat racism (Silva, E. 2018; Brandino, 2019). In line with that, influential black voices such as the former Human Rights Minister between 2015-2016, Nilma Lino Gomes, shows concerns with the current conservative approach that tends to reduce the importance of demands such as combating racism claiming that this sort of subject matter is simply a left-wing concern rather than a larger social issue (Fernandes and Martinelli, 2019). Actually, there are signs that, oftentimes, extreme far-right governments, such as in the case of Brazil nowadays, tend to adopt a binary standpoint that leaves vulnerable social groups (e.g. indigenous peoples, LGBT community, and ethnic minorities) unattended since their demands usually are not aligned with conservative values and, consequently, failing to leave room for reducing inequalities (Trindade, 2020b).

Thus, in conclusion, the overall scenario suggests that in addition to challenging Brazil's enduring ingrained racism, the organised black movement might find itself facing other equally difficult battlefronts. First, to endure efforts to maintain the important achievements reached over the past decades such as, for example, affirmative actions, since there are signs that it might be affected in the near future (Lempp, 2019; Heringer, 2020). Second, if the current political scenario does not present itself favourable enough for substantial new signs of progress towards greater racial equality, try at least to avoid considerable setbacks. And, finally, keep the efforts to revert the phenomenon of excessive killings of young black men, before it becomes so naturalised that the society does not find them surprising and/or alarming anymore.

Chapter 3

Race joking, social media
and the legal landscape

Introduction

Three major elements contribute to our understanding of the phenomenon of online racism in Brazil. First, over the years, the Brazilian derogatory laughter has been reproducing and reinforcing an oppositional duality between black and white people. Whilst blacks are oftentimes ridiculed and considered a source of mockery, whites are praised as smart and flawless. Moreover, the constant use of diminutives to express affection and short social distance allows the jokers to navigate as smoothly as possible; claiming that their humour is harmless and exempt from prejudice. Second, the proponents of racist ideologies have turned major social media platforms into a breeding ground for the dissemination of their values and beliefs and, besides, to connect with like-minded people. Within that, the third distinct element comprises the users' belief that online anonymity bestows them with implied permission to unleash different sorts of bigotry and without being held accountable for their attitudes.

Evolving from this reflection, analysing the growing emergence of online racism in Brazil naturally triggers questions concerning the country's anti-racism legal framework. What can be observed is that the deep-seated belief in the whitening ideology and 'racial democracy' has contributed to postponing over many decades the implementation of social policies aiming at tackling racism. Additionally, despite the recognised value of such policies, they contain legal loopholes that the proponents of racist ideologies take advantage. Finally, given that Facebook has become a breeding ground for construction and dissemination of online racism in Brazil, how does the corporation deal with it? What is their approach concerning this growing phenomenon?

Different studies reveal that the corporation has been employing both human and technological resources to remove inappropriate content (i.e. which violates its Community Standards). However, there are two important problems. First, many voices reveal that the corporation's response time to remove inappropriate content is considerably slow. Consequently, racist content circulates freely in the platform and reach a wide audience. Second, given the fact that their resources (personnel + algorithms) are unable to track all the content posted, the responsibility is transferred to the users' shoulders in identifying them and flagging as inappropriate to Facebook.

Disparagement humour: key concepts and debates

Disparagement humour (also called derogatory humour and race joking by some authors) is considered as "any form of humour that derogates or provides negative information about someone or something" (Janes and Olson, 2000, p. 474). As for Ford and Ferguson (2004, p. 79) "disparagement humour is humour that denigrates, belittles, or maligns a person or social group". Moreover, Weaver (2011b, p. 1) advocates that [racist] humour can "permit, legitimate and exonerates an insult". Thus, this type of humour conveys messages that disqualify and/or depreciate a particular social group, and its construction and dissemination encompass three social agents:

1. The jokers who construct and/or disseminate the derogatory messages, oftentimes, claiming that they are for amusement purpose only; what would indirectly grant them implicit permission to mock.

2. The subject or recipient of the joke who is left with the options to either endure the discourse as something natural and acceptable or challenge and deconstruct it, but with the risk of being discredited or considered to be taking things too seriously when they should not.

3. The audience, which can be one or more people witnessing the mockery and being exposed to that message which, in many occasions, endorses or finds amusement in the race joking.

Within these social agents, the jokers play an active role and their disparagement humour discourse poses a challenging circumstance to the subject of the mockery. There is evidence indicating that "in some societies, there is strong pressure for individuals to conform to jokes; individuals who negatively react to humour insults are told they 'can't take a joke'" (Sue and Golash-Boza, 2013, p. 1586). Moreover, "when jokers are challenged, they have the capacity to retreat into the defensive excuse 'I was only joking'" (Billig, 2001, p. 269). Finally, "the phrase 'only joking' presumes that words can be used without serious intent and that they are not intended to cause offense" (Howitt and Owusu-Bempah, 2005, p. 46). In effect, one of the strategies usually employed by people to deny racism is the "intention-denial [approach], saying, 'I did not mean that' or 'you got me wrong'" (van Dijk, 1992, p. 92).

Nevertheless, "humour is far from trivial" (Lockyer and Pickering, 2008, p. 809) and from the perspective of the recipient of race joking, it may not be as harmless or amusing as claimed by the jokers. In reality, the excuse of 'it is only a joke', also plays the role of silencing and discrediting the subjects of mockery whenever they manifest disagreements with it. Furthermore, the persistent dissemination of race joking can foster the acceptability or naturalisation of negative ethnic stereotypes by the audience as well as subtly, and skilfully, displaying and reinforcing an unbalanced system of power relations influenced by racist beliefs (Billig, 2001; Sue and Golash-Boza, 2013).

An important sociological study on humour was conducted by Stephenson (1951) where the author developed an examination of the conflict and control functions of humour in American society. The author has focused his analysis primarily on jokes addressing differences in social status, claiming that "such jokes function as control mechanisms expressing the common value system" shared by one social group regarding others (Stephenson, 1951, p. 569). What is also significant in this study is the contrasting stereotypes embedded in the jokes analysed. The author argues that characteristics perceived as negative or undesirable, such as laziness and stubbornness, are attributed, respectively, to black and Irish people, but not to the white American working man, even if they share the same social status.

Additionally, another distinct study aimed at bringing to the surface a broader perspective for the study of disparagement humour was developed by the sociologist Davies (1990), who conducted a comparative analysis of ethnic humour across 35 nations. The focus of the study was to investigate how different nations characterise ethnic groups (mainly immigrants, but not exclusively) concerning their attributed lack of cleverness and, in contrast, which peoples are characterised as wise. Interesting to highlight in this particular comparative analysis is the fact that the jokes convey a concealed message of contrasting privileged or unprivileged social positioning and sense of belonging in alignment with the ideas advocated by Stephenson (1951). Evidence of this perception is found in the argumentation that "the jokes thus indicate who is at the centre of a culture and who is at the edge" (Davies, 1990, p. 322), what is also observed in the dynamic found in the Brazilian racial hierarchy system as discussed in Chapter 1.

Whilst the construction and dissemination of disparagement humour towards ethnic minority groups it is not a new phenomenon, as evidenced in the literature, it can be identified that, in the recent past, these discourses have been increasingly conveyed on social media platforms, where they have found a breeding ground to be spread and transmitted to a variety of audiences (Trindade, 2018b). In effect, "while overt racist discourse has declined from public view since the civil rights era [in the US], it continues to reside in private contexts or has become coded and covert in public" (Pérez, 2017, p. 956). Moreover, it can be observed that "racist humour on the internet is not hard to find" (Weaver, 2011a, p. 417) and, on top of that, "the internet has developed as an unfettered site for the expression of racism, and its global reach allows for the spread and connection of racist ideologies" (Weaver, 2013, p. 484).

This trend of the online dissemination of race joking towards ethnic minority groups has been analysed under different perspectives such as messages conveyed through private e-mail (Boxman-Shabtai and Shifman, 2015), through specialized websites or blogs displaying derogatory jokes (Billig, 2001; Kuipers, 2002; Weaver, 2010; 2011a; 2013) and on social media platforms such as Orkut (Andrade, 2012) and Facebook (Laudone, 2010; Arango, 2013).

The review of these studies reveals that although they are focused on different online platforms, they share two common characteristics. First, the evidence that the online racist discourse replicates the dualistic ideology found in the offline environment, comprising the social inclusion of the dominant group in contrast to the marginalization or exclusion of 'the other'. However, it is oftentimes manifested more incisively and aggressively regarding the vocabulary used to convey the messages. The second common characteristic, which, actually, it is intertwined with the previous one, is the fact that they do not address the joker's belief in protection granted by their alleged anonymity. The relevance of this aspect lays in the fact that "studies have shown that people tend to disclose more information online than offline because they feel relatively safe and protected by the anonymity" (Denissen *et al.*, 2010, p. 572).

Consequently, this sense of protection and anonymity, combined with the so-called implicit permission to mock, contribute to explaining or understanding the harsher racist behaviour people express online. It means that they might feel safe and out of reach of the authorities to openly convey their ideologies and fearless of being caught or identified. Accordingly, if in ordinary face-to-face daily interactions, the jokers may refrain from the impulse to openly convey racist discourses due to social convention constraints; in the virtual environment, they might feel at ease to circumvent this boundary.

What makes race joking 'funny'?

An important question that must be brought to the surface is what makes race joking a laughable matter. To address this question, first, it is relevant to understand that jokes have the pleasurable effect of providing people with liberating moments of relief; what means without restraints enforced by the unconscious mind (Freud, 1963). Second, laughter arises predominantly from behavioural contrast, given humans' natural trend to behave spontaneously, involuntary or unexpectedly in moments of rigid behaviour would trigger laughter (Bergson, 1914). Then, whilst "rigidity is comic, laughter is its corrective" (Bergson, 1914, p. 9a). However, there are different points of view on this topic. Rather than assuming the possibility of identifying a structure of ideas characteristic of humour, "joke form rarely lies in the utterance alone, but it can be identified in the social situation" (Douglas, 1968, p. 363).

Nonetheless, despite Douglas' criticisms to Bergson and Freud, and the fact that none of the three authors answers directly what makes jokes funny, there are important clues in both Bergson's and Freud's studies that help us to address the question. Freud (1963), for instance, argues that jokes' pleasurable effects derive from aspects such as repetition and familiarity with the picture depicted in jokes. As for Bergson (1914, p. 5b), "laughter must answer certain requirements of life in common. It must have a social signification". In complement to this reflection, Douglas (1968) provides supporting clues in this direction highlighting the importance of the social context to give meaning to jokes.

Consequently, the mechanism of repetition is one of the core elements in making race joking 'funny' because it contributes towards the naturalisation, reinforcement and acceptance of the ridiculing portrayal of 'the other'. Furthermore, the social context where the race jokes are enacted and disseminated is equally important in this dynamic. It provides meaning and relevance to jokes that are easily recognised and decoded by people in that social setting (i.e. they become familiar, as argued by Freud). In effect, this argument coalesces with the idea advocated by Stephenson (1951) in the sense that jokes convey a certain dominant system of shared values. In other words, the jokers (and consequently, also their audience) find their disparagement humour 'funny' first because they are built on top of shared beliefs of contrasting dualities, such as superior *vs* inferior, core *vs* marginal, normal *vs* deviant, modern *vs* backward, beautiful *vs* ugly, and so forth. Second, because the repetition contributes to turning them into normal and acceptable verbal expressions; and, finally, the social context where they are enacted and disseminated provide shared meaning to them.

Characteristics of Brazilian race joking

It has become clear that the combination of repetition and the social context where disparagement humour is enacted encompass the core elements responsible for making race joking 'funny'. In line with that, it is important to understand the particular circumstances sustaining the Brazilian disparagement humour targeted at black people.

Race joking is not a new phenomenon in the Americas. In the early nineteenth-century-Cuba, blackface and comic performances were already present in that society (Lane, 2005). Moreover, before the emancipation of slaves in the US in 1863, "'blackface minstrel shows' were one of the prominent forms of humour in American society in which humour functioned to subordinate black Americans" (Pérez, 2013, p. 481). Nevertheless, in Brazil, the literature seems to reveal a picture slightly different. Fonseca (1994) suggests that, most probably, black Brazilians might have started to become the subject of mockery only after the emancipation of the slaves in 1888. The author claims that "jokes centred on black people were something practically non-existent in the slave society because they were considered merchandise, devoid of participation and competitiveness in society's power spheres" (Fonseca, 1994, p. 56). In effect, examining the work of many authors that have described the social life in colonial Brazil (e.g., Atkins, 1735; Koster, 1816; von Spix *et al.*, 1824; Debret, 1839; Ewbank, 1856; Agassiz, 1868), it is not possible to find accounts reporting jokes or situations of derogatory humour targeted towards black slaves. Instead, assertions tend to emphasize the objectified condition of black slaves. As addressed in Chapter 1, in 1816, a French cotton buyer claimed that slaves "were nothing but cattle" (Conrad, 1983, p. 63). Additionally, there is also evidence indicating that, in the colonial society, slaves were considered "an empty shell, utterly devoid of speech" (Camargo, 1988, p. 36). Thus, this picture suggests that as mere slaves, black people were not seen to represent a disturbing element in the established social structure. However, once they were emancipated, the balance was affected and, consequently, "the jokes have served the purpose to reposition the black people in 'their place', to produce a tacit collective fantasy that restores societal order and the distinct places for blacks and whites" (Dahia, 2008, p. 712).

Evolving from this point, there is an important Brazilian cultural trait that influences everyday social interactions and intertwines with the informal nature of humorous discourses. It is called *jeitinho* (knack, artifice), and the concept was introduced by the Brazilian anthropologist DaMatta (1986). *Jeitinho* then, as a form of social navigation, means first that people somehow find creative ways to overcome a situation that initially seemed devoid of solution. That is to say that *jeitinho* is strongly related to flexibility, improvisation, and circumvent social conventions (Vieira *et al.*, 1982; Motta and Alcadipani, 1999). Second, *jeitinho* is also related to personalising everyday social interactions, shortening formal distances or hierarchies to achieve a goal or to obtain some degree of personal advantage (DaMatta, 1986; Rega, 2000). Within that, a common verbal manifestation of this phenomenon in everyday social interaction is the frequent use of the diminutive form (adding the suffix *inho* to many verbs, nouns and names) to convey affection, emotion or social proximity. In line with that, rather than addressing someone as *preto* or *negro*, the use of the diminutive form (*pretinho* or *neguinho*) tends to lessen the impact of the racial terminology (Goldstein, 2003).

Consequently, *jeitinho* and the frequent use of the diminutive form encompass influential elements in the process of creating depreciative discourses embedded in race joking, since they provide a convenient social navigation strategy for jokers. Thus, if an attitude such as reciting racist jokes is challenged by the subject of mockery, the jokers oftentimes claim that their humour represents nothing but harmless jests (*brincadeirinha* in Portuguese) or simple expressions of affection. That is, they skilfully dodge from complaints and avoid being held accountable for their attitude.

As such, a successful Brazilian TV comedy programme that conveyed a stereotypical representation of black people was *Os Trapalhões* (The Clumsy), which was aired from 1966 to 1997. One of its four comic characters was a black man called *Mussum*, who always spoke Portuguese incorrectly, he was portrayed as uneducated, lazy, untidy, an alcoholic, and a *samba* singer. In contrast, the white leader of the group (named *Didi Mocó*) was depicted as the smartest of the four; with the other two characters also being white men (Travaglia, 1989; D'Oliveira and Vergueiro, 2011). To a certain extent, *Mussum* strongly resembles *Memín Pinguín* in Mexican comics and the Peruvian *Negro Mama*, who is "from humble origins; and his lack of social and intellectual acumen is highlighted for the purpose of humour" (Sue and Golash-Boza, 2013, p. 1583). This particular form of show is highly symbolic in the context of race joking in Brazil, first, due to its longevity of more than 30 years. Second, due to its strong influence on the subsequent generations of Brazilian humourists, reinforcing their continued tendency to employ such stereotyped portrayals of black people. Finally, the way it used to depict black people has contributed to naturalize such representations in the collective mindset, especially for young people.

In a press interview a few years ago, the leader of this group of humourists (Renato Aragão, who played the character *Didi Mocó*), was questioned about the sort of jokes he used to make towards *Mussum*, and he expressed his view on the topic.

> "Back then, we did that as a playful joke. It was a kind of circus jest between *Mussum* and I. We were sort of two children fooling around. There was no intention to offend anyone. People did not get offended because they knew the jokes were harmless" (Jorge, 2015, p. 12).

Nevertheless, there are many opposing voices claiming that, in reality, blacks were offended by the jokes conveyed in *Os Trapalhões*. However, since they did not have a voice, they were unable to stop such jokes from being openly recited for several years (Czech, 2015). Besides, the discourse of this leading figure in the country's comedy scene, with a career spanning for more than 50 years, has helped to convey the convenient and common claim made by jokers that their humour message is meant only to entertain (Billig, 2001; Howitt and Owusu-Bempah, 2005; Sue and Golash-Boza, 2013). In effect, the protective shield of 'it is just a joke' adopted by the jokers transfers responsibility to the subject of the mockery, implying that they lack a sense of humour and are unable to appreciate the supposed absence of offensiveness or depreciative portrayal (Howitt and Owusu-Bempah, 2005). Hence, both the joker and the audience "implicitly accept the stereotyped assumptions about the nature of the other" (Billig, 2001, p. 277).

Social media and the emergence of racist discourses

In the early stages of the internet, many voices advocated that this technology would be a colour-blind environment and a virtual space that would allow people to escape race, racism, sexism, class inequalities, xenophobia, and racial inequality (Turkle, 1995; Rheingold, 2000; Lévy, 2001; Poster, 2001; Hansen, 2006). One of these authors advocated that "by suspending the automatic ascription of racial signifiers according to visible traits, online environment can, in a certain sense, be said to subject everyone to what I shall call a 'zero degree' of racial difference" (Hansen, 2006, p. 141). Nevertheless, Daniels (2009, p. 17) strongly disagrees with this argumentation and says that this belief is nothing but a "pervasive myth". In a subsequent study, Daniels (2013) complements her disagreement explaining that one of the flaws in the colour-blind argument is that it relied on a text-only internet that no longer exists. In effect, what Daniels (2009) advocates is that with the technological evolution, the internet has become a breeding ground for the awakening of 'cyber racism', or what she calls, 'white supremacy online'. It means that "white supremacy online exploits uniquely web-based mechanisms to undermine civil rights and values of racial equality with overtly racist and anti-Semitic speech" (Daniels, 2009, p. 20).

In line with this standpoint, Kettrey and Laster (2014) argue that the internet is not a colour-blind territory but rather the space where both race and racism are markedly significant. In complement, the authors also say that "the web is a white space that grants easier access and greater power to white users than users of colour" (Kettrey and Laster, 2014, p. 257). Their understanding is that, in the US social context, whites' greater economic and cultural capital than that of Afro-American's equip them to have increased access to the internet. Consequently, whites have greater symbolic power and privileges in the online environment, and also disseminate and enforce their views, values, and beliefs about themselves and 'the others'. Another interesting line of research challenging racial blindness encompasses studies exploring the ubiquitous search engines such as Google. On this regard, Noble (2018) argues that, contrary to what is published, powerful and influential search engines do not offer an egalitarian field for the dissemination of different forms of ideas, identities and activities. In fact, complements the author, discrimination is a very real problem. The combination of private interests in promoting certain websites, as well as the monopolising status of a small number of search engines, leads to a set of biased search results that favour whiteness over blackness, and in particular disadvantaging black women. In line with this reflection, Silva (2019) defends the concept of 'algorithmic racism'. According to the author, this construct is defined as interfaces and automated systems, such as social media platforms, which can not only reinforce but also hide racist dynamics of the societies where they are employed and widely disseminated.

Having said that, in the Brazilian social context, there is data in alignment with the picture just described, revealing that whites have twice as much access to the internet as blacks, contributing to their greater symbolic power and privileges concerning the use of this modern technology (Waiselfisz, 2007). Besides, in a more recent study addressing racial inequalities in Brazil and Colombia, Roshani (2016) reveals that Afro-descendant youth in both countries experience great information asymmetry given that their white counterparts have the privilege of a greater online presence.

In its initial stages, the internet did not offer too many possibilities or technical capabilities for any type of interaction amongst its users. This configuration has been called text-only internet, web 1.0 or one-to-one communication (boyd, 2015; Fleming and Morris, 2015). However, in the early 2000s emerged the so-called web 2.0 (also called by some authors as many-to-many communication) enabling enhanced communication possibilities, varied forms of interaction between groups of people, collaborations and dynamic networks amongst users (Fuchs, 2008; Castells, 2010). Consequently, Facebook, Instagram, Orkut, Twitter, YouTube and alike became viable enterprises due to this shift in the broad technological scenario, since they rely on massive networking capabilities amongst their users. In effect, not by chance, these major social media platforms were established between 2004 and 2010 (Trindade, 2020a). This new technological scenario enabled users to construct and disseminate not only text but also images, audio and video content amongst a wide audience.

However, there is evidence indicating that concomitant with the emergence of the major social media platforms during this timeframe hate speech has also increased considerably in different societies. Within that, it is possible to observe that 2012 represents an important milestone regarding the phenomenon of online hate speech. It is the year that Facebook reached one billion active monthly users and, since then, online hate speech has become a highly frequent subject matter across several media outlets globally (Trindade, 2020a). The worrisome consequence of this picture is the possible consolidation of a new 'world order' where hate speech becomes a natural component of the digital landscape and also in people's daily lives.

The influence of social media in the shaping of social relations

In June 2013 erupted in Brazil a series of massive street demonstrations in several cities across the country (Mattos, 2013; Winter, 2013; Quaresma, 2014). Briefly, what has triggered the protests that mobilized millions of ordinary citizens to the streets were demands such as to end corruption scandals, against police brutality, in favour of improved public services, as well as in opposition to the huge public expenditure to host FIFA's World Cup in 2014 and the Summer Olympic Games in 2016 (Mattos, 2013; Watts, 2013). Within this context, there was a vital element enabling the mobilization in ways, in magnitude and speed not previously seen in Brazil's political history: social media platforms; especially Facebook and Twitter (Stauffer, 2013; Holston, 2014).

However, at the same time that social media enabled people to organise the demonstrations without the leadership of any established political party, it has also revealed people's need to express that they wanted their voice to be heard beyond the social media realm. On the one hand, technology has empowered people in such a way that they no longer needed an individual leader telling them what to do or where to go. In effect, they were mostly led by common goals and ideologies, rather than a particular person or any evident organised social group at the foreground. This innovative configuration of social movement was so unique and unusual that the federal government did not know how to relate to them since there was not a central leading figure with whom to talk or negotiate. Moreover, technology has also enabled them to find and establish connections with a large audience of like-minded people and, together, they have composed a new type of unity advocating shared ideologies and beliefs.

On the other hand, that context also revealed that people were actively sharing their street engagement on social media, and uploading content in real-time (e.g. pictures, videos, audios, memes and text messages). This move demonstrates that social media represented an important arena to legitimise and reverberate their cause. Furthermore, sharing their participation online also played the important symbolic role of 'recruiting' and engaging additional like-minded people to come out of the virtual environment and join them on the streets. In other words, the online environment contributed towards creating the conditions for offline demonstrations, while the latter returned online, feeding it back in an almost endless and growing looping movement.

An emblematic image illustrating this phenomenon encompasses placards bearing messages such as 'we have come out of Facebook' and 'come to the streets', held by many protesters (Assis, 2013; Holston, 2014). This singular aspect was captured by the lenses of different photojournalists and caught the attention of Brazil's mainstream media organisations. In effect, the phenomenon can be characterised as a type of two-way road (Silva and Silva,

2015). Namely, online and offline 'worlds' are constantly intersecting and overlapping, in such a way that people's voices were amplified and reverberated in both arenas (social media and the streets). In other words, one contributed towards the reinforcement of the other. The people mobilised online to go to the streets and speak up their mind against the *status quo*, while their demonstrations also fed social media posts in real-time in an attempt to increase the relevance and legitimacy of their demands. Thus, this event contributes to demonstrating that online and offline 'worlds' are not dissociated from each other, and they compose a complex and dynamic intertwined reality (Daniels, 2013; Silva and Silva, 2015).

Nonetheless, at the same time that major social media platforms have given voice to people demand social change in Brazil and other social contexts, they have also become powerful tools for the enactment of hate speech. Different studies contribute to support this argument. In the Australian social context, for example, Jane (2017) has explored the dissemination of strong misogynistic discourses more broadly over the internet, but also across Facebook and Twitter. Arango (2013) has developed a critical discourse analysis of racist comments on Facebook and Twitter triggered by a post made by a mainstream magazine bearing an unbalanced social representation of black Colombians. Finally, Laudone (2010) has developed a qualitative study aimed at exploring the extent and the ways in which racism, racial meanings and messages are conveyed on Facebook in the US social context.

Regarding the Brazilian social context, there is a comprehensive quantitative study addressing different forms of bigotry and racism across Facebook, Instagram and Twitter (Pereira *et al.*, 2016). This study monitored social media in Brazil from April to June 2016 and managed to capture 32,376 mentions of racial terminologies, being 97.6% of them employed negatively to expressing bigotry, prejudice or discrimination towards black people.

Consequently, these studies reveal that social media has become a breeding ground for people to distil all sorts of racist discourses targeted towards certain social groups. The technology has provided them with the capability to not only constructing such discourses but also disseminate them to a wider audience. In other words, social media enables like-minded people to connect among themselves composing a new type of unity that disseminates their shared ideologies, beliefs, and values through the platform. Within this context, "social media platforms not only reproduce but also allow the emergence of new discourses, new ways of expressing discriminatory ideas supported by colonial thinking" (Arango, 2013, p. 637). Additionally, major social media platforms have enabled the amplification of latent hate speech in Brazilian society. Actually, "when people post or share hate speech on social media, they are simply reinforcing and reaffirming an ingrained prejudice towards the target subject" (Pereira *et al.*, 2016, p. 8). This picture also reveals that people's attitude online is not completely detached from the offline environment, in such a way that their values and beliefs are also mirrored or replicated on social media (Daniels, 2013). Finally, "race matters in cyberspace precisely because all of us who spend time online are already shaped by the ways in which race matter offline, and we cannot help bring our own knowledge, experiences, and values with us when we log on" (Kolko *et al.*, 2000, p. 5).

Racist ideologies empowered by online anonymity

With more than 2.1 billion users worldwide, Facebook is currently the world's leading and ubiquitous social media platform (Kemp, 2019), and creating an account is very simple, straightforward and free of charge. The only requirements are that users be above 13 years old and provide some basic personal information (e.g. name, date of birth, gender and a valid e-mail address), and create a password (Caers *et al.*, 2013). However, no technical barriers prevent a user from setting up an account with an alias or pseudonym rather than their real identification to remain anonymous in their communication (Halfeld, 2013). Moreover, it is not difficult to find online tutorials explaining step-by-step how to set up anonymous or even fake accounts[1]. Having said that, anonymity is understood as "a condition where the sender or source of information is absent or not identifiable" (Misoch, 2015, p. 536). Whilst it can have a clear, well-defined and justifiable purpose, it can also open up an avenue for a myriad of questionable aims such as the enactment of hate speech (Kling *et al.*, 1999).

The technological evolution of the internet, from text-only to a more dynamic and interactive virtual space, has enabled online anonymity being used to masquerade attitudes that the person not necessarily would take in an ordinary offline social setting. On this regard, Hughey and Daniels (2013) present an interesting study addressing online versions of a range of US newspapers[2] in the early 2000s that had started to allow the readers to add comments in some of their news and articles. The strategy behind this move was an attempt to engage the readers with the available content and to attract new ones that, eventually, could become paid subscribers. However, what the newspapers' editors did not envision, and were unprepared to deal with, was the rise of slurs and racist comments, even when the news did not correlate with racial issues. In this particular study, the authors were interested in investigating the racist

---

[1] To support this claim, I have conducted a search on Google in March 2020 and found over 147 million results related to this topic.
[2] Boston Globe, Buffalo News, Raleigh News & Observer, Reuters, San Diego Union Tribute, The New York Times, The Wall Street Journal, and USA Today.

language only and, consequently, it is not possible to understand whether the news has also triggered other types of comments such as misogynist, xenophobic and so on. However, given the fact that online newspapers allowed anonymous comments, many people had conveniently hidden behind this feature to conveying their rude comments fearless of any social convention constraints or being blocked by the newspapers. Thus, online anonymity can act as a convenient shield 'protecting' (or preventing) the people from being identified right away and allowing them to speak their minds without any type of restraints (Younge, 2012; Pereira *et al.*, 2016).

This type of behaviour coalesces with Philp G. Zimbardo's 'Theory of Deindividuation', which states that "under anonymous conditions, people lose, or give up, their sense of self and their adherence to norms and expectations of others, whereby their behaviour becomes intensely emotional, impulsive, irrational – that is, unrestrained" (Malmqvist, 2015, p. 735). Nevertheless, "people have a false illusion that they can speak whatever they want [online] because there is no legal consequence. It is a wrong assumption because it is perfectly possible to go after them" if necessary (Rodrigues, 2015, p. 3). Moreover, "it is important for people to be aware that the internet is not a sea of impunity. Oftentimes users get behind the computer screen, log on with an alias and think that they cannot be reached; and that is a big mistake because the authorities can indeed reach them" to enforce the rule of law (Soares, W. 2016, p. 2).

Understanding Facebook's approach to racist content

In addition to the debates regarding the role played by social media platforms in the dissemination of racist discourses, there is another relevant reflection to be made, and usually not addressed in the literature. It is related to the approach adopted by the corporation Facebook concerning the dissemination of racist posts on its social media platform. Given the fact that, to date, Facebook represents the most successful social media platform (owner also of Instagram and WhatsApp), the positioning adopted by them is considerably relevant to understanding corporations' approach towards this phenomenon.

There is data revealing that Facebook employs a global workforce of 7,500 people exclusively dedicated to moderating content posted on its platform and removing anything considered inappropriate (Koebler and Cox, 2018; Lagorio-Chafkin, 2018; Madrigal, 2018). Nevertheless, not long ago, this global workforce amounted to 4,500 people worldwide (Chaykowski, 2017; Kuchler, 2017). Thus, the corporation's decision to increase this dedicated workforce by almost 67% in the past few years sends some signs to society. First, the corporation recognises the growing trend in the dissemination of inappropriate content on its platform. Second, because the increase may have been the result of pressures made by the civil society and policymakers in different countries, rather than a spontaneous initiative (Balmer, 2017; BBC, 2017; Valenti, 2017; Boffey, 2018; Hogan, 2018). Moreover, given the fact that 1.3 million posts in multiple languages are shared every minute on the platform, it makes the task for the 7,500 content moderators highly challenging; and they are left with something such as just 10 seconds to make a decision (Hopkins, 2017).

Hence, the inappropriate content to be reviewed by the team of content moderators is either flagged by users or automatically captured by powerful algorithms (Solon, 2017). This picture reveals that, indeed, the moderating process comprehends a shared responsibility approach. On the one hand, the corporation provides a large team of content moderators, combined with its powerful algorithms for tracking the content posted by its users. On the other hand, Facebook also relies on its users to flag what is potentially inappropriate and which, eventually, may not have been spotted by its internal mechanisms.

Regarding the removal of inappropriate content, in 2011 in the US, Facebook has rejected blocking groups disseminating messages denying the horrors of the Holocaust and claiming that it did not exist. The argument used in support of the rejection was that refusing to take down the content "allows people to see that the sites' proponents are stupid" (Citron and Norton, 2011, p. 1475). However, the corporation missed the opportunity to build constructive counter-narratives to combat hate speech.

In the Brazilian context, there are not too many publicly known cases of racist content flagged by users as inappropriate and removed by the corporation. In one of them, the context encompassed a humorous post published in 2013 using a picture of the movie 'Rise of the Planet of the Apes' to mocking of affirmative action initiatives in Brazilian public universities. Facebook's response to the claimant was that the post did not violate its 'Community Standards' on bullying and harassment (G1, 2013). The second case took place in 2015 when many users complained across different Facebook communities about a specific page conveying several depreciative comments about dating black women (Araujo, 2015). It took around 10 days for Facebook respond to the users' demand and take the effective action to block the page for violating its 'Community Standards'. However, in a matter of a few days afterwards, the administrator in charge of that community created new pages with different names but displaying the same content that had been previously blocked (Araújo, T. 2015; Romão, 2015). Hence, these examples contribute to revealing that the corporation's response lacks agility and that there are loopholes where people engaged in bigotry can take advantage.

Actually, the cases discussed also represent important elements evidencing the complexity and, oftentimes, not so clear and straightforward guidelines concerning the corporation's policies to tackling inappropriate content. The guidelines provided by Facebook to its users are regarded as very simplistic and they do leave room for doubts (Hopkins, 2017). In contrast, the corporation's internal manuals, although much more robust, also make the work of its thousands of content moderators very difficult and highly stressful (Hopkins, 2017; Solon, 2017). In line with that, the analysis of the corporation's 'Community Standards'[3] reveals some intriguing aspects. The document says that "Facebook removes hate speech, which includes content that directly attacks people based on their: race; ethnicity; national origin; religious affiliation; sexual orientation; sex; gender or gender identity; or serious disabilities or diseases" (Help, 2017, p. 2). However, the policy continues, people are allowed to use the social media platform "to challenge ideas, institutions and practices" (Help, 2017, p.2). Within this process, they can also use "humour, satire or social commentary related to the topics" (Help, 2017, p. 3). In the last paragraph of the policy, the corporation says that "while we work hard to remove hate speech, we also give you tools to avoid distasteful or offensive content" (Help, 2017, p. 3).

Thus, the corporation has put in place considerable resources to tackling inappropriate content (both human and technological resources). Nevertheless, it has transferred a great deal of responsibility to its users' shoulders. They are left with the options of either flag what they consider inappropriate or using functionalities to avoid being exposed to this type of content. However, the downside is that this last approach does not prevent any person from potentially being the subject of mockery and/or discrimination somewhere across the social media platform, even if they block content with such characteristics. In other words, people can, eventually, chose to block being exposed to discriminatory content but, if they are the subject of the bigotry, their image will still be circulating across the platform.

Furthermore, the corporation faces a huge identity dilemma because, to date, it is unclear whether it is a technology company or a media organization. Consequently, navigating over this grey area opens room for people posting content that, potentially, can be harmful and distasteful to certain social groups. However, posing as a technology company, Facebook does not consider that they have any responsibility regarding what people post. They argue that they are just providing a tool for people to engage with each other across a network. On the other hand, as a media corporation, they would be held accountable for what is published, and have to comply with certain clearer

---

[3] The policy is the same globally. It is translated from English to the local language and it is a three-pages long document available online at Facebook's Help Centre.

editorial guidelines and much tighter government regulations (Ingram, 2016; Castillo, 2018; Kelly, 2018; Collins *et al.*, 2019).

Overview of the Brazilian anti-racism legal landscape

The analysis of studies addressing the construction and dissemination of racist discourses in the online environment triggers some natural questions: a) what the legal boundaries in Brazil are concerning racial insults; b) how effective are the policies in place aimed at tackling racist attitudes both online and offline. They are relevant because they evidence a contrasting picture. Namely, despite the existence of several social policies, there is data revealing the growing trend of reported cases of online racism in Brazil (Pereira *et al.*, 2016; Angioleto, 2017; Boehm, 2018; Tavares, 2018; Trindade, 2018b). Consequently, this picture indicates that there must be some loopholes in the legal framework where the proponents of racist ideologies potentially take advantage.

Regarding the institutional combat to racism in Brazil, it is relatively recent and four major milestones evidence this fact:

1. The enactment of the Law number 7,716 in 1989, establishing the 'crime of racism',

2. In 2003 the senate approved to update a paragraph in the 1940s Penal Code including the 'crime of racial injury',

3. Also, in 2003, the national 'Secretariat for the Promotion of Racial Equality Policies' was established,

4. After over 10 years of parliamentary debates, in 2010 the Federal Law number 12,288 known as 'Statute of Racial Equality' was enacted.

On the one hand, the establishment of these distinctive milestones represents substantial institutional-level improvements towards tackling the enduring racial inequalities in Brazil. However, on the other hand, they also make apparent the long delay for their implementation, taking into account the emancipation of slaves in 1888, and the historical negative legacy of 3.5 centuries of enslavement of African people. Moreover, as addressed in Chapter 1, few years after the emancipation of slaves, the government had put in place social policies to foster white European immigration, whereas none was implemented to support the integration of blacks into the emerging class society. In reality, the aforementioned distinctive milestones are mostly the result of demands of the black movement over many decades, rather than spontaneous government initiatives (Domingues, 2007; Gomes and Santos, 2016).

Nonetheless, despite their unquestionable value and symbolic relevance, it is also possible to observe that when it comes to the enforcement of these laws, they do not seem to be as effective as society expected them to be. Namely, certain voices claim that racism is almost a 'perfect crime' in Brazil, since the perpetrators are seldom punished and when it happens the punishment is considered to be mild (Neto and Lettry, 2013; Pacheco *et al.*, 2016). Briefly, what has been advocated is that anti-racism laws are important to combat the discrimination against black Brazilians, but they are not enough given that, oftentimes, there are no punishments to offenders, and to a certain extent, there is a natural acceptance concerning the subtle racist discourses in Brazilian society.

It cannot be disregarded the possibility that the criticisms might reflect more people's perceptions than objective facts regarding the Brazilian anti-racism legal landscape. But, based on an independent international report called 'Rule of Law Index', it is possible to notice that, objectively speaking, the judicial system in Brazil is, actually, lagging behind in many aspects. The mentioned report analysed data from 113 countries according to eight factors: 1) constraints on government powers, 2) absence of corruption, 3) open government, 4) fundamental rights, 5) order & security, 6) regulatory enforcement, 7) civil justice, and 8) criminal justice. The country's overall ranking is the 52nd place and concerning specifically these eight factors, the one closely related to racism fits into 'the fundamental rights' category. This factor measures the protection of fundamental human rights, including the elimination of discrimination and racism, and the position Brazil has achieved on this factor is also the 52nd place (Botero *et al.*, 2016). This data contributes to illustrating the long road ahead towards achieving greater racial equality and enhanced defence of basic rights. Besides, it also contributes to the understanding that, indeed, the negative perceptions raised by different opinion-makers in Brazil is aligned with the findings of this independent international report.

Thus, two distinctive relevant aspects can potentially influence society's perception of the high level of impunity regarding racist practices, and consequent negative views of the legal system. Firstly, people with greater economic capital may benefit from legal loopholes not available to ordinary citizens and, secondly, that the judicial system is considered to be over-complex and sluggish in its decision process. Within this context, it is considered that "in Brazil, the law is strict and punitive against some people, in particular, the most deprived; whilst for others more influential and affluent it is lenient. It all depends on who the defendant is" (Junges, 2011, p. 3). Moreover, there is also the understanding that "people are treated differently according to their social position, skin colour and financial status. The combination of these aspects plays an enormous role in the judicial system and especially regarding impunity" (Zampier, 2013, p. 1).

A reflex of this differentiated treatment according to the person's class positioning or social influence, can be observed in many cases of racism on social media. Oftentimes when the victim is a leading public figure, the investigations are tirelessly conducted until the users are identified and brought to justice; whilst for many ordinary voiceless citizens, the same level of effort and dedication is not seen (Araújo, P. 2015).

Finally, concerning the complexity of the anti-racism legislation, there is a dual classification capable of causing misunderstandings in peoples' interpretation of the rule of law, to contribute to fuel the perception of impunity, and also that racism is a sort of 'perfect crime'. According to the Brazilian National Council of Justice, the legal concepts of 'crime of racism' and 'racial injury' are different. The first one (regulated by the Law number 7,716/1989) refers to acts addressed towards an unspecified cohort of people, discriminating the whole of a racial group, whilst 'racial injury' (regulated by the Law number 2,848, article 140, paragraph 3) consists of offending one's honour by referring to race, colour, ethnicity, religion, or origin (Santos, 2011; CNJ, 2015). However, the problem is the fact that whilst the 'crime of racism' can lead to up to five years of imprisonment to the offender, 'racial injury' can lead to no more than six months of incarceration, or even be replaced by a fine or community service at the judge's discretion. Given the fact that the majority of the cases of racism on social media are interpreted by the authorities as 'racial injury' rather than 'crime of racism', the offenders, when convicted, oftentimes receive mild punishments and that fuels peoples' perception of impunity, the inefficiency of the judiciary system and a system that contributes to the perpetuation of unequal privileges.

In complement to that, although there is a lack of nationwide consolidated data regarding cases of racism effectively brought to court, there are two sets of revealing data from Brasília and Rio de Janeiro. During the first semester of 2015, there were 352 reported cases of racism registered in Brasília's judiciary system. Within that, only three were considered, in fact, crime of racism by the judges, whilst the remaining 349 were considered racial injury whose punishment is considered mild (Diniz, 2015). In Rio de Janeiro, from 1988 to 2017 (i.e. a timeframe of almost 30 years) there were only 244 cases of racism reaching the courts and 40% of them were dismissed by the judges in the civil area, whilst in the criminal area, the defendants were acquitted in 24% of the cases (G1, 2017). Consequently, these cases evidence that, in Brazil, racism is a type of crime that conveniently hides behind the 'blankets' of the rule of law (Diniz, 2015).

Therefore, in conclusion, it is possible to highlight the three major aspects of the Brazilian anti-racism legal framework. First, that the deep-seated denial of the existence of racism in Brazilian society, influenced by the whitening ideology and 'racial democracy', has contributed towards the postponement of the implementation of institutional-level social policies for a long time. In effect, studies reveal that they have been implemented only after enduring social pressure led by the organised black movement. Second, despite the value and symbolic relevance of the social policies, it is evident that given the dual classification regarding racist attitudes, and their respective distinct levels of punishments, it provides legal loopholes of which people take advantage. Finally, and intertwined with the second aspect, the lack of serious consequences to racist attitudes contributes to fuel civil society's disbelief in the legal framework and, besides, the perception that such attitudes are exempt of serious legal consequences.

Internet regulations in Brazil

The issue of internet regulation has been the subject of a global debate over several years, encompassing not only divergent views regarding the level of control or supervision over the content uploaded and conveyed through it but also different approaches across the nations. Within that, the international organisation Internet Society proposes that "the internet is an open platform for innovation and sharing of ideas", and that "it cannot be regulated in a top-down manner, but its governance should be based on processes that are inclusive and driven by consensus" (Society, 2016, p. 1). Similarly, Delacourt (1997, p. 234) also advocates in favour of non-regulation but he recognises that it would be "the ideal alternative, [but] it is no longer realistic in light of the strength of political forces aligned against it". On the opposite pole of the conversation, Hughes (2015, p. 1) argues that "a clear regulatory framework is fundamental for the promotion and protection of rights in the digital context".

Thus, according to a study conducted by Ang (1997) analysing the regulatory framework in six countries[4], there are five types of content regulations usually adopted by countries: 1) individual self-regulation, 2) second part controllers, 3) non-hierarchically organised social forces, 4) hierarchically organised non-governmental organisations, and 5) governments. Additionally, the author continues, oftentimes, "countries with a longer and stronger tradition of free press would tend to use the first three types of regulations", implying a correlation between the level of freedom experienced by the press and the regulatory framework imposed towards the internet (Ang, 1997, p. 6).

Within the Brazilian context, there have been also many debates around this subject matter since 2007 triggered by an influential newspaper article by Lemos (2007) that, ultimately, has contributed to parliamentary discussions

---

[4] China, France, Germany, Singapore, South Korea, US.

two years later towards the regulatory framework model to be adopted (O'Maley, 2015; Solagna, 2015). After three years of public consultations, adjustments and parliamentary debates, the Law number 12,965, known as *Marco Civil da Internet*, was enacted (Mari, 2014; Solagna, 2015) which, in accordance to the categories of the regulatory framework developed by Ang (1997) positions Brazil in the fifth type (i.e. government regulated).

Thus, it is possible to notice the existence of a sensitive contrasting balance: freedom of expression *vs* respect to social norms. Namely, oftentimes people who engage in controversial comments of derogatory nature in the online environment claim that they have the constitutional right to freedom of expression and speech. Within that, any initiative towards questioning such contents would represent censorship. Nonetheless, the flaw embedded in this argument is that freedom of expression does not make people exempt from responsibilities and compliance to social norms, and the very same Law number 12,965 makes it clear that the social agents shall be held accountable for their online activities in accordance with the rule of law (Rousseff *et al.*, 2014).

Hence, whilst freedom of expression and speech, both online and offline, are considered by different authors (Rossini *et al.*, 2015; Dunham, 2016; Kelly *et al.*, 2016) as one of the fundamental pillars of democratic societies; it is also relevant to incorporate in the discussion the fact that, oftentimes, people who engage in offensive comments online try to shield themselves behind this argument (Younge, 2012). Within this context, in Germany, for example, "freedom of speech is a central tenet of their view of democracy, and their interpretation of this right includes bans on certain forms of white supremacy online" (Daniels, 2009, p. 163). This debate is relevant and meaningful to societies because words are embedded with power and they have the capability to engage people either in pleasant or unpleasant thoughts, feelings, ideas and beliefs (Daniels, 2009).

In line with this argument, despite the unquestionable importance of freedom of expression and speech towards the strengthening of Brazilian democracy, this cannot be used as a convenient excuse to equipping people to spread hate, racism and discriminatory offences in either the online or offline environments (Castro, 2014). Furthermore, rather than a manifestation of freedom of expression and speech, the dissemination of offensive comments on the internet works against the formation of a democratic and fairer society (Gomes, 2015; Trindade, 2019). Consequently, on the one hand, freedom of expression and speech represent important democratic tools that contribute towards people's empowerment. However, on the other hand, it cannot be disregarded that people are not exempt from their responsibilities and compliance with social norms since words can potentially have negative impacts and effects on others.

Chapter 4

Anatomy of racism on social media

Introduction

The analysis of the Facebook data gathered for the present study has enabled the identification of four major intertwined elements composing the anatomy of racism on social media platforms (see Figure 4.1). Combined, they contribute to our understanding of both the most salient mechanisms of the phenomenon of enactment of racist discourses, and as well as the role played by users and the technology.

Figure 4.1: Anatomy of racism on social media platforms

- Predominant geographical distribution.
- Reasons to becoming targets.

Element I: The primary target

Element II: The proponents of white supremacy ideologies

- Users' general profile.
- Users' major motivations.
- Key events prior to the action to post the content.
- Users' approach towards online anonymity

Element III: The long tail of social media posts

Element IV: What's in a name of online communities

- The long tail of posts and the echo chamber effect.
- The long tail of posts: how it works.

- § Blatant aggressive.
- § Mild terminologies.

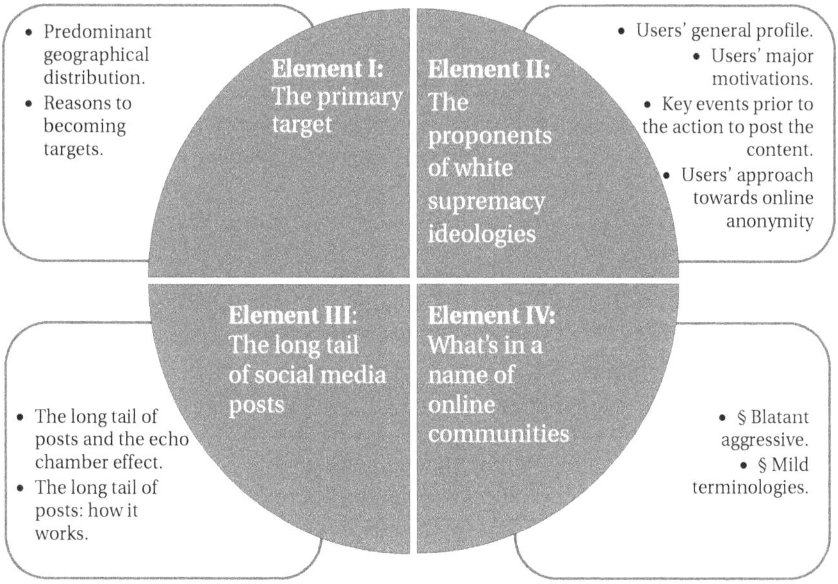

Having said that, three main intertwined arguments are raised in this chapter. First, racism on social media in Brazil is strongly gendered, given that black women comprise the primary target of this practice. Moreover, contrary to fallacious belief that 'money whitens', black women's successful upward social mobility does not shield them from experiences of racism.

Second, the proponents of white supremacy are predominantly men, oftentimes, employing harsh language to belittle black women. Additionally, their core motivation to engage in this practice is fuelled by a deep-seated belief in the whitening ideology.

Finally, major social media platforms (in)directly contribute towards the increase of the phenomenon of online racism in Brazil. The technology provides white supremacists with capabilities that enable them not only to enact racist ideologies but also to attract like-minded people, amplifying the reach and reverberation of their voices to a wide audience, as an endless echo in cyberspace.

Element I: the primary target of online racism

Detailed analysis of the 224 news articles gathered during the online search for the present study reveals important aspects regarding racist discourses enacted on social media in Brazil. These secondary data cover the timeframe 2012-2016 and address 42 different cases of racist discourses enacted specifically on Facebook across 13 Brazilian states. Certainly, this number of cases represent only a fragment of what happens on Facebook in Brazil, since the reported cases of racism on this social media platform have soared from 2,038 in 2011 to 11,090 cases in 2014 (Safernet, 2015). Moreover, these 42 cases also represent the ones who have been captured by the radar of the mainstream media; whilst hundreds of others certainly did not make news headlines. Nevertheless, despite this fact, these 42 cases do contribute to bringing to the surface some relevant pieces of evidence for the development of qualitative analyses concerning the phenomenon of online racist discourses in Brazil.

First, the available data reveals that racism on social media in Brazil is strongly gendered, given that the majority of the victims within the analysed cases are black women (81% in contrast to 19% cases involving black men), and aged between 20 to 35 years (64.7%). This finding coalesces with the argument that lived experiences of racism in Brazil are not even between the two genres. In fact, "of all Brazilian social groups, black women are the most profoundly impacted by discrimination and prejudice" (Caldwell, 2003, p. 21). Second, this finding also represents additional evidence corroborating the argument developed by other authors that the online environment is far from being a colour-blind territory (Daniels, 2009; Noble, 2018; Silva, 2019). Finally, regarding the geographical distribution of the cases, they are scattered across 13 out of Brazil's 26 states. However, the majority of them (ca. 60%) are concentrated in the states of Rio de Janeiro (14 cases), São Paulo (seven cases), and Bahia (four cases).

Geographical concentration of cases of racism

The concentration of cases in Rio de Janeiro and São Paulo warrants further critical reflection to understand the reasons leading towards this phenomenon. An important clue to shed some light on this aspect is found in the occupation of the identified victims in the cases analysed. In Rio de Janeiro, 50% of the victims were either actresses or singers, and 21.4% were university students. The city of Rio de Janeiro hosts the country's leading TV network (an important employer in the entertainment industry) and, consequently, there is a higher proportion of prominent actresses living there than in São Paulo, or in many other locations as well. The relevance of this finding is that, in Brazil, Rio de Janeiro is also well-known as a place where there are bigger chances of ordinary citizens meet celebrities in ordinary daily contexts such as, for example, on the beach, bars, restaurants, theatre, and shopping malls (Ortiz, 2011; Ribeiro, 2014; Mulher, 2018). Namely, these public figures are more exposed in Rio de Janeiro than in several other cities across the country.

Thus, two inferences can be made. First, the fact that these prominent figures are 'more accessible' (i.e. proportionally easier to be seen in ordinary daily circumstances) in Rio de Janeiro than in other Brazilian cities, this aspect may trigger on social media users the perception of reduced social distance in relation to the celebrities. Namely, the celebrities' more privileged social position, granted by their occupations, does not seem like a sturdy barrier to many social media users, or a huge social distance. Being relatively 'more accessible' may be interpreted by users that the reduced social distance would imply permission to convey their derogatory discourses also towards them. In other words, being 'within their reach' would turn the celebrities into almost ordinary citizens, and then also capable of being targeted like everybody else. However, given the celebrities' differentiated social position, social media users benefit from the technology to amplify the reverberation of their discourses.

Different from that, in São Paulo, the proportion of actresses and singers as victims, in the analysed cases, is lower than in Rio de Janeiro (only 28.6%), whilst journalists represent another 28.6%. São Paulo's urban atmosphere differs considerably from Rio's and, oftentimes, the prominent figures live and circulate predominantly in neighbourhoods that are more exclusive than the average citizen is used to navigating (i.e. the social distance seems to be more clearly established). However, the qualified exposure granted by the mentioned occupations (especially on TV) is associated with success and symbolic positions of privilege, which also makes them an appealing target for social media users.

The second inference is that the qualitative exposure achieved by these successful black women in mainstream media both in Rio de Janeiro and in São Paulo, contributes to turning them into a convenient target for social media users, regardless of social distance. Supporting evidence corroborating this argument is found on the statement made by a man arrested by the police a few years ago charged for racial injury against a well-known black actress.

> The members of my Facebook community aimed at becoming famous [amongst our Facebook peers]. We have spread an attack towards a prominent black female figure because we thought that a racist attack would be the easiest way to achieving the desired fame (source: G1, 2015).

In effect, the data reveals that social distance between the Facebook users and the victims of racism does not represent a hindrance to them, given that in 76.2% of the cases analysed, the users had no previous relationship with the victims. They did not know the victims either in the offline or online context. This finding has two major implications. First, these users tend to feel at ease to convey their discourse towards people that, in an offline context, they might not have access or relationship. Second, this lack of social connection might also contribute to them expressing their views employing harsh language.

Young black women: why they have been targeted

The evidence that black women aged 20 to 35 years have been the primary target of racism on Facebook in Brazil is intriguing. What explains this phenomenon? Why this age range in particular? Three major aspects explain this phenomenon: 1) the increasing number of black women with university degree challenges the ingrained belief that they are 'destined' to perform solely domestic work, 2) the proponents of white supremacy consider that young black women's visibility and exposure is a threat to Brazil's whitened national identity, and 3) in reproductive age, their potential motherhood postpones Brazilian modernity.

The social roles commonly attributed to black Brazilian women are oftentimes associated with subservient and unskilled occupations such as, for instance, room maid, helper, house cleaner, cook, and domestic worker (Burdick, 1998; Gillam, 2017). This perception represents a legacy of colonial society. The occupations performed by black female slaves in the Big House were room maid, wet nurse, cook and house cleaner. Within that, "colonial period in Brazil left an inheritance in people's mind that black women are useful solely for domestic work or exhibiting their bodies" (Antonieta, 2013, p. 20). In line with that, a history teacher and social media activist, who used to perform domestic work herself up to 2009, says, "unfortunately, for black women, domestic work is inherited from one generation to another. My mum, my aunt, and my grandma were domestic workers. It is impossible to dissociate it from our slavery past" (Barrucho, 2016, p. 3).

However, despite this deep-seated colonial legacy, studies reveal that, currently, black women have greater access to higher education (in comparison to previous generations), and they are receiving degrees in a variety of disciplines, including medicine, journalism, law, business administration, among many others (Artes and Ricoldi, 2015). Indeed, they are still lagging behind their white female counterparts, as other studies reveal, but there have been considerable improvements over the past three decades (Vieira, 2015; Queiroz and Santos, 2016). What can be inferred is that this trend of an increasing number of black women in higher education might shatter the deep-seated belief that they were 'destined' to perform only domestic and low-skilled occupations. Consequently, rather than engaging solely in subservient social roles, many black Brazilian women are becoming medical doctors, dentists, business managers, journalists, etc., and this might upset the proponents of white supremacy because it goes against their ingrained perception regarding black women's 'legitimate' social place.

Another distinct characteristic of the cohort of black Brazilian women targeted on Facebook is the fact that most of them are well-educated and upwardly mobile. The available secondary data do not reveal objective information concerning, for instance, their income level. Nevertheless, their reported educational level and occupation contribute to support the inference that most of them belong, at least, to middle-class (Rocha, 2015). Within that, the secondary data reveals that 53% of the black female victims are either university students or engaged in occupations that require a university degree (e.g., journalist, anthropologist, dentist, and medical doctor). Moreover, another 26.5% of them are engaged in the entertainment business (acting or singing) and professional sports; being several of them recognised national celebrities and quite successful in their chosen careers. Thus, this picture contributes to demonstrating that, in effect, the majority of the black women belittled on Facebook in Brazil are socially well-positioned.

Evolving from this reflection, and as addressed in Chapter 1, since the early years of the twentieth century, the country's proud visible face (both domestically and overseas) has been built and reinforced on top of white women's beauty standards. A contemporary example illustrating the perpetuation of this ideology was the opening ceremony of the 2016 Summer Olympic Games in Rio de Janeiro. Rather than a leading black or even miscegenated woman, the organisers chose the blonde, blue-eyed, white supermodel Gisele Bündchen to perform a catwalk and represent Brazilianness before the eyes of the world. In effect, it can be observed that this choice also resembles the recommendation made by the Brazilian president Epitácio

Pessoa in 1921 regarding the national team. As discussed in Chapter 1 in the topic addressing national identity, he did not want black or mulatto players in the team because Brazil should portray its best image possible abroad (Filho, 1947; Máximo, 1999; Santos, J. 2019) Consequently, the unique Brazilian race-mixing, proposed by Gilberto Freyre and the modernists, has not been chosen to represent Brazil because the Eurocentric modernity aspiration remains prevalent amidst the Brazilian elite and the collective mid-set. Hence, under the perspective of the proponents of white supremacy ideologies, black women achieving qualified exposure represents a type of 'transgression' (or trespassing) of the racial hierarchy boundaries. What does qualified mean in this context? It stands for the engagement with careers that historically have been associated with white male privilege (e.g. medicine, journalism, law, etc.) and this type of engagement challenges black women 'expected' subservient occupations (e.g. room maid, cook, cleaner, etc.).

Within this context, given the fact that the 'transgression' shatters the 'original' balance of Brazilianness; this 'delinquent act' would then be subjected to some type of 'punishment' aiming at re-establishing the 'original' balance. In the past colonial society, African enslaved people who misbehaved or failed to comply with their masters' expectations and commands were subjected to severe public punishments on the *pelourinhos*[1]. Therefore, for the proponents of white supremacy in Brazil, Facebook has become their modern-day *pelourinho*, whilst race joking represents a form of virtual whipping. They inflict 'exemplary' public punishments against black women. Thus, the aim is not only to discredit and disqualify their achievements but also to discourage others from following suit and re-establishing the 'original' racial hierarchy boundaries and the whitened national identity.

Regarding the fact that these black women aged 20 to 35 years are within their reproductive age is also intriguing. For a long time in the Brazilian social context, black motherhood has been subjected to race joking. Examples of this include the following:

> What does a black pregnant woman have in common with a car that has a flat tire? They are both expecting a monkey. [2]

---

[1] This word stands for pillory. In Brazilian colonial society, it represented the public place, such as a small central square, where 'justice' was practised through physical punishment towards *Negro* people and anyone else considered criminal. The punishments were always performed with whipping (Moura, 2004)

[2] In Portuguese, car jack is popularly known as 'monkey'.

Why a black woman expecting triplets was arrested? Because she was charged with gang formation.

Soon after finishing the caesarean procedure, the white doctor slaps at the black baby until he cries. Since he does not stop beating at the baby, the black mother pleads him to stop. Then the doctor says: 'tell him to give my watch back'.

Combined, these jokes convey two powerful embedded discourses disqualifying black motherhood. First, by comparing their offspring with an animal, the joke removes the humanity of both the mother and the baby. Moreover, it also places them underneath the lowest position in the racial hierarchy, since their humanity has been removed. Second, the jokes imply that delinquency is innate to black people from birth, inherited from the mother, and passed on from one generation to another. Furthermore, potential black motherhood indirectly upsets the whitening ideology, since their offspring might not be white but rather *preto* or *pardo* (black or brown). Consequently, under the perspective of the proponents of white supremacy ideologies, their reproductive potential represents the postponement of achieving the desired modernity embedded in the whitening of the population. In other words, black motherhood represents the perpetuation of Brazil's backwardness, since whitening ideology has contributed to establishing this association with black people.

Racism and sexism in Brazil

Whilst the previous topic has explored the major reasons contributing to turning young black women the predominant target of racism on social media, it is also pertinent to understand why black men are less affected by this practice. First, as argued in Chapter 1, Brazilian society has been shaped on top of a patriarchal mode brought by the Portuguese settlers, and it has remained predominantly this way to the present day. Actually, on this aspect, Alves (2018, p. 1) argues that "Brazil has a history and culture founded on racism and sexism, with deep marks that are still perfectly visible today". In line with that, the Brazilian racial and social hierarchy structure (as discussed in Chapter 1), positions people according to the following order of relevance: 1) white men at the top, 2) white women in second, 3) black men in third, and 4) black women at the bottom. Thus, this overall picture reveals that the social position of black Brazilian women is often associated with inferiority, including lower salaries, lower professional acknowledgement, and marginalisation (Flor, 2019).

In corroboration with this argumentation, a recent study conducted by IBGE (2019) reveals that the intersection of race, class and gender continues to affect the social condition of black women. The study evidence, for example, that on average, black women earn only 44.4% of white men's income. Moreover, among the four social groups analysed (white men, white women, black men, and black women), whilst only 34.4% of white men are engaged in informal occupations, 47.8% of black women are in this precarious working condition (IBGE, 2019). Although these data are considerably alarming, this overall picture of racial and class inequality is not a new phenomenon in Brazil. A decade earlier, S. Santos (2009) already argued that black women's working conditions are usually the most vulnerable, precarious and that they are absent in leadership positions in most corporations. And, before that, there were also many other studies revealing this same picture of disadvantaged social condition for black women (e.g., Dzidzienyo, 1971; Fernandes, 1972; Gonzalez and Hasenbalg, 1982; Caldwell, 2000).

Thus, it is possible to observe that, not by chance, Essed (1991) had already theorised that the living experiences of racism between black men and women are not the same. That is, in addition to the intersecting dimensions of race and class, sexism amplifies considerably the lived experiences of racism for black women. In line with this reflection, although black men are also subjected to many lived experiences of racism, their relational hierarchical position in comparison to black women (i.e. being positioned one step above) contributes towards their reduced participation as the target of racism on social media. In other words, the paradoxical explanation is that, since there is a weaker link (i.e. black women), it suggests that, by exclusion, black men seem to be spared from massive disparagement on social media.

Another distinct aspect to take into consideration lays in the fact that not only racism but also misogynist values have become naturalised in Brazilian society. An emblematic example in support for this argumentation comprises the episode discussed in Chapter 2 regarding the 1st National Encounter of Black Women in 1988, which was classified as a 'lesbians' encounter' by some black males. That is, even within the organised black movement, black women were belittled. Consequently, "discriminatory practices such as sexism, racism, lesbophobia, religious intolerance, and sexual and psychological violence can be identified in a broader context as situations that are part of black Brazilian women's lived experiences of racism" (Santos, S. 2009, p. 279).

Thus, in conclusion, although "the internet did not invent sexism, it is amplifying it in unprecedent ways" (Jane, 2017, p. 3). And, in the case of social media in Brazil, it becomes evident that this virtual environment is also allowing the reproduction and reinforcement of the sexist behaviour observed in the offline context, however, amplified due to its networking capabilities that can potentially engage a large number of like-minded people.

Element II: the profile of proponents of white supremacy

Depicting a picture of the proponents of white supremacy on social media consists of an intriguing and, at the same time, challenging task. It is intriguing because reading the threads of disparagement posts and their associated comments naturally raises some questions such as: a) who are engaging in publishing them online, and b) what drives these people to write this type of content. The task is also challenging because there are no previous studies in the Brazilian social science literature addressing this topic and nor there is a wealth of secondary data available.

One of the reasons for the lack of secondary data is that, oftentimes, the people arrested and charged for racial injury in Brazil deny the requests to be interviewed. Hence, to address this topic, it has been adopted a combination of evidence revealed by the research participants interviewed for the study, evidence emerged from the 217 public Facebook pages gathered for the study, and secondary data available in the 224 news articles.

The proponents' general profile

Within the public Facebook pages gathered for the study, it was possible to identify a total of 27,065 unique users and, within this cohort, 65.6% of them were men, 28.6% women and the remaining small proportion of 5.8% it was not possible to identify their gender. This finding reveals an interesting picture. Whilst the majority of the victims of racist discourses on Facebook are black women, this finding indicates that their offenders are, predominantly, men. It is also raises to explain that since the study has used solely publicly available Facebook pages, the inherent limitation is that it was not possible to investigate the users' racial category. To have access to this sort of demographic data it would demand formal consent from each one of these 27,065 unique users, what it was beyond the scope of the research project.

Another distinct aspect emerged from the data is the fact that male users are more prone to use swear words than women which, to a certain extent, replicates an unwritten social convention in Brazil establishing that this type of language is more socially acceptable to be employed by men than by women. That is to say that, for men, the use of swear words is 'normalised' and it also represents a reinforcing element of their masculinity and expression of relative power (Silva, 2017). Nevertheless, this explanation must not be interpreted as a flawless rule, since there are also many female users on Facebook employing male-like harsh language. In the US social context, for example, the use of swear words and harsh language on Facebook is quite frequent, and there are different terms employed by male and female users and also across different age groups (Kirk, 2013).

Regarding the Brazilian social context, there is no equivalent study addressing the use of swear words on social media; however, the secondary data gathered for the present book has revealed interesting aspects. First, male users are more prone to use swear words that refer to male genitalia and, oftentimes, in active ways such as: a) suck my dick, b) I'm gonna bang your ass, c) fuck you, d) fuck, e) you deserve to be fucked up, f) asshole, g) faggot, and h) son of a bitch. Second, the female users, in turn, do not employ the same array of swear words referring to male genitalia, although they are also found sometimes. However, they are more prone to employ terms that question other women's moral integrity such as: a) fuck you, b) bitch, c) cow, d) whore, e) you need a black cock in your ass, f) son of a bitch, and g) chicken.

This finding is relevant because it is intertwined with the fact that 76.2% of the proponents of white supremacy on social media in Brazil disregard any social distance that might exist between themselves and the victims of their mockery (Trindade, 2018b). Thus, this indicates that disregarding social distance, they might as well feel at ease in expressing their views employing this type of language in unrestricted ways. Since there is no previous relationship between the parts (proponents and victims), there is no embarrassment in using them. Ultimately, paraphrasing Billig (2001), these people have no *crise de conscience* in expressing their racist discourses employing either race joking to disqualify and belittle others.

Motivations of the proponents of white supremacy

The ideal way to unpack users' motivations to engage in the practice of constructing and disseminating racist discourses on social media platforms, would certainly be interviewing them directly. Nevertheless, in practice, this access proved to be extremely difficult and unfeasible. The secondary data gathered for this book provides clear evidence in support of this assertion, given that very rarely journalists have managed to hear their point of view. In effect, in the interview I have conducted with Moacyr Netto, one of the producers of a 2016 awareness video campaign called 'Mirrors of Racism', has also confirmed this fact. The campaign comprises a five-minute-long video aimed at fostering constructive debates about the social consequences of virtual racism in Brazil (W3Haus, 2016b). The executive has reported that, during the video's production stage, they had identified and contacted dozens of social media users who had previously posted racist content against black women, to grant them the chance to freely speak their mind. In the end, just one of them accepted to participate but, differently from his online 'eloquence', in the final shot, he verbalised just a few short sentences and practically monosyllabically.

Therefore, given these natural restrictions beyond the researcher's control, I have tried to understand their motivations through the lenses of other social actors. The interviews, conducted in the summer of 2016 in Brazil with eight social actors, have shown different views concerning their interpretation of users' motivations. Nevertheless, despite that, they have proved to be rich qualitative data because, rather than conflicting standpoints, they are, indeed, complementary. The critical discourse analysis of their statements has enabled the emergence of users' four main motivational categories as follow: 1) uneasiness with black women's upward social mobility, 2) masquerading ideologies, 3) sensation of impunity, and 4) intersectionality of gender, race and class.

Talking with Djamila Ribeiro, then a representative of São Paulo's Secretariat of Human Rights, has advocated that it is inconceivable that users are not fully aware of what they are doing online; and conveniently framing their attitude as a mere joke. Besides, Djamila Ribeiro argues, the users' aim is, actually, to outrage black women; and to cause harm to them because the users feel uncomfortable with black women's successful upward social mobility. A similar point of view is advocated by Elaine Aparecida Dias, then the coordinator of São Paulo-based public service 'SOS Racismo'. She believes that the people who engage in this type of practice are trying to make black women step back, to give up their achievements, to stop attending tertiary education and progressing socially.

Regarding masquerading ideologies, Maria Lúcia da Silva, director of the NGO 'Instituto Amma Psique Negritude', believes that people use social media as a sort of stage, where they can wear a mask to be who they really are; however, it is a persona that oftentimes cannot be revealed in public. In complement to that, Djamila Ribeiro says that since being openly racist in public can be embarrassing and inappropriate, they instead unleash their ideologies online.

Indeed, intertwined with this second category, the impunity sensation has also been highlighted by the interviewees. The users' impunity's sensation is fuelled by a perception that their attitudes are exempt of any serious consequence, and that nothing can be inflicted upon them. On this regard, Jurema Werneck, then managing director of the Rio de Janeiro-based NGO 'Criola', has said that people write this sort of thing on social media first because they consider normal and acceptable. Second, because they believe that nothing can happen to them. In alignment with this standpoint, Maria Lúcia da Silva considers that, since most of the time, no one is arrested or charged by the authorities, they keep doing it. Moreover, Maria Lúcia da Silva adds, when they are rarely caught and brought before justice, the legal consequences are mild or practically irrelevant. In effect, interviewing Moacyr Netto, then the CEO of the advertising agency W3Haus in

São Paulo, specialised in digital marketing, stated that, as long as no effective move is made towards changing society's perception of the absence of legal consequences of online racism, there must always be users willing to engage in this type of practice on social media.

Finally, the intersectionality of gender, race and class, as one of the users' motivations has been raised by another interviewee. A black female social activist[3] argues that racial hierarchy based on skin colour is very strong in the collective mindset. According to her understanding, since oftentimes the Brazilian elite positions black women at the bottom of the social pyramid, they become vulnerable and easy targets for racist users on social media. In other words, the intersection of gender, race and attributed disqualified social position, represent elements that amplify their likelihood of becoming subject of racist discourses on social media.

What triggers the posting of derogatory content on social media?

Besides users' general profile and their four major motivations to engage in the practice of enacting racist discourses online, another distinct aspect needs to be addressed. Namely, which are the predominant events triggering the action to post the derogatory content. In other words, what are the 'sparks' that lead them to effectively take the action to write the sort of thing they do on social media platforms. For this purpose, the analysis of both the primary and secondary data has revealed eight major categories of triggering events which, in turn, can also be combined into two groups, as shown in Table 4.1.

The first group gathers categories of triggering events that represent distinctive symbolic markers of black women belonging to social spaces associated with privilege and power. As for the second group, it encompasses symbols conveying black women's clear ethnic identity, political positioning, and assurance in their own choices.

These eight categories of events have triggered two types of attitudes by the proponents of white supremacy: a) active or b) reactive. The 'active' user comprises people who deliberately post negative and derogatory comments against black women, apparently for no specific or particular reason. Namely, it is not possible to identify any clear and explicit evidence that a post made by a victim would possibly trigger the derogatory comment. Regarding the 'reactive' comment, it is commonly made to counterpoint something that the victim has said, done or achieved. However, the data reveals that the 'reactive' posts are oftentimes done aggressively, discrediting, disqualifying and reducing the value of the victim and/or their achievement, appearance, ideas, etc.

---

[3] She requested to be anonymized in the study.

Table 4.1: Major triggering events prior to derogatory posts

Belonging to positions of privilege and power	Symbols of identity and political positioning
▪ Performing leading position in successful TV programmes either as host or guest.	▪ Interracial relationship.
▪ Enjoying vacation abroad.	▪ Rejection of dating proposition.
▪ Winning beauty contest.	▪ Expressing a disagreement with a previous post or comments made by somebody else, which the victim considered inappropriate.
▪ Evidence of professional or academic engagement with 'prestigious' careers (e.g. medicine or journalism).	▪ Praising and/or using Afro hairstyle.

The first group gathers categories of triggering events that represent distinctive symbolic markers of black women belonging to social spaces associated with privilege and power. As for the second group, it encompasses symbols conveying black women's clear ethnic identity, political positioning, and assurance in their own choices.

These eight categories of events have triggered two types of attitudes by the proponents of white supremacy: a) active or b) reactive. The 'active' user comprises people who deliberately post negative and derogatory comments against black women, apparently for no specific or particular reason. Namely, it is not possible to identify any clear and explicit evidence that a post made by a victim would possibly trigger the derogatory comment. Regarding the 'reactive' comment, it is commonly made to counterpoint something that the victim has said, done or achieved. However, the data reveals that the 'reactive' posts are oftentimes done aggressively, discrediting, disqualifying and reducing the value of the victim and/or their achievement, appearance, ideas, etc.

On top of that, the data has also revealed the occurrence of a greater proportion of 'reactive' posts (64.3%), in comparison to 'active' derogatory posts (35.7%). Thus, it can be inferred that the reactive posts are subtly expressing 'how dare you to occupy this privileged social space that was not meant for you?' Alternatively, 'how dare you to speak your mind, and take a clear and strong positioning about something when you are supposed to be subservient and engaged in less qualified occupations?' Additionally, it can also be said that this reflection coalesces with the first motivational category previously discussed (uneasiness with black women's upward social mobility).

Within this context, Elaine Aparecida Dias (SOS Racismo) has argued that users try to make black women step back and give up their achievements. As for Djamila Ribeiro (São Paulo's Secretariat of Human Rights), black women's upward social mobility is uncomfortable for the proponents of white supremacy. Consequently, it means that the greater proportion of 'reactive' posts mirrors the attitude of challenging black women's social advancements and creating additional obstacles on their way upward. In other words, such achievements represent a threat both to the 'original' racial hierarchy boundaries and to the whitened national identity, triggering then a variety of race jokes and associated comments.

Users' approach regarding online anonymity

There is evidence emerged from the secondary data and the interviews, demonstrating that online anonymity plays a relevant role in the process of posting race joking on social media. Hidden behind this technical capability, the proponents of white supremacy in Brazil, oftentimes, feel at ease and empowered to unleash their beliefs and ideologies unrestrictedly. This perception leads users to understand that they are 'protected' from being held accountable for their attitudes on social media. Actually, they tend to believe that the online and the offline environment are detached from each other. This reflection leads us to question whether this alleged 'protection' granted by online anonymity is for real, or rather, resulting from a perception built on top of unsubstantiated assumptions.

Experts in digital technologies argue that people can easily create anonymous profiles on social media platforms; and this capability enables users to convey views, beliefs and ideologies free from social convention constraints (Hill, 2014; Perez, 2016). However, there is evidence revealing that this alleged 'protection' is, in fact, a fallacious perception, as the following example illustrates. The posts were extracted from a publicly available Facebook community whose members are predominantly university students. At a certain point in the thread of conversations (published in 2015), a black woman expressed her disagreement with some disparagement racist comments conveyed by other users. In retaliation, other users have published a series of offensive posts against her, such as the examples shown below.

Post #1:   Get an abortion black bitch. The baby deserves that.

Post #2:   She alleges to be pregnant but, in reality, she has swallowed a baby. Soldiers get ready. We have the mission to remove the baby from inside this whale immediately.

Post #3:   Hi guys. Do not worry. The comments have been made online, and within six months, any legal complaint of this nature prescribes. For the authorities grant confidentiality breach takes much longer than that. The only issue would be the print screens. Delete everything that involves her in the conversation, and it will be fine. Believe me, am a law student.

The conversation suggests that there is no problem in insulting the black woman because there would be no legal consequences. Although there is no factual evidence corroborating the claim made by the user in Post #3, this discourse is quite emblematic, because it aims, first, at providing peace of mind to the users who had offended the victim. Second, to assure that, as long as they follow some simple rules such as deleting the conversations, they would be safeguarded.

Another illustrative example encompasses an emerging young white male singer who, along 2011 and 2012, used to publish on social media dozens of posts classified as xenophobic, racist and misogynistic. They came to the surface mostly along 2016 as the singer became very successful and got involved in a controversial disrespectful behaviour with a female journalist. As his old social media posts reached the news headlines, the singer deleted his social media accounts and claimed that they were nothing but jests (Belloni, 2016; Ferrari and Finco, 2016).

Thus, what can be observed, is the fact that there is a strong incongruence in the behaviour of many users because the moment their offences reach the news headlines, they oftentimes take at least one of four attitudes: 1) shift the status of their social media account from public to private; 2) delete the derogatory post; 3) delete their social media profile; and 4) claim that the post was meant to be a harmless joke. In other words, the incongruence lays in the fact that, before their attitude becomes public, they feel empowered and shielded from the external world behind the computer screen. However, the possibility of being effectively found and exposed, as a result of what they have done, concerns them, indicating that the imagined shield is not as impenetrable as originally conceived in their minds. Besides, there is data revealing that 83% of Facebook users in Brazil engaged in posting derogatory comments against black people delete their account once their comments become subject of news articles (W3Haus, 2016a; 2016b).

Furthermore, there are different voices in Brazil arguing that, contrary to users' belief, online anonymity does not prevent people from being identified, if necessary, to enforce the rule of law (Rodrigues, 2015; Lopes and Ricci, 2016; Soares, W. 2016). Namely, whilst technology grants people the possibility to navigate anonymously in the online environment, it can also be used to track and locate the person when needed. Consequently, in conclusion, the combination of the four attitudes taken by users once their comments reach the news headlines represent strong indicative that, in reality, they might have a clear idea of the negative impact of their derogatory post and that they are concerned that they can, actually, be reached by the authorities and be held accountable for their actions.

Element III: the long tail of social media posts

Briefly, the long tail of social media posts means that a particular post published on a given date can, potentially, engage people (both new and recurring users) from several months up to three years after its publication. Besides, it also means that rather than ceasing the conversation soon after the publication, the engagement keeps the derogatory talk active for a long period. Thus, this element plays a relevant role in attracting like-minded people to the same conversation for a long time and keeping it active.

The long tail of posts and the echo chamber effect

Many studies have addressed the subject matter of echo chamber effect in the context of social media platform (e.g., Harris and Harrigan, 2015; Bessi *et al.*, 2017; Ingrams, 2017; Takikawa and Nagayoshi, 2017; Justwan *et al.*, 2018). Amongst them, two major characteristics call our attention. First, they are all relatively recent, which contributes to reinforcing the understanding of the impacts of social media platforms in contemporary societies. Second, they predominantly address the subject matter of echo chamber effect under the perspective of electoral process and political polarization. Having said that, some authors argue that the repeated dissemination of analogous standpoints on social media platforms tends to reinforce them and leave no room for opposing views (Takikawa and Nagayoshi, 2017). Moreover, once people are attracted to engaging in an echo chamber, they tend to remain there, and to persuade them to come out of the echo chamber, one must deconstruct the ideology that ties them together (Bessi *et al.*, 2017). This reflection is relevant because it indicates that one of the ways to combat racist discourses enacted on social media in Brazil might demand the deconstruction of the deep-seated colonial-like ideology fuelling their enactment. Consequently, this aspect contributes to reinforcing the relevance of the anti-racist discursive strategies and initiatives as discussed in Chapter 2.

In effect, echo chambers are considered as "ideologically congruent and homogenous environments in which political views are not debated but instead reinforced and amplified" (Justwan *et al.*, 2018, p. 2). Hence, following this line of reflection, it becomes clear that ideological homogeneity encompasses the core element in any echo chamber. Likewise, the long tail of posts revealed by the data shows this same core element. Namely, the continuation of the derogatory conversation on social media represents the repetition of many verbal insults towards the same person or social group for a long period. Figuratively speaking, it is like a hammer repeatedly hitting a nail. While in an ordinary offline social context, oftentimes, the users would refrain from verbalising the same type of racist comment they do online, on social media they are provided with tools that allow them to do that and connect to many others like-minded people who contribute towards its reinforcement and amplification (i.e. the hammer becomes bigger, heavier and stronger).

The long tail of posts: how it works

Social media platforms are built on top of powerful networks of nodes (i.e., users) that expand rapidly at exponential rates. Within that, users can connect to a wide number of other people sharing common ideologies, values, beliefs and, consequently, amplifying their voices in large proportions. On this context, a network formed, for instance, with only five members can provide 10 connections among them; another one with 10 members can generate 45 connections, and one with 15 members rise to 105 connections (Cann *et al.*, 2011). Thus, this explanation contributes to illustrate the potential amplifying reach of discourses disseminated on social media platforms.

Having said that, the Facebook data gathered for the present book reveals many cases where a particular derogatory post towards a black person, kept engaging users for the same conversation for up to three years. Oftentimes, there is a strong concentration of users' interaction soon after the post original publication date (on average, around 30-45 days). Then, there is a considerable reduction in the intensity but, even so, it keeps attracting users for a long time afterwards (see Figure 4.2).

Within that, it has also been possible to observe the occurrence of three important aspects in the long tail of posts: 1) the proportion of unique users, 2) the continuity, and 3) a small gap between interactions. The data reveals that, in most of the cases of a long tail of posts (i.e. posts that trigger users' interaction for, at least, six months after its publication), at least two-thirds of the audience is formed by unique users. The remaining one-third is formed by recurrent users who interact more than once. This aspect is intertwined with the second (continuity), and it helps us to understand the length of the long tail, given the fact that the original posts keep attracting not only recurrent users but mostly new ones to the derogatory conversation. Finally, it has also been possible to observe that, rather than scattered users' interaction over time, in fact, after the initial concentration, the subsequent interactions tend to happen in small intervals usually fewer than 30 days (Trindade, 2018b).

Figure 4.2: Concept of the long tail of social media posts

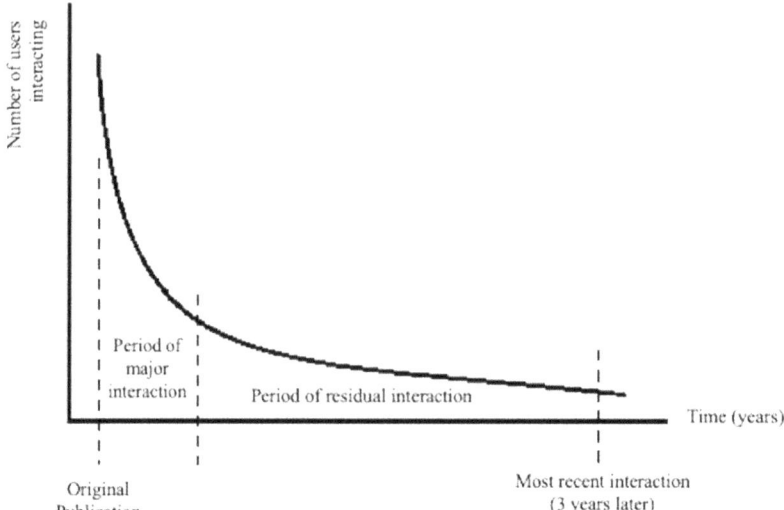

Within that, it has also been possible to observe the occurrence of three important aspects in the long tail of posts: 1) the proportion of unique users, 2) the continuity, and 3) a small gap between interactions. The data reveals that, in most of the cases of a long tail of posts (i.e. posts that trigger users' interaction for, at least, six months after its publication), at least two-thirds of the audience is formed by unique users. The remaining one-third is formed by recurrent users who interact more than once. This aspect is intertwined with the second (continuity), and it helps us to understand the length of the long tail, given the fact that the original posts keep attracting not only recurrent users but mostly new ones to the derogatory conversation. Finally, it has also been possible to observe that, rather than scattered users' interaction over time, in fact, after the initial concentration, the subsequent interactions tend to happen in small intervals usually fewer than 30 days (Trindade, 2018b).

The overall picture revealed by this long tail of posts is the fact that race joking posted on social media (and hate speech in general), do not fade away soon after their publication. First, they oftentimes attract a large audience once they are published. Second, they remain imprinted in the online environment for a long time available to anyone to see them and, finally, they act as magnets regularly attracting new audience for that content. As previously addressed, humour involves three social agents: 1) the joker, 2) the subject of the mockery, and 3) the audience. Within that, in the context of a long tail of posts, the audience is composed by the unique users attracted by the original disparagement post; and their continuous interaction can represent a form of endorsement and reinforcement of the embedded message in the race joking.

Furthermore, although the study has predominantly adopted publicly available Facebook pages as research data, it cannot be disregarded the fact that it is not uncommon that such content migrates across different social media platforms. In other words, a particular disparagement post can be originally published on Facebook, but it can also circulate, for instance, on Twitter or Instagram and vice-versa. Thus, it cannot also be disregarded, first, that Facebook, Instagram and WhatsApp are all part of the same corporation and, second, that the technological integration amongst the three platforms is increasing. Consequently, the circulation of this sort of content across the different platforms can become even easier in the near future and amplifying even more the social impacts of this practice (Hern, 2019; Isaac, 2019).

Thus, the dynamic of the long tail of posts, in combination with the potential circulation of racist discourses across different social media platforms, compose a challenging scenario for the victims. As the content remains active online for a long time, such as an endless echo in cyberspace, it can potentially inflict great harm on them.

Element IV: what's in a name of online communities

The data gathered for the study has revealed that there is a large array of Facebook communities displaying disparagement content targeted towards different social groups. Whilst one group encompasses communities more aggressive regarding their content, the other is relatively mild. Within that, what calls our attention is the fact that, rather than a trivial aspect, their choices of vocabulary to compose the communities' titles also reveals a great deal about them (see Table 4.2).

As for the communities adopting blatant aggressive vocabulary to compose their titles, it has been possible to observe that, oftentimes, the language employed by most of the users tend to follow this same pattern. That is to say that they employ vocabulary considered rude, impolite and inappropriate in many ordinary social contexts. Indeed, they can be more frequently employed in situations of conflict and aggravated tension (Bartel, 2014). On the other hand, in more formal social settings or with people that do not share close ties, it is not expected to see them being employed. However, the data demonstrate that, in the context of social media platforms, users do not feel constrained by any social convention. In reality, they rather subvert and disregard such conventions. Moreover, they also tend to disregard social distances and openly employ rude vocabulary without any type of concern. Furthermore, it has also been possible to observe that the harsher the combination of vocabulary adopted in the title of many of these Facebook communities, the more comfortable users feel to unleash an equivalent level of aggressiveness in their language. Most probably, this behaviour is fuelled by a nurtured belief that online anonymity provides them with a 'protective' shield that would grant them implicit permission to behave this way.

Table 4.2: Sample of vocabulary adopted in the title of Facebook communities

Blatant aggressive	Mild terminology
▪ Assassin …	▪ Humour …
▪ Cursed …	▪ Joke …
▪ Scoundrel…	▪ Fun…
▪ Son of a bitch…	▪ Funny…
▪ Your mother…	▪ Playful…
▪ I defy you to sue me…	▪ Jest…
Major characteristics	
▪ Users also make use of rude and aggressive language on their posts and comments. ▪ To a certain extent, they feel embedded with implicit permission to be rude with others.	▪ Oftentimes, the vocabulary is not as rude as in the other category. However, they enable users to explore a wide array of targets of their humour (e.g., blonde women, blacks, LGBT community, immigrants, overweight people, etc.)

As for the communities adopting blatant aggressive vocabulary to compose their titles, it has been possible to observe that, oftentimes, the language employed by most of the users tend to follow this same pattern. That is to say that they employ vocabulary considered rude, impolite and inappropriate in many ordinary social contexts. Indeed, they can be more frequently employed in situations of conflict and aggravated tension (Bartel, 2014). On the other hand, in more formal social settings or with people that do not share close ties, it is not expected to see them being employed. However, the data demonstrate that, in the context of social media platforms, users do not feel constrained by any social convention. In reality, they rather subvert and disregard such conventions. Moreover, they also tend to disregard social distances and openly employ rude vocabulary without any type of concern. Furthermore, it has also been possible to observe that the harsher the combination of vocabulary adopted in the title of many of these Facebook communities, the more comfortable users feel to unleash an equivalent level of aggressiveness in their language. Most probably, this behaviour is fuelled by a nurtured belief that online anonymity provides them with a 'protective' shield that would grant them implicit permission to behave this way.

The adoption of strong swear words and unusual terminologies to composing the titles of the Facebook communities may also contribute to conveying upfront to anyone interested, an idea of their nature and the type of content on display. Thus, the content may become more appealing to certain social groups than to others, given that "the person with the loudest, most inflammatory opinion gets the most attention" on social media platforms (Manfred, 2012, p. 2). Additionally, the users who engage in these communities might share common values, beliefs and ideologies, in alignment with homophilic characteristics; meaning that "contact between similar people occurs at a higher-level rate than among dissimilar people" (McPherson *et al.*, 2001, p. 416). In line with this argument, there are also voices advocating that homophilic ties represent one of the major building blocks of echo chambers (Takikawa and Nagayoshi, 2017). Consequently, just as disparagement racist discourses can potentially act as magnets attracting like-minded people, the adoption of strong swear words and rude vocabulary might have similar effects, establishing strong bonds amongst users in these Facebook communities.

What concerns the group of Facebook communities adopting an array of mild terminologies to compose the titles of their pages, the language employed is more socially acceptable than swear words. Nevertheless, this does not mean that they are exempt from impact in people's lives. On the one hand, the Facebook communities adopting swear words and unusual terminologies to compose their titles, oftentimes, target their disparagement humour towards single specific social groups. On the other hand, the group of Facebook communities adopting mild vocabulary, are much wider in scope. Consequently, rather than targeting solely black people, they disseminate disparagement humour towards many other social groups. They can encompass, for example: a) blonde women, b) the LGBT community, c) Brazilian North-eastern immigrants, d) Portuguese citizens, e) overweight people, f) Jews, g) followers of religions of African ancestry, and h) supporters of certain football teams.

This picture leads to the inference that, targeting a wider number of social groups, the embedded message is that there would be no reason for complaints since practically everyone has become subject of mockery. Actually, in one of such communities, a user has expressed his endorsement concerning a joke about black people with the following statement: 'a joke is a joke, guys. There are jokes about blonde women, jokes about mothers-in-law, and so forth. There is no big deal'. Besides, the disclaimer in another Facebook community says that 'it is not the intention to create and to foster prejudice and discriminatory attitudes, but rather to entertain'. Nonetheless, what these communities are, actually constructing and disseminating, is the spectacle of 'the other' for the amusement of few. Moreover, as the audience finds amusement in race joking, they are (in)directly endorsing and naturalising the stereotyped assumptions about the nature and 'deviant' characteristics of the non-hegemonic group.

Chapter 5

The embedded meaning of race joking
on social media

Introduction

In the context of social media in Brazil, the dissemination of racist discourses aims at disqualifying improved symbolic social spaces achieved by black women and repositioning them back to their 'original' place of inferiority. Over time, the Brazilian racism, constructed on the grounds of 'racial democracy' and the whitening ideology, has been internalised in the collective mindset (including that of non-white people), in such a way that discursive racist manifestations have been naturalised and also conveyed through a variety of forms, including race joking. This dynamic, combined with the racial hierarchy system, establishes strict boundaries of belonging, it legitimates a whitened national identity and, consequently, establishing differentiated social spaces for blacks and whites.

Within this picture, social media as a sort of modern-day pillory enables the proponents of white supremacist ideologies to perform and engage in a form of virtual whipping through race joking and their associated comments. In other words, joking is employed as a "socially acceptable way to articulate beliefs publicly and reproduce white supremacy and black inferiority" (Twine, 1998, p. 136). Thus, the proponents' desired outcome with this practice consists of legitimising the enduring racial hierarchical boundaries, whilst undermining the collective achievements of black Brazilian women. To achieve this goal, the predominant derogatory discourses on social media not only challenge the improved social spaces of black women, but they also convey white supremacist ideologies aiming at reinforcing the 'genuine' Brazilianness. Moreover, they disqualify black Brazilian women's achievements through expressions of laughter and jeer and, finally, they silence the opposing voices, which means that they delegitimise demands for greater racial equality.

Having said that, this chapter addresses five major narratives emerging from the data that allow us to understand the embedded meaning of the race joking enacted on social media in Brazil; which in essence articulates the perpetuation of racism in Brazilian society. These salient narratives are: 1) ridiculing the 'trespasser' of the white space, 2) black women as 'perpetrators' in a white space, 3) discourses challenging black women's schooling, 4) laughter as an endorser of whitening ideologies, and 5) delegitimising anti-racist discourses.

Ridiculing the 'trespasser' of white space

As previously addressed, the development of the whitening ideology in Brazil has established the distinction between social spaces associated with privilege, progress and modernity; in contrast to spaces of backwardness and inferiority. As such, the former space is considered a 'legitimate' white space whilst the latter is 'destined' to black people. This sort of perception is ingrained in the collective mind-set and naturalized both in race joking and in racial insults, in such a way that when black women make their way upwards into social spaces associated with white privilege, their achievement is ridiculed and disqualified as shown in the examples below. The posts were gathered from a publicly available Facebook page belonging to a black woman (actress, 31 years old, 2015). She had published a series of pictures of herself together with her white male partner travelling across some European cities while on vacation. Analysis of the posts reveals a discourse conveying the idea that the black woman has unduly 'trespassed' into a white space which, consequently, represents an incongruence that needs to be ridiculed.

Post #1:   The black woman's place is in the fields harvesting cotton, and not travelling across Europe.

Post #2:   She is pretty but, unfortunately, blacks are not on sale anymore.

Post #3:   Have you got official permission from the environmental authorities to walk around with an ape?

Post #4:   In the event of a blackout, the only thing you can see is the teeth.

Post #5:   How much does it cost for a *N...* to board on a ship?

Post #6:   I did not purchase a colour computer screen to see pictures in black and white.

Post #7:   It is already time that we put an end to this racism issue. It is time for both of us (humans and blacks) to live in peace.

First, harvesting cotton in the fields (Post #1) represents the idea of engagement in any subservient and unskilled occupation, in alignment with a colonial-like ideology. In that time, blacks were considered mere 'slaves of sickle and hoe' (Bethel, 1984), which implies that they were useful solely for unskilled manual labour in the plantations. Post #2 highlights a similar ideological element as the user claims that 'blacks are not on sale anymore'; once again referencing the colonial society that enslaved Africans and sold them as merchandise. Of course, the act of 'selling' black people in Post #2 cannot be taken literally. Rather, it represents a way of reducing the subject's value as an individual and attempts to highlight the black woman's inferiority. Objectifying a person can be deemed as an indirect way of removing their humanity and, consequently, their power and agency. Actually, Post #3, Post #5 and Post #7 also work to remove the black woman's humanity in various ways. First, Post #3 reduces her to an animalistic condition. Second, her agency is eroded by comments that simultaneously evoke the image of the slave ships and imply that she could not possibly afford a flight from Brazil to Europe (Post #5). As for Post #7, it is tricky because it starts developing an argument that, initially, seems to propose breaking the flow of derogatory jokes but, in effect, it endorses them by stripping the humanity from the black woman. It is a different type of discursive construction but, in essence, it still conveys the same colonial-like white supremacist ideologies manifested in many other social media posts.

Furthermore, returning to Post #1, in this discourse 'Europe' is presented as embodying the idea of modernity and civilization, as widely advocated from the early twentieth century, whereas blackness in Brazil has since been considered to represent the opposite of such values (Andrews, 1997; Twine, 1998; Wade, 2010). Consequently, Post #1 conveys a belief that 'Europe' is not the right place for black Brazilian women, since it is associated with the summit of white space. In this context, the meaning attributed to 'Europe' transcends the physical, geographical space; it embodies an element of the whitening ideology and, hence, under the users' perspective, a black woman in such 'privileged' social space is inconceivable. Moreover, given the fact that the construction of Brazilian national identity has been established on top of a whitening ideology that, for many decades, displayed white female beauty as the country's proud international public face, a black woman in Europe is not considered legitimate enough. Then, for the proponents of this ideology, the black woman 'trespassing' this social space contributes towards the postponement of Brazil achieving the desired modernity.

In effect, the combination of these posts conveys colonial-like white supremacist ideologies with the aim to establish distinct boundaries of social belonging. Such boundaries delineate who are the legitimate occupants of the core of Brazilian society, and who should stay at the margin. Conversely to what users oftentimes claim, such race joking is not exempt from social impacts and meant for entertainment purposes only. In reality, they serve the purpose of constructing, disseminating and reinforcing ascribed differentiated social spaces to whites and blacks in Brazilian society. On top of that, racist discourses conveyed through race joking also represent symbolic punishment to black women who dare 'trespassing' the boundaries of their assigned social spaces associated with inferiority and subservience. Within this context, social media platforms play the role of enabling people to perform and articulate colonial-like racist attitudes in different ways found in ordinary offline social contexts (Trindade, 2018b).

   Therefore, racist discourses in Brazil have not dramatically evolved in form over time, as the derogatory jokes previously analysed have been circulating in Brazilian society for a long time. Nevertheless, the proponents of such white supremacist ideologies have adapted themselves to contemporary social circumstances by shifting their arena towards the online environment. The consequence of this shift is that through social media they can reverberate their voice to a wider audience and for a long period (in some cases, up to three years, as discussed in Chapter 4). Furthermore, by presenting these jokes as harmless *brincadeirinha*, the social media users enjoy a convenient and socially acceptable escape route, whilst neglecting the legitimacy of demands for greater racial equality. By ridiculing 'the other', the white supremacists reduce the relevance of demands raised by the black community and aim to ensure that the dominant racial hierarchy system remains unchallenged and unchanged.

Black women as 'perpetrators' in a white space

According to a study conducted by Guimarães (2003) addressing categories of racial insults in Brazil, those exploring moral defects (e.g., stealing and delinquency) are among the most common. Probably not by chance, there are also many jokes circulating in Brazil associating blackness and criminality, such as the following examples.

   'Why blacks do not pay the bus fare? Because in a police car there is no fare taker.'

   'Why there is no black food? Because it would steal its nutrients.'

   'What shines most in a black? The handcuffs, when he is not holding a knife to rob the bank.'

Similar to what has already been argued by Weaver (2011a) and Pérez (2017), this sort of racist joke is easily found on the internet in Brazil both in websites dedicated to humour and also on major social media platforms. Actually, this delinquency stereotype comprises another element of the colonial legacy in shaping contemporary society's perception regarding black Brazilians. As argued in Chapter 1, in that social context, "Africans were considered strangers, pagans, thought to be untrustworthy or dangerous" (Schwartz, 1985, p. 330). Additionally, this type of joke "contains stereotypes that inferiorise inside a rhetorical comic device that, in certain readings, becomes more than 'just a joke' that can support racism through making the stereotype appear truthful and less or not ambivalent" (Weaver, 2011b, p. 95). Within this context, black women's successful upward social mobility can be undermined on social media through discourses reinforcing the moral defect stereotype, as shown in the subsequent examples. They were extracted from a publicly available Facebook page belonging to a black woman (business manager, 28 years old, 2016). She had posted several pictures of herself whilst skiing abroad during her vacation, and soon after that, many racist posts appeared on her page.

Post #1:   Are you also going to steal the snow?

Post# 2:   You have stolen even the white snow, ape.

Post #3:   Wait until the snow melts down and use the water to do the dishes.

Post #4:   At a certain moment there were a white guy and a black, then… Gosh! Where's the fuck my wallet?

Post #5:   A *N…* meets a hot blonde woman in a party. They go to her place and there he finds out that she is well off. He gets nuts. They go to her bedroom where there is a large full-HD flat TV. The woman lays down on the bed completely naked and says to him; 'come my *N…* and do what you know how to do better than anyone else, making justice to your race'. He then grabs the flat TV and runs away.

For most Brazilian citizens, long-lasting and thick snowy landscapes are associated predominantly with Northern Hemisphere countries. Over time, this association has been amplified by images and discourses fostered in many TV news programmes, movies and popular culture of people elegantly dressed and enjoying winter sports, which are associated with refinement and wealth (such as skiing, for example). Thus, both Post #1 and Post #2 establish the association between blackness and delinquency alongside the suggestion that, since thick snow is not something very common in Brazil, a black woman would probably steal it.

If we adjudge that stealing essentially can be defined as forcefully or skilfully taking ownership of something that originally did not belong to the person, 'stealing the snow' represents reaching a social space that does not belong to the subject. Consequently, the subject's presence in that social space is delegitimised. Besides, 'white snow' may initially sound redundant, given that it must be common knowledge that snow is naturally white. However, it can be inferred that the joker aims to amplify the embedded whitening ideology by including this detail, reinforcing the belief that such places (snowy international destinations) are meant only for white people.

In Post #3, it is once again possible to observe a challenge to black women's 'rightful' social space in Brazilian society, albeit by adopting a different figure of speech. The black woman is assumed to be performing some sort of subservient and unskilled occupation such as a cleaner, rather than travelling across 'white' and/or snowy international destinations. In sum, posts #1 to #3 coalesce contrasting notions of white and black women's boundaries of belonging and expectations of the later regarding occupations (unskilled and subservient), moral traits (delinquent), and appearance (ape or animalistic).

As for Post #4, it conveys the discourse that blacks are prone to stealing things, get involved in delinquent acts, or once they are around things might simply 'disappear'. In reality, the association 'blackness = delinquency' encompasses deep-seated ideas in the collective mind-set in Brazil, and this stereotyped association conveys the idea of social deviance. Namely, fostering this type of association through humour, the user establishes differentiated social belongings by contrasting positions. Within that, the 'anomalous' delinquent black woman belongs to the margin of society, rather than in a white social space since the latter embodies the 'normality'. In Post #5, in essence, the user has engaged with the mockery conveyed in the antecedent posts, and added his endorsement, sharing an additional joke to reinforce the racist discourse that presents black people as contumacious perpetrators.

Discourses challenging black women's schooling

Historically, careers such as law, medicine, and engineering have been considered 'noble' and prestigious occupations in Brazilian society and have , associated with middle- and upper-class white men. This assumption was established in the colonial period when no universities existed in Brazil and only the male sons of Portuguese settlers were able (and allowed) to access such educational level in Portugal; whilst white women were instead prepared to become housewives (McCoy, 1959; Cunha, 2000). Thus, this notion of access to a 'privileged' tertiary education and a prestigious career being restricted to white men has endured to this day (Ruffato, 2016; Filipak and Pacheco, 2017; Passarelli, 2019). Moreover, the colonial Brazilian Constitution established that "primary education was mandatory to all Brazilians, except people with any contagious disease, the ones not vaccinated and the enslaved" (Fonseca, 2012, p. 87).

Consequently, not only did the government compare enslavement with a contagious disease, but it also denied black people the possibility of attaining better conditions in the emerging class society in the early years of the Republic (Fonseca, 2012). Within that, nowadays it is not difficult to find jokes that deride black people's relative lack of formal education, such as, 'When does a black go to school? When it is under construction'. This joke not only challenges the plausibility of black people receiving an education but also conveys the belief that they are prone to be engaged in merely unskilled and low-paid occupations such as bricklayer. The examples of Facebook posts below have been constructed based on this same logic. The posts have been extracted from a publicly available Facebook page belonging to a black woman (medical doctor, 33 years old, 2016). She had posted a comment on her page in support of an elderly illiterate male patient who had been the subject of mockery by a white male doctor on Facebook because this particular patient of his was unable to write 'pneumonia' correctly. However, by expressing her disagreement with the behaviour of this white male doctor, she received dozens of racist comments such as the ones above displayed.

Post #1:   It is amazing this eco-friendly hairstyle. There must be even a baby ape hidden in there.

Post #2:   What the fuck? Are you really a medical doctor? I bet you are specialised only in removing lice out of homeless' hair.

Post #3:   What is the name of this bloody bastard? Does she really know how to use a stethoscope?

Post #4:   Wow, I had no idea that a *N…* could become a medical doctor. Who fancy taking the chances of a consultation?

Post #5:   I would never.

Post #6:   A *N…* Wait a minute, let me get my whip.

Post #7:   Say hi to your cellmates.

What can be observed is that the posts clearly challenge her engagement in the medical profession (Post #2, Post #3, and Post #4) and they also cast doubts on her actual professional competence (Post #4 and Post #5). They are fuelled by the deep-seated belief that such a 'noble' and prestigious career should be off-limits for blacks in general, and black women in particular. In effect, the presence of blacks in medical school is relatively reduced in Brazil in comparison to whites, and oftentimes, they are perceived as outsiders in this predominantly white male space (Santana, J. 2015).

The trend of an increasing number of black women in higher education over the past decades (Artes and Ricoldi, 2015) seems to shatter the ingrained belief that they would be 'destined' to perform only domestic work. Rather than engaging solely in subservient social roles, many black women are becoming medical doctors, dentists, business managers, journalists, etc., and this fact might upset the proponents of the whitening ideology because it clashes with their perception regarding black women's 'legitimate' limited social space. As for Post #1, the mocking of female Afro hairstyle represents, in fact, a visible facet of enduring ingrained negative perceptions around black beauty. A woman's hairstyle is an important element of femininity, beauty, and self-esteem, and also a racial marker (Caldwell, 2003). Consequently, mocking the Afro hairstyle of this woman intersects with both gender and race dimensions, meaning that the humour discourse not only erodes black aesthetic value but also positions the subject in a condition of inferiority in comparison to her white female counterparts. Moreover, by ridiculing her Afro hairstyle, the user also indirectly reinforces the legitimacy of a whitened beauty standard and disqualifies what is considered deviant from such a pattern.

Regarding Post #6, the user has adopted the symbolic figure of a whip not only to discredit or disqualify the black woman but also mainly to allocate her in a different social space. In other words, the discourse is that the black woman's 'natural' social space is at the *senzala* being punished rather than performing medicine. *Senzala*, as it has been previously addressed, is not only a physical depriving space used as accommodation for the slaves in colonial society but also a symbolic representation of lack of power, lack of agency and limited life prospects. During colonialism, as discussed in Chapter 1, misbehaviours such as running away from captivity or not complying with the master's commands represented sufficient reasons for public 'exemplary' punishment as a means to discourage others from following suit. Consequently, in the context of Post #6, it can be inferred that before the eyes of the user, the black woman committed a 'transgression' worthy of punishment by engaging in the noble medicine career. Within that, this sort of race joking represents the modern-day whips inflicting 'exemplary' punishments on the black women daring to 'trespass' a white space through tertiary education. Finally, in Post #7, once again, it is possible to notice a common manifestation associating blackness with delinquency, implying that prison would be the black woman's 'natural' social space.

Laughter as an endorser of whitening ideology

As I have explained in Chapter 3, repetition and the social context where racist humour is enacted contribute to turning it 'funny'. The mechanism of regular and constant repetition contributes towards the naturalisation, reinforcement and acceptance of the ridiculed portrayal of 'the other'. As for the social context, it provides shared meanings and decoding elements that enable people to find amusement with the enacted humour. Having said that, it has emerged from the data that laughter represents an important manifestation of both endorsement and amusement with the disparagement racist humour displayed on social media in Brazil. Within that, rather than explicitly verbalising their views after derogatory posts, it is not uncommon to identify that many social media users employ some sort of onomatopoeia to suggest the sound of laughter and jeer such as, for example: a) kkkk; b) rrrrr; c) rsrsrsrs; c) ahahaha; d) LOL; and e) the use of graphic icons known as emojis.

Laughter manifestation in the online environment (also called 'lulz' or 'lolling' by some authors) is an important form of discourse because it contributes to concealing identification with discriminatory ideologies without sounding blatantly racist. Moreover, laughter provides a convenient escape route for people expressing what it might not be appropriate to be openly verbalised (Dahia, 2010). Laughter also represents a detachment between the person and the subject of mockery, meaning that they stand at a higher position than the subject of the humour (Halfeld, 2013). Moreover, "humour and laughter are created from, and convey, a sense of superiority over the object of laughter" (Weaver, 2011b, p. 14).

Thus, the following set of four posts, in combination with their respective associated comments, contributes to illustrate the manifestation of this type of discourse. They were extracted from a publicly available Facebook page displaying many jokes about black people published in 2016. Each one of them is followed by comments where the users manifest their endorsement with a variety of onomatopoeia[1] suggesting their amusement with the disparagement humour.

---

[1] For the sake of analytical accuracy, all the onomatopoeia expressions reproduced here follow exactly the same spelling and length employed by social media users.

Post #1:   Why there is no black food? Because it would steal its nutrients.

Comment #1: LOL!

Post #2:   A black man passed away, and soon after arriving in heaven, an angel asks for his name. In reply, he says 'Leonardo Di Caprio'. The angel then says 'come on, you are pulling my leg! Tell me the truth'. However, as the black man insists, the angel calls the head office enquiring: can you confirm if the Titanic sank or went on fire?

Comment #1: kkkkkkkkkk

Comment #2: I have enjoyed the joke! kkkkkkkkkkkkkkkkkkkkkk

Post #3:   A *N...* meets a hot blonde woman in a party. They go to her place and there he finds that she is well off. He gets nuts. They go to her bedroom where there is a large full-HD flat TV. The woman lays down on the bed completely naked and says to him; 'come my *N...* and do what you know how to do better than anyone else, making justice to your race'. He then grabs the flat TV and runs away.

Comment #1: That was amazingly funny. kkkkkk

Comment #2: kkkkkkkkkkkkkkk

Post #4:   Why a black pregnant woman expecting triplets was arrested? She was charged for gang formation.

Comment #1: Even my mother found it funny. Kkkkkkkkkkkkkkkkkkkkk

Comment #2: ahahahahahahahahahahahahahah

The seven comments above displayed, triggered by the four-race jokes, reveal clear evidence of the expression of amusement by the users. Moreover, as it can be recognised, Post #3 and Post #4 repeat jokes already seen and analysed in previous topics in this book. Thus, their repetition here in another Facebook page contributes to evidence the persistent internalisation of certain racial stereotyping in the collective mindset and also their reinforcement. Moreover, it can also be observed that the longer the onomatopoeia employed by them, the funnier it might have sounded for the person. These expressions of laughter are challenging to interpret because they can be ambiguous. On the one hand, they can represent that the person has simply enjoyed the joke that has been posted and considered it amusing and harmless. However, on the other hand, they can also represent an endorsement of the discourse embedded in the disparagement humour. Actually, "the person finding [this type of] joke funny is implicitly accepting those stereotyped assumptions about the nature of the other" (Billig, 2001, p. 277). In other words, the person is expressing agreement with the disqualified and caricature depiction of 'the other' embedded in the joke, or taking that portrayal as natural, acceptable and consistent with reality.

Within this context, according to Freud's psychological theory of relief, people laugh "to release emotional or psychic tension and this produces pleasure" (Watson, 2015, p. 410). In effect, this is a possible analytical approach to users' laughter manifestations after a race joke. However, it does not change the fact that users' 'source of relief' to unleash their psychic tensions and achieve pleasure is comprised of ridiculed black people. Additionally, "mocking of someone is equivalent to turn the person powerless, make him/her weaker and infantilised" (Dahia, 2008, p. 705).

Consequently, the laughter of these users represents a subtle and not verbalised agreement with the derogating discourses embedded in the humorous posts. Moreover, the laughter also represents a peculiar form of manifestation because, given its ambiguity, it provides users with a convenient escape route. It means that they cannot be immediately pointed out as supporters of that discourse. This convenient escape route is consistent with the easy social navigation in Brazil provided by the *jeitinho* (knack, artifice). Concisely, it means that people skilfully dodge themselves from complaints of this type of attitude claiming that they were simply 'friendly' and harmless jest (*brincadeirinha* in Portuguese). Thus, this picture resembles the paradoxical circumstance coined by Bonilla-Silva (2006) as 'racism without racists', where the racist act is identified and acknowledged by society, but the agent is 'absent'.

In complement to this analysis, another intriguing aspect emerged from the data encompasses the influential effect of people's laughter on other users. This is said because if one perceives that somebody else has considered the post funny and amusing, they can feel at ease to express their jeer as well, fearless of any rebuke since they are not the only one laughing about the content. Actually, to a certain extent, this behaviour coalesces with the neuroscience concept known as 'laughter is contagious', meaning that individuals tend to mimic other people's gestures and behaviours and, with that, reinforce social bonds (Thompson, 2006; Bergland, 2017). Clear evidence in this direction lays in the fact that it is not difficult to find that laughable comments conveyed through the aforementioned onomatopoeic expressions are followed suit by many others in the sequence, which ultimately can represent a different facet of the endless echo in the cyberspace of racist discourses. To illustrate this aspect, the following post and sample of associated comments were extracted from a publicly available Facebook page displaying dozens of examples of race joking. The post has triggered a total of 38 comments ranging from the publication date on 02 November 2013 up to 07 November 2016, and 21 of them (i.e. more than half) were simply expressions of laughter.

Post #1:   A vulture had swallowed a diamond and the owner of the precious stone hired a man to kill the bird and retrieve it. When the man arrived to kill the bird, there were hundreds of them flocking together and just one apart. Then he shot exactly that lone bird and it happens that it had been the one who had swallowed the diamond. The owner was surprised and asked how he could have known that. The man replied that when black becomes rich, he does not mingle with his peers. Kkkkkkkkkkkk

Comment #1: It is just a joke. Kkk

Comment #2: That was awesome! Kkkkkkkkk

Comment #3: Cool! Kkkk

Comment #4: kkkkkkkkk

Comment #5: kkkkkkkkkkkkk

Comment #6: I love this joke! Kkkkkkkkkkkkkkkkkkkkkkkk

Comment #7: kkkkkkkkkkkk

Comment #8: kkkkkk

Comment #9: Although I am a black man myself, I love jokes about blacks. One thing is to be racist, and other is to find amusement in a joke. How long does it take for a black woman take the trash out of the house? Nine months. Kkkkkkkkkkkkkkkkkkkk

Two major aspects call our attention in the above thread of comments. First, the combination of the joker's discourse (i.e. Post #1) and the audience (i.e. the nine subsequent comments) turn black people into a subject of mockery and ridicule. Additionally, the fact that a single race joke has enabled to keep engaging users over a three years period, coalesces with the concept of the long tail of posts previously discussed in Chapter 4. In other words, the continuation of this laugh echoing for such a long period in the online environment contributes towards the naturalisation of the stereotyped portrayal of black Brazilians, and the reinforcement of their condition of laughable subjects.

The second major aspect encompasses Comment #9, which displays three discursive endorsement manifestations. However, rather than conflicting they, in fact, coalesce and complement each other. First, by self-declaring black, the user aims at neutralising claims of embedded racism in Post #1. Second, to strengthen the argument of the absence of racism, the user adds another derogatory joke to the conversation. Finally, there is the long onomatopoeia expressing laughter, which not only echoes the ones present in the antecedent comments but also endorses his humorous post.

This particular Comment #9 also leads us towards another relevant reflection. It contributes to demonstrating that not every person who engages in the construction and dissemination of racist disparagement humour in Brazil is white. In reality, race joking on social media might rather be enacted by 'whitened' people. In other words, it means to say that colonial-like white supremacist ideology has been internalised across different racial groups in Brazilian society. Hence, it has also become naturalised in people's discourses, including the self-declared black man in Comment #9 above.

Consequently, in conclusion, it seems that in the context of social media platforms, the relevance of the person's racial group is reduced because the whitening ideology is at the core of the construction and dissemination of race joking. This way, people of different racial groups, including non-whites, not only find amusement in the derogatory jokes but they also naturalise and grant legitimacy to them. Besides, granting legitimacy to the mockery provides a navigation strategy to the non-whites across the colour continuum in such a way to allow them to maintain some distance from the lower end of the racial hierarchy scale (black) and get closer to the upper end (white), as previously illustrated in Figure 1.2.

Delegitimising anti-racist discourses

There is evidence revealing that, overall, the internet is a white space, meaning that whites have greater access to this digital technology than blacks (Waiselfisz, 2007; Kettrey and Laster, 2014; Roshani, 2016). However, what concerns the context of social media platforms in Brazil, more important than a white space, the data reveals that this digital technology is, in fact, a 'whitened' space. Within that, one of its most important characteristics comprises the approach towards delegitimising the relevance of opposing voices. In other words, to keep intact the supporting pillars of Brazil's enduring racism, it is important to disqualify and silence voices that reveal the ingrained racist discourses in Brazilian society. In fact, "whenever a black speaks out [about racism], they become disturbing and annoying" (Oliveira, 2017, p. 3). Additionally, the moment a black person verbalises the persistence of racist discourses in Brazilian society, they are discredited by the dominant elite and, oftentimes, the black's argument is coined as mere whining or over-victimisation complaint (Vitorino, 2018).

Within this context, the data reveals many situations on social media where expressions of disagreement with disparagement discourses against black people are strongly delegitimised by 'whitened' users. The following example was extracted from a public Facebook page displaying dozens of jokes about black people (published in 2014). At a certain point, a black female user expressed her disagreement with the content and, her comment triggered a series of other reactive posts displaying disdain regarding her opinion and also endorsements for the derogatory jokes.

> Post #1:   'Why do black people only eat white chocolate in the cinema? To avoid biting their own finger.'
>
> 'What shines most in a black? The handcuffs, when he is not holding a knife to rob the bank.'
>
> 'Why blacks do not attend evening school? To avoiding failing due absence.'
>
> 'What is the difference between a tin full of shit and a black? The tin.'
>
> 'A dog entered the church and peed on the altar. What colour is the dog? White, because if it was black, it would have shit.'
>
> Comment #1: How disgusting. What did you have in your mind when you published this offensive post?
>
> Comment #2: Today's best! Kkkk

Comment #3: Fuck off *negona*[2] and stop whining. I am just playing around.

Comment #4: Where is the racism here? It is just a joke.

Comment #5: kkkkkkkkkkkkkkk

Comment #6: Fuck you!

Comment #7: I cannot stop laughing!

Comment #8: Too much *mimimi.*

Comment #9: Here it goes again a black woman playing the victim card. Stop with this victimisation. Enough is enough.

Comment #10: Racism lays within your mind, and not in other people's. Enough with this shit.

The scenario above depicted by the sample of reactive comments reveals that, by challenging racist discourses on social media, blacks face disdain from the proponents of white supremacist ideologies. The disdain becomes evident, first, by the strong language employing swear words (Comments #3, #6 and #10); which either attempt to end the debate before it even starts, or to incite an escalation with equivalent language. Second, the disdain is also manifested by expressions of laughter and jeer (Comments #2, #5, #7 and #8), which play the double role of endorsing the race joking and reducing the relevance of the complaint raised by the black woman. Third, there are discourses manifesting denial of embedded racism in the jokes (Comments #4, #9 and #10), alongside the common claim that 'it is only a joke' or *brincadeirinha* (Comments #3 and #4). As previously addressed in this book, the 'it is only a joke' excuse, provides a convenient social navigation tool for the proponents of race joking. It is a clear manifestation of Brazil's *jeitinho*, meaning that claiming the post represents simply a 'harmless' jest, the user expects to dodge from complaints and disarm opponent voices (i.e. weaken the counter-narratives).

Concerning the denial of embedded racism, the posts reveal a dualistic discursive strategy. First, they employ a direct and straightforward challenge to

---

[2] *Negona* stands for an informal racial terminology in Portuguese (usually impolite) to talk about black women. Additionally, it is also the augmentative form of *nega*, whilst the diminutive form is *neguinha*, which in most circumstances are quite pejorative.

black people ('where is the racism here?', in Comment #4), which could potentially trigger the opportunity for a constructive debate. Nevertheless, given the pattern of subsequent aggressive comments, most probably, that arena might not be the most appropriate space for this initiative. Actually, on social media platforms, "the person with the loudest, most inflammatory opinion gets the most attention" (Manfred, 2012, p. 2).

The second discursive strategy shifts the responsibility of any racist content towards the blacks (Comments #9 and #10), claiming that since racism lays solely on black's minds, this leads them to develop a permanent state of victimisation. This discursive strategy aims to remove any trace of legitimacy in anti-racist discourse raised by black Brazilians. The logic is since the 'alleged' issue has been individualised (i.e. it is within the person's mind and nowhere else), it does not represent a wider social issue worthy of attention or credibility.

Finally, and intertwined with the previous aspects discussed, there are also discourses classifying anti-racist narratives as mere whining manifestations (Comments #8, #9, and #10). By framing the black woman's complaint as a whining manifestation, users convey the discourse that opposing standpoints are worthless, infantile and, consequently, do not deserve attention. Thus, whatever is verbalised by anti-racist voices are regarded simply as *mimimi*. The interesting aspect regarding this particular minimalist verbal expression *mimimi* is the fact that, in Portuguese, it is nothing more than a sort of onomatopoeia to convey the idea of disdain and irrelevance of other people's demands, complaints and opinions. Hence, by encapsulating anti-racist discourse into this *mimimi* box, ultimately, the proponents of white supremacist ideologies are saying that blacks' demands are equally meaningless.

Having said that, there is another example that contributes to illustrate discursive strategies aimed at delegitimising anti-racist discourses on social media. The following posts were extracted from a publicly available Facebook page displaying the picture of five white girls with blackface make-up. The five girls were undergraduate students of medicine and the post was published in 2015. Within the Brazilian social context, blackface jokes and performances are considered offensive and highly disrespectful by the black community (Bechara, 2017; Dias, 2017; Nascimento, 2017). Given this context, at a certain point, a black woman challenged the blackface post with the five white girls highlighting its racist and disrespectful content.

Post #1:   This type of behaviour is not expected from future female medical doctors. It is completely inappropriate.

Post #2:	Honey, I know why you took it personally and you are mad about it. You are fat and dating a black guy. Therefore, you should, in fact, feel offended. I understand. Kkkkkkkkkkkk.
Post #3:	Do you know what irony means, stupid? The girls are just playing around. For sure, you must be black.
Post #4:	These black people complain about everything.
Post #5:	Do you see? Lots of *mimimi* leads to that my dear: reaction!

The reactive posts bring several elements aiming at discrediting, reducing and delegitimising the value and relevance of the anti-racist discourse enacted by the black woman. To start with, in Post #2, the user (a white woman) makes use of a linguistic resource to reduce the black woman's attractiveness potential. By asserting that the black woman might by overweight, the user is recalling the Brazilian hegemonic beauty standard (white, straight blonde hair, clear eyes, and slim) and implying that the black woman does not fit within this pattern. In contrast, the user might consider herself to be closer to the hegemonic beauty standard and, consequently, above the black woman in the racial hierarchy. Additionally, by suggesting that the black woman dates a black man, it aims to reinforce her position of racial and social inferiority. As such, in this condition of inferiority, the expectation is that the black woman should be voiceless. Finally, the long onomatopoeia expression of laughter represents the final touch of disdain and irrelevance concerning the complaint raised by the black woman.

The subsequent posts, again, make evident the use of discursive strategies that, first, shift the responsibility of the perceived racist content towards the claimant. Besides, they also bring the recurring 'it is only a joke' excuse that bestows implied permission to be disrespectful towards other people. Finally, the black woman's voice is disqualified, delegitimised and striped of any relevance (Posts #4 and #5). Ultimately, these posts reveal that in strongly 'whitened' spaces (i.e. influenced by colonial-like racist ideologies), voices enacting anti-racist arguments are not heard, acknowledged or taken seriously. Under the perspective of the proponents of white supremacist ideologies, such discourses become simply inconvenient and out of place arguments.

Major differences between online and offline racism

A pertinent question that emerges when analysing the enactment of race joking on social media, is how it differs from ordinary offline contexts. First, it can be observed that, in contrast to the offline environment, users in the online environment tend to disregard any social distance between themselves and the victims of mockery. Thus, people who engage in posting and commenting on derogatory content can convey their discourses towards people with whom they might not have previously met. In this regard, as previously discussed in Chapter 4, the data reveals that in 76.2% of the cases of online racism analysed, users had no previous relationship or proximity to the victims, whether in real life or online. Second, social media platforms also enable like-minded people to connect among themselves, thus amplifying the reach and reverberation of their voices in more aggressive ways than found in an ordinary offline social context. Furthermore, studies highlight five elements that contribute to differentiating online from offline hate speech: a) anonymity, b) invisibility, c) community, d) instantaneousness, and e) harm. Their combination turns the practice of online hate speech different from the offline context and more problematic (Brown, 2017).

On top of that, the critical analysis developed in this book has allowed the identification of two major differentiation aspects between online and offline racism in Brazil: 1) the circumstances triggering the racist attitudes, and 2) their reach and reverberation. Racist insults against black people in ordinary daily circumstances are not a new phenomenon in Brazilian society. Already in the 1930s, several newspapers used to openly disparage black people (Levine, 1973). Moreover, different authors reveal that racist insults still happen in a variety of ordinary daily contexts (Guimarães, 2003; Oliveira and Barreto, 2003; Bartel, 2014; Machado *et al.*, 2016). In other words, these authors are evidencing that racist insults against black Brazilians are, actually, an enduring social practice rather than one that recently emerged with social media platforms. Additionally, other distinct aspect emerged from the analysis is the fact that the language style identified in the race joking posts coalesces with the offline racial insults found in the aforementioned studies. Consequently, this finding corroborates this enduring social practice and illustrates that the embedded ideologies nurturing the insults have also been reproduced for a long time and continue to circulate and being reinforced.

Nevertheless, different from what happens on social media, the triggers of racist insults in ordinary offline social contexts are predominantly situations of conflict (e.g. argument between neighbours, disagreements in the workplace, argument after car collisions, argument at parties, etc.). Supporting evidence for this claim is found in a study where the authors have analysed 2,061 cases of racism brought to court across nine Brazilian states (Machado *et al.*, 2016).

The authors advocate that "when racial insults operate in a conflictive way, [negative] stereotypes are employed to disqualify the person and, quite frequently, animalise the black person. The court cases refer much more significantly to situations of conflict" than other circumstances (Machado *et al.*, 2016, p. 23).

Thus, does it mean that racial insults are not verbalised in other non-conflictive circumstances? Most probably, that is not the case. However, nowadays, people do not verbalise everything that comes to their mind indistinctively or without pondering the place where they are (Silva, L. 2003). Likewise, in the US social context for example, "while overt racist discourse has declined from public view since the civil rights era, it continues to reside in private contexts or has become coded and covert in public" (Pérez, 2017, p. 956). In other words, this picture reveals that, apart from conflict situations where oftentimes the racial offences emerge more easily, people might refrain to be openly racist in other circumstances due to social convention constraints. However, since on social media the proponents of white supremacy circumvent offline conventions, they do not feel constrained in unleashing racialized insults.

The second difference between the context of social media and ordinary daily context encompasses the reach and reverberation of the racist insults. The aforementioned studies addressing racist insults in Brazil provide no evidence that the ordinary offline social context engages a multitude of people and nor that they trigger long-lasting conversations. This does not mean to say that they do not reverberate or cause an impact on the parties involved. However, oftentimes, their reach is more limited when compared with the online environment. On social media, for example, the long tail of posts reveals that race joking is capable of reaching a wide audience, keep the derogatory conversation flowing for a long period, and attracting other people to the same dialogue. Consequently, this explains why social media platforms enable people to construct, disseminate and reinforce racist ideologies in different ways found in ordinary offline social contexts. Ultimately, racist insults against black Brazilians have not changed their form considerably over time, as the perpetuation of the vocabulary employed indicates. Nevertheless, social media platforms enable the proponents of white supremacist ideologies to convey their values and beliefs differently from what it is seen in offline social contexts.

Chapter 6

Examining the anti-racist
discursive strategies

Introduction

The previous chapters have revealed that, in Brazil, white supremacist ideologies remain very strong and vivid in the collective mindset. Additionally, such ideologies are transmitted across different generations, reproduced and reinforced in an echo chamber effect. Within that, the data has also revealed that upwardly mobile black Brazilian women comprise the preferred target of colonial-like racist ideologies on social media platforms. Consequently, this picture leads us to question which anti-racist narratives are being enacted by black Brazilian women. Actually, as discussed in Chapter 4, to persuade people to come out of echo chambers, it is necessary to deconstruct the ideology that ties people together (Bessi *et al.*, 2017). Having said that, in alignment with the discussion developed in Chapter 2, there is evidence revealing that Afro hairstyle embodies the most distinctive political response to racism (Lima, 2015; Lima, 2016; Oliveira, 2016; Alvez, 2017).

The Afro hairstyle serves the purpose of challenging not only Brazil's 'whitened' hegemonic aesthetics ideals but also white supremacist ideologies. The resistance discourses grounded on Afro hairstyle aims, first, to convey a renewed perception of black aesthetics as something worthy of being celebrated and a source of ethnic pride. In second place, it grants the necessary legitimacy and agency to black women as an important and genuine constituent of Brazilian society and, finally, it represents an important symbolic element to praise their upward social mobility. Furthermore, it is also interesting to notice that this type of discursive strategy adopted by black Brazilian women is found also in different social contexts. In Italy, for instance, young black women are "contesting the racialisation and degradation that targets their bodies and lives" by fostering on the internet the political symbology of their Afro hairstyle (Frisina and Hawthorne, 2018, p. 719).

Having said that, the data set gathered for the study was explored inductively and deductively aiming at allowing the emergence of the most relevant anti-racist narratives constructed by the users. This process led to the identification of the following key themes: 1) Afro hairstyle as a symbolic marker of political positioning, 2) praising black beauty to boost individual and collective self-esteem, 3) empowering through sharing similar lived experiences of racism, and 4) conveying the idea that black women are no longer voiceless as they used to be in the past.

Afro hairstyle as a symbol of resistance

Within the Brazilian social context, Afro hairstyle represents a distinct symbolic tension point where ambivalent ideologies are manifested. On the one hand, for a long period, it has been a sort of magnet of many disqualifying associations and negative portrayals that have reduced its aesthetic value (Xavier, 2013; Quadrado, 2015). Within that, the list of pejorative names employed to describe Afro hairstyle is immense, including[1]: a) hard hair, b) kinky hair, c) witch's broom hair, d) steel wool hair, e) hopeless hair, f) poorly kept hair, g) messy hair, and h) untamed hair (Caldwell, 2003; Edmonds, 2007; Oliveira, 2016). This myriad of terminologies is oftentimes employed against both black men and women, but the latter represents the preferred target of such insults because the hairstyle is an important element of femininity, beauty, self-esteem and also a racial marker (Souza, 1990; Caldwell, 2003). Consequently, insulting Afro hairstyle intersects with gender, race and beauty pattern, meaning that the insult not only delegitimises the black female aesthetic but also places them in a position of inferiority in comparison to their white female counterparts. Moreover, disqualifying Afro hairstyle contributes towards reinforcing the deviant aspect of 'the other' whilst indirectly reinforcing the normative role played by the hegemonic 'whitened' beauty standard.

On the other hand, Facebook data reveals that the female Afro hairstyle also represents the most important element of empowerment for black Brazilian women in challenging colonial-like racist discourse. Supporting evidence for this argumentation is found in a political movement led mostly by black female bloggers called 'My hair, my crown', where they aim to convey the message that their hairstyle represents a symbol of their power and agency (Lima, 2015; Lima, 2016; Alvez, 2017). Furthermore, interviewing Maria Lúcia da Silva (director of *Instituto Amma Psique Negritude*) has said that currently in Brazil, Afro hairstyle embodies the symbol of an empowerment movement where you hear black women verbalising that they are going through a transition process. However, Maria Lúcia da Silva added, the interesting aspect is that more than an aesthetic hair transition they are, in fact, experiencing an inner transition.

---

[1] Their respective meanings in Portuguese are: a) cabelo duro; b) cabelo crespo; c) cabelo vassoura de bruxa; d) cabelo de Bombril; e) cabelo sem jeito; f) cabelo malcuidado; g) cabelo bagunçado; and h) cabelo indomável.

Within that, black women have been at the foreground of adopting Afro hairstyle as an empowered resistance element, conveying a clear political positioning and resisting Brazilian ingrained racism. Hence, praising and accepting their natural hairstyle goes beyond an aesthetic choice and conveys strong political symbolic meanings (Oliveira, 2016). Within this context, the following set of eight Facebook posts contributes to illustrate this inner transition process just addressed. The posts were extracted from three publicly available Facebook pages focused on empowering black women through the acceptance of their natural curled hair. In Facebook page "A", the following posts call our attention.

Post #1.A: It is not only your hair that changes when you accept it naturally curled. We also change as an individual… and a lot. (*user: D.O., 22 years old, undergraduate student, posted on 01/08/2016*).

Post #2.A: My self-discovery process started three years ago. The first step encompassed accepting my natural Afro hairstyle, and only now that I have been admitted into university, my social position as a young black woman became more salient to me. My university is a predominantly white environment and, therefore, being a woman, black, poor and beneficiary of affirmative action programmes represents a challenging scenario to me. (*user: A.P., 21 years old, undergraduate student, posted on 09/02/2015*).

Regarding Post #1.A, it conveys an idea that the transformation experienced by the female user, identified as D.O., has gone beyond the aesthetic layer and reached her in a deeper level as a person going through a process of self-discovery. Moreover, her statement also conveys a message of ethnic identification embedded in the acceptance of her naturally curled hair. Actually, over the years, the ambivalent discourses about natural Afro hairstyle in Brazil have constructed a very challenging scenario for black women, where many of them have manifested dissatisfaction with their curled hair since childhood, as revealed by different authors (e.g., Souza, 1990; Caldwell, 2003; Mikulak, 2011). Consequently, accepting it and praising its beauty contributes towards breaking this damaging equation where Afro hairstyle embodies a myriad of negative attributes.

Moreover, Afro hairstyle also challenges the hegemonic 'whitened' Eurocentric beauty standard that grants legitimacy only to straight blonde hair and, simultaneously, reveals a renewed perception of what it means to be black in Brazil. Within that, there is an interesting reflection raised by Souza (1990) where the author argues that being black in Brazil is not simply granted by birth. In fact, the author explains, a person 'becomes' black through the acceptance of their ethnic identity, values and historical roots. Ultimately, the acceptance of these elements is what validates the process of 'becoming' a black person.

In alignment with this argumentation, a person's cultural identity (rooted in meaningful historic legacies) is what makes possible the person to 'becoming' who they are (Hall, 1990). This idea implies a proactive role to be played by the person, rather than passive, meaning that one's ethnic identity is not simply naturally granted, but developed over time and conquered. Besides, in the study 'When I discovered myself black', B. Santana (2015) shares her own ethnic identity self-discovery process. The author says that since her childhood, she has lived a conflictive relation with her Afro hairstyle because her grandmother used to comb them in such a way to avoid looking like '*neguinha*' (a pejorative diminutive form of black women in Portuguese). It is for this same reason that the internal transformation experienced by the black female user identified as D.O. in Post #1.A matters to her.

As with Post #2.A, the female user identified as A.P. also reveals that she has gone through a self-discovery process by accepting her natural Afro hairstyle. However, she brings to the surface a different array of distinctive elements in her statement. First, accepting her hairstyle not only contributed to her self-discovery as a black woman but also to what symbolic social space she might belong. Thus, her social position becomes more evident to her as she navigates in a social space that embodies different levels of symbolic social privileges and, besides, in that social space (i.e. at the university) she realises that she is the exception, rather than the rule. In other words, since she is not the norm in that social space, she might indirectly embody 'otherness' before her peers.

This reflection leads us towards the second distinct element that the same black female user identified as A.P. in Post #2.A brings to the surface: the intersection of gender, race, class and the means that contributed to her admission in the university. The combination of these dimensions composes a challenging scenario for her because they (in)directly reinforce her 'original' symbolic social space that might differ from most of her peers. However, discovering herself as a black woman through the natural Afro hairstyle contributes to her positioning within that social context and the development of navigation strategies. Consequently, her self-discovery process transcends aesthetic aspects and embodies strong symbolic, material and political positioning, playing an important role for her to succeed in that social context, regardless of the intersectional dimensions she points out.

In effect, corroborating previous studies (Souza, 1990; Caldwell, 2003; Mikulak, 2011), the data reveals that negative perceptions concerning Afro hairstyle are learned since childhood. On top of that, they are learned within the black family realm, which indicates that such beliefs are passed on across generations. Within that, in the public Facebook page "B" (2015), the following posts contribute to illustrate this reflection.

Post #1.B: I grew up just like many other black girls, who have been taught to reject our complexion, our hairstyle and our identity. I did not understand my mother's reason for constantly teasing me about my hair. However, I remember two things clearly. First, the pain of the straightening process she made me go through on a regular basis. Second, her warnings that, if I did not do that, I would become ugly and unattractive [to men]. Nevertheless, do you want to know something? My days of whitening my identity are over. I have decided to empower myself starting with my natural Afro hairstyle. (*user: D.C., 30 years old, secretary, posted on 29/06/2015*).

Post #2.B: A couple of years ago I faced a self-discovery process of becoming myself a black woman through my Afro hairstyle, that nowadays I am aware that it is curled, rather than hard, as I got used to hearing. I have been taught to hate my wide nose and Afro hairstyle since my childhood, but I was unable to hate my skin tone. Nevertheless, the moment I realised that my blackness is present beyond my skin tone, and encompasses all my features, my natural Afro hairstyle got a renewed and empowered meaning to me. (*user: T.A., 29 years old, business analyst, posted on 23/03/2016*).

Post #3.B: The black woman's hair embodies the symbol of our blackness. (*user: T.R., 25 years old, saleswoman, posted on 22/04/2014*).

Analysing the powerful accounts of these black women identified as D.C. and T.A., respectively in Post #1.B and #2.B, it is possible to identify elements of ingrained negative perceptions regarding Afro hairstyle. In Post #1.B, for example, the black woman's mother justified the need to straighten her hair because she was concerned with the daughter's future female attractive potential. However, the embedded discourse is that, since the mother was unable to remove any other characteristic black trait from the daughter (e.g. skin tone or wide nose), she adopted the only strategy within her reach (i.e. straightening the Afro hair). Consequently, the aim was to lessen, as much as possible, an evident racial marker represented by the Afro hairstyle and to enable the daughter to navigate within Brazil's colour continuum closer to the upper end of the racial hierarchy, and as far as possible from the lower end (as previously illustrated in Figure 1.2). Thus, this picture also reveals that the negative perceptions around black aesthetics are ingrained not only in the mind of racist people but also within the mind of 'whitened' persons, such as the mother of the black woman identified as D.C. in Post #1.B.

Moreover, in Post #1.B, it becomes evident that the black woman identified as D.C. was taught since her childhood to despise her black features and indirectly embrace the hegemonic white female aesthetic patterns. This demonstrates how negative perceptions become naturalised in the Brazilian social context and transmitted across different generations over time. In fact, in addition to the naturalisation of such perceptions within the family realm, the process reaches the wider society through its incorporation into popular culture. On this regard, different studies reveal the dissemination and reinforcement of many negative attributes regarding Afro hairstyle on successful popular songs (Caldwell, 2003; Trotta and Santos, 2012), in race joking (Fonseca, 1994; Dahia, 2008; 2010; Fonseca, 2012; Trindade, 2018b) and on TV comedy shows (Machado and Muniz, 2013). Therefore, the transition of such pejorative and derogatory discourses from popular culture towards social media represents the continuation of this naturalisation process and the reinforcement of the negative attributes.

Another important element emerged from Post #1.B and Post #2.B encompasses the respective black female users D.C. and T.A. conscious decision to cease fostering the 'whitened' beauty ideal that they have been taught to give credit to since their childhood. These black women have said 'enough' for themselves and, indirectly, for the people around them and posting these comments publicly on social media demonstrates that they are willing to share their decision with a wider audience. Moreover, another interesting aspect of the decision taken by these black women, from Post #1.A to Post #2.B is that they have reported having taken their decision in recent past. The user identified as A.P. in Post #2.A, for example, says that her self-discovery process started three years before publishing the comment, whilst the user identified as T.A. in Post #2.B says that the decision had been taken in a couple of years before the post. In alignment with that, B. Santana (2015, p. 20) shares a similar experience saying that "I am 30 years old, but it has been only 10 years that I have become black. Before that I was *morena*". This picture reveals that, given the fact that these black women have been taught since an early age to dislike their natural Afro hairstyle, breaking the chains of this internalised belief, might require a considerable amount of energy and self-confidence. Moreover, it contributes towards the reinforcement of the argument that the process of 'becoming' black might also require a great deal of maturity and understanding. Consequently, making sense of (or re-signifying) historic legacies takes time, and most probably comes at an adult age.

Finally, in Post #3.B, the black woman identified as T.R. attributes a strong symbolic power to female Afro hairstyle as a genuine representation of the racial group, highlighting its relevance. Additionally, the woman's statement also implies a need to adopt a defining symbol to embody all aspects related to blackness in Brazil. Consequently, Post #3.B conveys not only the acceptance of 'becoming' black but also, indirectly, classifying the whitening ideology as an illegitimate value to black women.

In complement to the analysis developed up to this point, the next three posts (Facebook page "C") contribute to revealing another angle of the strong symbology embedded in Afro hairstyle. In this case, the black women are voicing the acceptance of their renewed ethnic identity first to themselves and then to the wider public.

> Post #1.C: I strongly believe that accepting your natural [Afro] hairstyle is a political attitude to expressing, firstly to yourself, and then to the world around you, that you accept your real identity. (*user: A.N.Z., 25 years old, student, posted on 22/06/2014*).

> Post #2.C: We have to accept the black component that it is within each one of us. (*user: N.A.P., 27 years old, saleswoman, posted on 05/05/2015*).

> Post #3.C: Independence comes primarily with self-acceptance of our ethnic identity. (*user: M.I.S., 22 years old, hairdresser, posted on 05/08/2015*).

First, the black woman identified as A.N.Z. in Post #1.C highlights the relevance of accepting her natural Afro hairstyle as a political positioning. However, what is particularly interesting in Post #1.C is the fact that the black woman stresses that the process is first directed towards oneself, and then to the external world. Namely, before responding to external disqualifying racist discourses on social media, black women might need first to provide an 'answer' to themselves before addressing the voices that aim at reducing their value. Considering that several of these black women have been brought up nurturing 'whitened' beauty standards, they would need first to mature their blackness. Ultimately, this process might allow them to deconstruct their own enduring internalised racism and, subsequently, challenge the ingrained racism of 'whitened' people.

Besides, in Post #2.C it is possible to find similar discourse where the black woman identified as N.A.P. shares her ethnic identity acceptance and suggests its presence in other black women as well. It can be inferred that including a wider audience in this process, she is addressing the African legacy in the formation of Brazilian society. This is relevant because Brazilians usually do not recognise their ethnic origins and have difficulties in accepting them. Instead of that, they prefer to avoid being associated with blackness (Arraes, 2015; Santana, B. 2015). In effect, in Brazil, Afro hairstyle plays a relevant role in this process of ethnic identification for black people because this element "has long been used as an indicator of racial background and a basis of racial classification" (Caldwell, 2003, p. 20). In other words, the self-recognition process voiced by these black women might also imply that the downside is that white supremacists will place them at the lower end of the Brazilian racial hierarchy scale (as previously illustrated in Figure 1.2).

Regarding Post #3.C, the black woman identified as M.I.S. stresses independence as a distinct element of ethnic self-acceptance. To a certain extent, this discourse coalesces with the previously mentioned argument developed by Souza (1990, p. 17) that "one of the ways of exercising autonomy is having a discourse about oneself". Consequently, these black women are effectively 'becoming' black by taking ownership of the discourse about themselves, rather than simply internalising what the world around them has provided and taught them from an early age.

Hence, the combined analysis of this set of eight posts (from A.1 to C.3) extracted from three different Facebook pages contributes to bringing to the surface three major aspects concerning the construction of anti-racist discourses based on female Afro hairstyle. First, that negative attributes and disqualified perceptions around Afro hairstyle are learned and internalised even by black women since their childhood in their family realm. Such beliefs, influenced by hegemonic 'whitened' beauty patterns are not only transmitted across different generations, but they have also been incorporated into popular culture and reinforced over time (e.g. songs, race joking, and on TV comedy shows). Consequently, circulating also on social media in Brazil, they amplify their reinforcement and perpetuation. Second, despite the picture just described, Afro hairstyle also embodies the most distinct element capable of challenging colonial-like white supremacist ideologies. The data reveals that through the acceptance of their natural Afro hairstyle, black women are (re)discovering their blackness and effectively 'becoming' black, rather than keeping nurturing 'whitened' beauty ideals inherited from their upbringing. Moreover, more than just an aesthetic choice, this process embodies a conscious political positioning. The outcome is that these women achieve greater awareness of their current symbolic social space in Brazil and also which legitimate social space they aim at achieving, regardless of different dimensions of intersecting challenges (especially race, gender and class). Finally, although social media has become a sort of modern-day pillory for the proponents of white supremacist ideologies, it has also enabled the emergence of different anti-racist narratives, such as nurturing the improved political significance of Afro hairstyle as the black women's genuine crown (Trindade, 2018b).

The rise of discourses praising black beauty

Another recurrent aspect emerging from the data encompasses different forms of narratives praising black beauty as a discursive strategy aimed at deconstructing and challenging racist ideologies. This discursive strategy aims mostly to raise black women's self-esteem, and grant legitimacy to black Brazilian beauty, rather than directly confronting white supremacists employing their language style. However, there is also an important aspect of this discursive strategy (most probably unbeknownst to their proponents) that indirectly contributes towards the reinforcement of stereotypes attached to blacks' over-sexualised physical attributes. This aspect is explored in texts and images praising what the users consider unique black assets such as, for example: a) sex appeal; b) virility; c) sexual appetite above average; and d) and irresistible black women's bodies. However, the problem is that they represent limited perceptions of the social navigation possibilities of the racial group and, ultimately, they do not grant influential social capital to them.

Having said that, the following set of seven social media posts were extracted from a publicly available Facebook page belonging to a black woman (actress, 38 years old, 2015). She had published a couple of pictures of herself displaying the new look of her Afro hairstyle, and she was heavily insulted by many users employing racially-based derogatory comments. However, many other users have expressed their support to her as shown in the sequence.

Post #1:   This black woman is beautiful, and her natural Afro hairstyle is amazing.

Post #2:   You are a beautiful black woman.

Post #3:   You are gorgeous in every way possible.

Post #4:   I just want to say that you are very pretty.

Post #5:   Disregard this type of negative comment, my dear. You are beautiful.

Post #6:   She is so beautiful. Why these mad people are doing that?

Post #7:   You are a wonderful black woman.

Initially, the embedded discourses in these seven posts might look relatively simple in comparison to many others discussed in this chapter. However, in reality, they are not. On the surface, they might not display very intricate linguistic constructions, but even so, their embedded meaning is representative. They are distinctive manifestations, first, because they have been triggered by a prior event of racism on social media that inspired users to post them in support of the victim. Namely, the fact that someone has been targeted on social media made users react to that event in this way. Consequently, rather than expressing their disagreement directly confronting the people who posted the derogatory content, the users have chosen instead to support the victims. Second, praising the victims' beauty also represents an attempt to lessen the possible pain and wounds the victims might have experienced in the modern-day *pelourinho* caused by the virtual whipping. Furthermore, the data also reveals that this type of manifestation praising black beauty comprises one of the most frequently employed by users who want to express their support to the victims of online racism.

Beauty patterns in Brazil represent important elements for the establishment of distinctions among different racial groups, and also the rules of qualified and disqualified social visibility (Quadrado, 2015). Namely, this dynamic establishes the elements composing the country's proud and legitimate visible face, in contrast to the features representing ugliness or the illegitimate beauty characteristics. Therefore, this argument demonstrates that beauty standards may represent an additional dimension influencing the establishment of differentiated social spaces for racial groups in Brazil. Within that, analysing the topic from a historical perspective, it is possible to discover other important aspects. While in the 1960s emerged in the US the political movement *'Black is Beautiful'* (Santos, 2000; Quadrado, 2015), its echoes took some considerable time to reach Brazilian leaders of the black movement. As previously discussed in Chapter 2, from 1964 to 1985, Brazil was under military ruling and, consequently, any attempt to go around praising black beauty would be strongly repressed. The reason is that the military leaders were against the emergence of ideas and social movements that could challenge not only the dictatorship regime but also shatter the racial 'balance' provided by the 'racial democracy' discourse (Gonzalez and Hasenbalg, 1982; Domingues, 2007; Nacked, 2012). Hence, within this scenario, bringing to the surface debates around racial inequalities was not legitimised and nor accepted by the country's ruling political elite. Consequently, only after the country's re-democratisation process in 1985 that openly praising black beauty became more feasible (Carneiro, 2003; Trotta and Santos, 2012).

Thus, the statements made by the users in the above sample of seven posts in support of the subjects of mockery on Facebook convey an adjacent political meaning. In other words, praising and/or giving value to black beauty conveys a message that challenges the hegemonic 'whitened' Brazilian beauty standard, widens the boundaries of social acceptance, and attempts to bring both racial groups in equal standing. In addition to this political facet, the discourses are also making an effort towards raising the victims' self-esteem. This argument is supported by accounts of a number of victims of racism on Facebook interviewed by newspapers and magazines. Many of them have revealed that soon after being subject of racialized posts on Facebook they were afraid of getting out of their homes, concerned that in addition to being recognised by people on the streets, they would also laugh at them. Therefore, praising their beauty becomes an important attitude not only in raising the person's self-esteem but also for them to develop confidence about the feasibility of being black and valued, rather than black and inferior.

Still, in this discursive strategy praising black beauty to challenge racist discourses, it is possible to identify that, in many occasions, the users construct their counter-racist argument over exploring the sensuality of the black body. Namely, rather than deconstructing old stereotyped objectified perceptions of the black body, the users indirectly contribute towards the reinforcement of the stereotypes. The users intended to praise what they consider unique black attributes but, actually, the highlighted 'differentiated' characteristics are based on enduring imaginary exaggerations of the black body. In other words, the users aim at empowering and supporting victims of racist discourses but without acknowledging that their posts are, in fact, fostering limited perceptions concerning blackness.

Within this context, there is an emblematic example emerged from the data that contributes to illustrate this reflection. The posts were published on a publicly available Facebook page of a mainstream daily newspaper in 2014. The following sample represents users' support to a black man who had been racially insulted by a white woman that had publicly called him an ape. She had done the insult in an upper-middle-class supermarket in a large metropolitan area because she was upset that this black man was taking too much time in the cashier to pay for his purchases.

Post #1:   Arrest this racist woman and put her in a prison cell with
                10 Afro-descendant men to see what happens to her.

Post #2:   These white racist women like to insult black men calling
                them ape and so forth but, in fact, what they love most is
                a big black cock.

Post #3:   In fact, this white bitch cannot wait to have her ass fucked
                up by a big black guy.

Post #4:   What needs to be done is to gather a bunch of black guys
                and do a gang bang on this bitch. I am sure that she is
                going to enjoy it.

As it can be observed in these sample of posts, to express their disagreement
with the white woman's attitude, users have explored over-sexualised
perceptions of black men. Within that, under users' perspective, the male
genitalia represents a type of 'corrective tool' to be used against misbehaving
white racist women.

It is possible to notice that in Post #1 the user displays a revealing
contradiction. The user attempts to sound polite adopting Afro-descendant as
a racial identifier, rather than *preto* or *negro*. However, the user associates the
racial group with delinquency by placing them in prison cells, which also
reveals the naturalisation of this association in people's minds (i.e. blackness =
delinquency). Furthermore, the number of people in the imagined cell also
conveys a subtle image of overcrowded prisons, given the fact that this
circumstance represents a common scenario in the Brazilian penitentiary
system (Adorno, 1991; Erdely, 2017). Within that, it is implied that if inmates are
held in overcrowded cells, chances are that their behaviour might be 'less
civilised', suggesting that if a white woman would be incarcerated in that
environment, most probably, she would be sexually abused by the group of
black inmates. Therefore, aiming at combating racism, the user ends up
conveying elements that reinforce many negative stereotypes about black
people (e.g. savagery, delinquency, and untamed sexual appetite).

On the one hand, Post #1 employs a language construction that subtly
suggests that black male genitalia might be an appropriate 'corrective tool' to
be applied against the white woman. On the other hand, in the subsequent Post
#2, Post #3 and Post #4, the users have rather employed explicit and graphic
language. What can be observed, is that the users are exploring an enduring
over-sexualised stereotyped construction of black men that removes their
humanity and reduces them to very limited characteristics of sexual nature;

that is a large penis and sexual performance above average (Nkosi, 2014; Ferreira, 2016). In fact, the over-sexualization of the black male body has created an imaginary idea that "a white woman who has had a Negro lover finds it difficult to return to white men" (Fanon, 1986, p. 132). In line with this reflection, recalling the race joke seen in Chapter 5 where a black man steals a full-HD flat TV, it can be observed that, before establishing the correlation between blackness and delinquency, the joke also explores an imaginary black males above-average sexual performance ('come and do what you know how to do better than anyone else, making justice to your race'). Consequently, once again, this particular type of humour contributes towards both the reinforcement and the naturalisation of such stereotyped social representation of black Brazilians.

Actually, most of the naturalisation of this over-sexualisation of the black male body in the collective mindset has been strongly influenced by cultural products such as the cinema and TV. Studies reveal the existence of five major black stereotypical social roles in most US movie productions: a) 'Tragic black', or the subject of all sorts of unfortunate events, b) 'Tom', or the obedient and loyal jack-for-all-trades servant, c) 'Coon', the simple-minded funny character, d) 'Mammy', or the over-weight dark-skinned woman, and e) 'Bucks', or the brutal and hypersexualised black man (Bogle, 2001).

Although these five major stereotyped social representations of black people are based on US movie productions, the picture is not that different in Brazilian movies. In effect, Rodrigues (1988) has also developed a similar study, identifying 12 categories of stereotyped social roles of black Brazilians in movies. Amongst them, 'bucks' is also equally present, displaying negative characteristics such as untamed sexual appetite, sexual savagery, and proneness to committing rape (Rodrigues, 1988). Over time, many Brazilian cultural products such as movies and soap operas have repeatedly explored this type of over-sexualised black roles and contributed towards their naturalisation in people's mind-set (Rodrigues, 1988; Araújo, 2000; Ferreira, 2016). Consequently, the embedded discourses observed in the above sample of posts are not only the reproduction of these stereotyped social representations but also their reinforcement.

Nevertheless, what drives users to construct anti-racist discourses exploring physical attributes of black bodies? In their attempt to highlighting the black beauty and challenge racism, the users aim at conveying a more concrete and tangible facet of beauty. In fact, the well-shaped black body would represent the materialisation of a beauty pattern that it would be difficult for detractors to deny its closeness to perfection. To a certain extent, by exploring the black body's features on social media (either by text and/or supporting images), the users are emulating the almost-perfect ancient Greek sculptures on display in museums. Actually, in Brazilian popular culture, it is well-known the colloquial expression 'Greek God/Goddess' concerning someone considered physically gorgeous. The expression circulates mostly in informal oral communication, but it can also be found in mainstream media and blogs (Rogerio, 2010; Extra, 2014; Borrelli, 2015; Fernandes, 2016). The implied message is that the features of the person are almost perfect, highly attractive and irresistible. However, this expression in Brazil is oftentimes employed mostly to describe whites, rather than black people. Therefore, by exploring well-shaped, 'desirable' and sexually attractive black bodies, it is possible to convey the message that blacks can be as beautiful as white Greek God/Goddess.

Furthermore, whilst black Brazilians are oftentimes absent from most power structures, the embedded message aims at challenging this scenario with elements that convey a different type of power. It is a manifestation aimed at triggering envy in the minds of their detractors. In fact, the imaginary above-average sexual performance of black men, for example, can cast doubts on the mind of white men, leading them to question their performance (Fanon, 1986). Namely, the users are trying to make evident that only being born black to be granted with that 'natural' set of physical attributes and sensuality not found in other racial groups. Thus, the set of "'natural' characteristics and abilities such as strength and sexuality, are commonly associated with blacks, whilst 'intellectual' or cultural activities are within the white's domain" (Corrêa, 2006, p. 88).

Consequently, empowering discourses praising black beauty as a means to challenge racist discourses may contribute towards raising the victims' self-esteem, their level of self-confidence, and convey a political positioning that symbolically levels whites and blacks in Brazil. Nevertheless, the moment the discourses are constructed on the grounds of elements highlighting predominantly black's 'natural' physical features, the side effect is the reinforcement of enduring ingrained limiting stereotypes. Furthermore, this type of discourse conveys a reductionist vision of black Brazilians, bringing only their physical attributes to the foreground, rather than amplifying society's perception about them and highlighting also elements of their cultural capital (Sousa, 2014). The latter is important because the power structures in Brazil are not under the domain of people with the greatest physical abilities or the most well-shaped bodies, but those with greater cultural and social capital.

Empowerment embedded in shared lived experiences of racism

Another distinctive form of anti-racist discourse emerged from the data encompasses manifestations of solidarity with the victims. To a certain extent, praising black beauty, as previously discussed, can also be considered as a form of solidarity. However, what calls our attention is a particular form of solidarity represented by the account of similar lived experiences of racism by many users. In reality, sharing these experiences plays the role of connecting like-minded black women through common pains. The accounts do not necessarily challenge the racist discourses directly, but they attempt to restore the victims' resilience by highlighting that they are not alone and that other people understand the dimension of their pain. Moreover, sharing their experience also contributes towards establishing bonds among black women and inspiring collective resistance against Brazilian racism. Finally, it also becomes evident that, in addition to sharing similar experiences of racism, social media enables black women to have an active voice in Brazilian society. Within that, they organise themselves into several virtual communities aimed at empowering themselves and resisting Brazilian racism both online and offline.

Having said that, the following set of Facebook posts contribute to illustrating this reflection. The context encompasses a post published in 2015 by a mother of a 12-year-old girl who was verbally abused in school by some of her fellow pupils. The pupils had made use of a series of racial slurs against the girl, such as: a) you dirty stinky black, b) I am in fact racist, and what do you have to do with that?, c) every time I meet you I am going to mock you mercilessly, and d) kinky hair. The mother explains, in a lengthy and detailed account on her public Facebook page, that the girl did not receive any type of appropriate support by the school and, instead, the principal made the girl apologise to her fellow pupils. According to the mother, the principal did that because she believed that the case was more of an annoyance to the school than a serious issue.

Comment #1: Only I know what I have gone through in my youth. Those were hard times. I was one of the very few black girls in my school and also overweight. My mom had two jobs, and she struggled to provide me with the best educational opportunities possible within her reach. Since she is lighter skinned than me, when she picked me up in school, my fellow pupils used to mock of me saying that my master had come to take me home. At school plays, the teachers always assigned me the roles of house cleaner, cook and maid. This type of discrimination hurts, and nothing takes it away from my memories.

Comment #2: When I had her age, I faced exactly the same experiences, and my fellow pupils called me several names. At a certain point, the school's principal said that she was fed up with that type of story and I was blamed instead. I missed the interest to attend school, but my mom pressured both the school and the city council's educational board.

Ultimately, the principal was replaced, and I was transferred to another class.

Comment #3: Only those who have already gone through this road are capable of fully understanding how much it hurts. It may look trivial, but after repeatedly listening that you have bad hair, for example, you internalise and give credit to this type of statement.

The posts reveal the construction of a discourse conveying the message: 'I know how much it hurts because I have also been wounded the same way'. Differently from the previous two categories of anti-racist discourses analysed, I do not find discursive elements aimed at deconstructing racist ideologies. What can be observed is an attempt to convey empathy with the victims and support them. In effect, it is also interesting to notice the manifestation of elements of internalised racism. The same way that black women are taught, since childhood, to dislike their Afro hairstyle, the above set of comments reveals that lived experiences of racism also took place in their childhood. Furthermore, analysing the tone and linguistic style of the racial slurs that were directed against the 12-years-old girl, it becomes evident that they reflect ideologies learned in the pupils' family realm. In other words, the pupils are not only reproducing racist ideologies learned from adults but also reinforcing and perpetuating them.

Consequently, the users' accounts evidence, first, that lived experiences of racism in Brazil display recurrent patterns across different generations. This is argued because the users are adult women revealing that they have experienced similar circumstances in their childhood. Second, given this repetition across different generations, they contribute to unveiling the naturalisation of these practices over time. Namely, they continue to happen the same way that these adult women have experienced in the past, demonstrating that people naturally replicate them to date. Moreover, they also reveal that such experiences are capable of leaving enduring marks on the people subjected to racism in Brazil. Finally, this type of account and other expressions of solidarity, bring to the surface that posting racist discourses on social media might be targeted towards a specific person, but the potential impact is not restricted to that person in particular. It can reverberate and affect many others as well.

Within this reverberation context, interviewing Maria Lúcia da Silva (director of *Instituto Amma Psique Negritude*), she says that when she reads news articles reporting cases of racism on social media, she also feels attacked. She argues that the user is not directly attacking her since he does not know her. However, she adds, the user is offending all black women, and, at this moment, she recalls all her painful past lived experiences of racism, especially during childhood. Moreover, Maurício Pestana (then serving as São Paulo's Secretary of Racial Equality) expressed a similar standpoint. He argues that it feels like the offence had been targeted towards himself. It could have been also towards his daughter or a family member and, as a black man, he believes to share similar pains before these violent acts. In conclusion, he says, the attitude is individualised, but it reaches the black community as a whole. Thus, the interviewees' accounts contribute towards reinforcing the evidence that experiences of racism in Brazil oftentimes start at an early age, leave enduring marks in people's lives, and such experiences may be painful to process. Besides, the interviewees' interpretation of the cases of racism on social media is that, on the surface, they are targeted towards a single person. However, underneath, they can potentially affect the entire racial group.

In complement to that, it is possible to observe that in Brazil whenever a white person commits any type of fault or mistake, the event is attributed solely to them at an individual level. Nevertheless, a black person in similar circumstance represents not only themselves but also the whole racial group, meaning that the fault and mistake are collectively attributed rather than individualised (Carone, 2003). Consequently, this argument contributes to understanding the dynamics behind the perception that the individualised event of racist discourse enacted against a specific black person is amplified towards the racial group.

However, what is the practical relevance of sharing lived experiences of racism on social media? These manifestations are important because they might inspire like-minded black women to gather among themselves and speaking out against racist attitudes. Within this context, social media platforms enable the emergence of many empowering communities that try to challenge Brazilian ingrained racism by evidencing the harm that it inflicts on black people. In line with this reflection, it is possible to notice the emergence of a number of distinctive initiatives over the recent past. Amongst them, four, in particular, call our attention.

First, Brito and Nascimento (2013) have organised a book called 'Black (in)confidences: not bullying. This is Racism'. The work gathers 21 testimonials of black women who have experienced situations of racism in the context of primary school and their strategies to cope with that scenario. It discusses the differences between bullying and racism in the Brazilian context and reveals black women's past lived experiences of suffering and humiliation and explores their strategies to navigate within that context.

In the second place, in 2015, the Rio de Janeiro-based black feminist NGO Criola promoted a nationwide awareness campaign called 'Virtual racism, real consequences'. The campaign was made up of dozens of billboards displayed across the country calling people's attention regarding the social impacts of online racist attitudes (BBC, 2015; Charlton, 2015). Such billboards were composed with a selection of Facebook racist posts and positioned around each users' neighbourhood (however with their names and pictures blurred to safeguard their privacy). In complement to this action, there was also the production of short videos posted on YouTube (Criola, 2015; Pakman, 2015). In third place, in the following year, this awareness campaign was expanded and triggered the production of other short videos called 'Mirrors of Racism' bringing the accounts of victims and the testimony of one user who had published racist posts on social media (W3Haus, 2016a; 2016b).

Finally, more recently, there has been the publication of a book called 'I have felt it on my skin: victims reports' (Xavier, 2017), where the author has gathered more than 100 accounts of black Brazilian victims of racism. What calls our attention in this particular work is the fact that it started with fewer than a dozen testimonies on the author's homonymous Facebook page in 2015. Within that, the author explains, the first testimonials brought to the surface exactly lived experiences of racism in the context of primary school (Deister, 2017), which coalesce with the context described in the three social media comments analysed in the present section. Thus, the combination of this sample of initiatives composes a different anti-racist approach. Rather than directly confronting offenders, the users create a sort of network of solidarity and affection with the victims to empower them.

In conclusion, sharing lived experiences of racism represents a form of expressing solidarity with the victims of racism on social media in Brazil. However, rather than directly challenging the proponents of white supremacist ideologies employing their same discursive strategy or language style, the users attempt at restoring black women's resilience and creating a sense of community (i.e., you are not alone). In other words, sharing similar lived experiences of racism conveys an embedded symbolic message of aggregation and union established through common pain. Besides, there is a perception that verbal abuses may transcend the individualised victim and reverberate on the racial group as a whole. Finally, the positive side effect of this painful circumstance is that it also contributes towards the emergence of connections amongst like-minded black women on social media. Consequently, black women can resist contemporary Brazilian racism in the same arena where it has been taking place.

Call to action: jumping off the social media page

The discussion addressing the influence of social media in the shaping of social relations (Chapter 3) revealed a two-way road. It means that both environments (online and offline) are not detached from each other, but rather intertwined. Thus, what people do online can reverberate offline and vice-versa. Given this scenario, it has emerged from the data that in many occasions, the victims of online racism are encouraged by other users to jump off the social media page and take practical action against their offenders. In other words, the embedded anti-racist message is for the victims to go after their legal and institutional citizens' rights in the offline environment, rather than simply enacting anti-racist discourses online.

Within that, the following sample of six posts displays this type of discourse that more than supporting the victims, aimed at driving them to take effective actions. The posts were published between 2015 and 2016 in support of a black woman (university student, 27 years old) who was the subject of a series of racial slurs on her page, such as: a) in here there is no room for stinky *N*... like yourself, and b) the place for blacks is either in *senzala* or six feet under.

Post #1:   It is imperative to denounce it [to the authorities] rather than stay quiet.

Post #2:   I suggest that you save a print screen of the racist post and file a police report because racial injury is a crime. It is not possible to put an end on this sort of crime if you are silent. These people will keep offending others the same way they have done with you.

Post #3:   It is necessary to speak out, disclose the names of the people who engage in racist attitudes. A post like this one can be forgotten after some time if nothing is done. Racism is a crime.

Post #4:   It is not enough reporting the case to Facebook. We know that the corporation is slow to reply to these cases. Besides, soon after the community is terminated [by Facebook], the administrator can create another one even worse than the original. Let us denounce it to the police.

Post #5:   You should not silence. File a formal case in the public ministry against the person. Racism is a crime.

Post #6:   Facebook campaign helps, but it does not solve the issue. The most appropriate reaction must come with the support of law enforcement actions.

The posts convey a straightforward message suggesting that the victim should take legal actions against the users. Nevertheless, it is more important to understand what is not so visible or apparent in these posts. As previously discussed in Chapter 3, people who engage in derogatory posts on social media strongly believe that online anonymity shields them from being held accountable for their attitudes. Moreover, oftentimes jokers argue that their humour is harmless, made for entertainment purpose only and that it should not be taken too seriously. Within that, one of Brazil's most successful TV comedian said that, in the past, "categories such as the ugly, black and homosexuals, did not get offended [by the jokes] because they knew they were harmless" (Jorge, 2015, p. 12). However, different scholars advocate that the jokes conveyed in the TV comedy programme did offend these social groups. The problem is that the non-hegemonic social groups did not have a voice to express their concern and disagreement (Czech, 2015). Therefore, 'voice' is what really represents the core element in the embedded discourse in the above set of six social media posts.

Based on this reflection, the call to action conveyed through the posts transcend the practical and legal aspects of denouncing the racial injury. In fact, they are conveying the idea that black women should no longer remain silent and feel voiceless in such circumstances. In the recent past, several legal mechanisms have been implemented in Brazil, aimed at giving voice to people subjected to different forms of abuse. Therefore, the posts aim at highlighting this aspect to the victims and suggesting that silencing may not be their best option.

Not by chance, silencing represents one of the key elements composing the Brazilian racist dynamic. On the one hand, it is considered as a sort of defensive mechanism by many black Brazilians. Within their family realm, black Brazilians are oftentimes taught since childhood to ignore insults and avoid open and direct confrontation with white supremacists. The idea behind this strategy is that by ignoring the insults, the subjects of mockery is not providing additional fuel to their offender and, eventually, at a certain point, that individual will naturally realise that their attitude does not find echo and stop verbalising it. On the other hand, the enduring ingrained racism in Brazilian society and the increasing trend of cases of racism on social media reveals that this strategy has not necessarily been effective enough. Whilst avoiding conflict seems to be "a preferred strategy for managing racism among Afro-Brazilians of all classes", the side effect is the maintenance of white supremacy and 'racial democracy' (Twine, 1998, p. 143). Furthermore, silencing also leads towards a challenging paradoxical scenario to black Brazilians. While Brazil silences and denies articulations of racism, black Brazilians continue experiencing everyday circumstances of racial discrimination. Within this context, black children tend to be brought up unequipped to deal with racism and unable to develop a strong sense of self-esteem (Gillam, 2017).

Having said that, there is also another important critical analysis to be done regarding speaking out about racism in Brazil. As previously discussed in Chapter 3, in the first place, there is a considerable lack of confidence in the effectiveness of the legal system. Namely, in many occasions, the victims do choose to silence not only as a defensive mechanism but mainly because they believe that the outcome might not be satisfactory in comparison to the energy dedicated to pushing the matter forward; and/or that it might take a long time for anything concrete to happen. Second, there is also an interplay between class position and voice power. Overall, black Brazilians have lower social and economic capital than whites. However, concerning the context of cases of racism on social media, it comes to the surface a distinctive differentiation amongst the victims. Namely, for affluent and well-known black Brazilians, is more feasible having their voices heard, than for underprivileged ordinary blacks.

Within that, two contrasting cases emerged from the data contribute to illustrate this reflection. The first one comprises an ordinary black woman (university student, 20 years old, 2015) who went to a police station to file a report after being racially insulted on Facebook. However, she was persuaded by the police officer not to follow this path because, according to him, it would not lead into an investigation and her case was nothing more than a water drop in the ocean. In contrast, another prominent black woman subject of racist insults, equally on Facebook (journalist, 37 years old, 2015), also went to a police station to file a report. Nevertheless, in a matter of a few months, the police had already made arrests and pressed charges against the suspects. Consequently, overall, black Brazilians are not as voiceless as they used to be in the past concerning speaking out against racist attitudes since there are several legal mechanisms at their disposal. However, that does not necessarily mean that their voices are evenly heard and/or given the appropriate credit. There is still a considerable chance, even amongst blacks, that their differentiated class positions may interfere with the process either positively (in case of well-off blacks) or negatively (when blacks belong to underprivileged social strata).

Conclusions

There is a famous African proverb which says, 'Until lions have their own historians, tales of the hunt shall always glorify the hunter' (Adagba, 2006). The proverb is also the subject of many regional variants across the African continent and globally depending on the language (Adagba, 2006; Maraire, 2015). However, despite these variants, I consider relevant to resort to this proverb to illustrate this book's concluding reflections.

Brazil's enslavement of African people and all its negative associated legacies to date (e.g. racism, discrimination, negative stereotyping, enduring racial and social inequalities, etc.), are considered inconvenient subject matters. As such, for a long time, there have been many institutional initiatives aiming at constructing a hegemonic narrative that, firstly, deny their existence. In this regard, it is emblematic to observe that, as addressed in Chapter 1, just two years after the emancipation of slaves, the Hymn of the Republic was already conveying the argument that 'we do not even believe that slaves once there have been in such a noble country' (Albuquerque and Miguez, 1890). And, moving forward in time, it is possible to observe that in the 1930s, the moviemaker James A. Fitzpatrick also claimed that Brazil was 'a heaven of tolerance for all races' (Fitzpatrick, 1932) and in the 1960's Thompson (1965a, p. 28) argued that "if discrimination do occur [in Brazil], they are economic, not racial; committed by foreigners, not Brazilians".

Furthermore, demands towards greater racial equality raised by black Brazilians are oftentimes delegitimised and considered whining manifestations and victimisation out of place by the elite. In line with this reflection, it is highly problematic, for example, when Brazil's current president publicly denies the existence of racism and frames the phenomenon as an unnecessary annoyance (Alfonso, 2019; Tavae, 2019). Given the symbology of his position as an elected political leader, this sort of statement carries a strong institutional weight and (in)directly endorsers many delegitimising discourses already circulating in Brazilian society. Thus, in addition to neglecting the relevance of the phenomenon, this sort of attitude aims to silence opposing voices and to foster the prevalence and perpetuation of the 'whitened' hegemonic narrative (Oliveira, 2017; Trindade, 2018a; Vitorino, 2018).

In line with the African proverb, Brazilian society has always glorified 'the hunter', whilst 'the lions' were kept either voiceless or discredited. Thus, as 'the lions' aim to narrate the tales from their standpoints, they are discouraged, challenged and undermined in their attempts. Within that, one of the mechanisms employed by white supremacists in Brazil to accomplish this goal (and safeguard their position of privilege), encompasses the construction of racial insults. They are constructed to highlight the 'deviant' nature of 'the other' and, by opposition, legitimise the oppressor's position of normality and superiority.

However, whilst in contemporary Brazilian society racial insults might seem out of place or inappropriate in many ordinary social circumstances, conversely, race joking is widely acceptable. Actually, the ambivalent characteristic of humour, and its ethereal border between genuine entertainment and concealed racism, is what turns it into a challenging discursive strategy. It is challenging because, on the one hand, it provides a convenient escape route for white supremacists to claim that the jokes are mere harmless jests (*brincadeirinhas*). On the other hand, it is challenging for the subjects of mockery because they are, oftentimes, characterised as whiners and over-victimisers. Nonetheless, the critical analysis of the dozens of race jokes and social media posts developed in this book, supported by a robust theoretical framework, breaks the ambivalence and unveils their embedded discourse.

It becomes evident that, combined with 'racial democracy' and the whitening ideology, one of the key supporting pillars of Brazilian racism is the deep-seated belief that 'blacks know their place' in Brazilian class society. This belief implies a tacit balance in Brazilian racial relations, meaning that, as long as blacks remain within the boundaries of social spaces associated with inferiority, racial tensions are absent. Consequently, the maintenance of this condition contributes to keeping the balance immutable and unchallenged. Furthermore, single successful case stories of upward social mobility achieved by black Brazilians are treated by the elite as a confirmation of the effectiveness of the 'racial democracy'. The exception is made up solely of blacks who engage in occupations that explore their 'natural' abilities, such as dancers, entertainers and footballers. Additionally, since 'money whitens', as advocated by the elite to justify their particular perception of meritocracy, these successful blacks would be exempt from circumstances of racism.

Nevertheless, over the past three to four decades, black Brazilians in general, and women in particular, as many studies reveal, have achieved better tertiary education than previous generations. As a consequence, they are increasingly engaging in more qualified occupations such as, for instance, medicine, journalism, engineering, law, and many others (Artes and Ricoldi, 2015). Thus, what the social media posts reveal is that the social advancement achieved by black Brazilian women shatters the 'original' balance of Brazilian racism. In other words, these women seem to knowingly be ignoring their 'original' place in class society and aiming at achieving many others and amplifying their social roles. However, fuelled by colonial-like ideologies, the white supremacists nurture, first, the belief that black women should remain indefinitely restrained in their 'original and legitimate' social space associated with inferiority and subservience. Second, that black women are not legitimate representatives of Brazilian long-desired 'whitened' national identity.

Within this context, there is a quote originally raised by a university-based black organisation which has been widely adopted by many other organisations and social activists, stating 'The Big House already snaps when the *senzala* learns to read, imagine when it engages into medicine' (Freire, 2016; Marques, 2017). The discursive construction in this quote explores the iconic colonial racial and social contrast between the masters and the slaves present in Gilberto Freyre's *Casa Grande & Senzala* (Freyre, 1987). The black organisation aim is to challenge Brazil's enduring racial inequalities and the elite's strong resistance to accepting blacks upward social mobility through greater access to tertiary education, especially in prestigious careers and selective educational institutions. This quote is relevant in the context of this book because it represents an appropriate figure of speech to symbolise the same contrasting picture conveyed on social media. That is, the successful upward social mobility of black women upsets white supremacists since, in their perspective, black women should not go beyond the *senzala*, and even less try to assume a distinctive agency in the *Casa Grande*.

Within that, the emergence of major social media platforms from the mid-2000s onwards, their exponential growth-rate, and their ubiquitous presence in peoples' lives, have contributed towards the surge of racism in the online environment (Trindade, 2020a). Due to the powerful networking characteristic of social media platforms, this digital technology enables white supremacists to construct and disseminate their racist discourses towards a wide audience. In line with that, they are also able to engage a large number of like-minded people, which amplifies the reverberation of their voices in ways not seen in the offline context. Finally, the data has also revealed that race joking on social media keeps engaging new users for around three years after the original publication, turning the derogatory conversation into an endless echo in cyberspace.

Ultimately, the consequence of this picture is the perpetuation, acceptance, and naturalisation of racism in Brazilian society as an inseparable element of the digital landscape. However, the greatest problem with the naturalisation of inequalities is the fact that it tends to hinder people's capacity to be alarmed and astonished by the phenomenon. Since it might become a natural component of the social fabric, why should people bother after all?

In fact, how does the perpetuation of racism operate in Brazil? Two major aspects contribute to this phenomenon: 1) the increasing trend of construction and dissemination of colonial-like racist ideologies on social media, and 2) the enduring denial of the pernicious impacts of Brazilian racism. Regarding the first aspect, reported cases of racist insults on social media have soared from 2,038 cases in 2011 to 11,090 cases in 2014 (Safernet, 2015). In 2016, other data revealed the occurrence of 32,376 mentions of racist terminologies on social media against black Brazilians (Pereira *et al.*, 2016). Additionally, in 2017, one-third of 63,698 reported cases of hate speech on the internet in Brazil were targeted also against black people (Boehm, 2018; Tavares, 2018). Regarding the second aspect, it has become evident that denial of the existence of racism in Brazil is strongly rooted in the political discourse (Alfonso, 2019; Tavae, 2019). Thus, the perpetuation of Brazilian racism, manifested in the combination of these two major aspects can cause: a) the effect of reducing the relevance of demands towards greater racial equality, b) fuelling the perpetuation of a myriad of negative perceptions regarding black Brazilians, c) reinforcing the fallacious idea of the existence of a post-racial society (i.e. a 'racial democracy') in the collective mindset, and d) attempts at delegitimising the opposing voices.

Hence, to address this challenging scenario and propose a 'tale' that reflects not only the 'hunter's side but the 'lion's perspective', the data reveals that many anti-racist narratives are being fostered in Brazil. It has become clear that black Brazilian women are either at the foreground in many of these initiatives or playing a decisive role in the process when they are led by black men.

In fact, as argued in Chapter 2, resistance to Brazilian racism and its negative impacts, has been taking place since colonial times with the establishment of *quilombo* communities and evolving up to the surge of NGOs established and led by black women in the 1980s. However, it is possible to observe two major aspects in the current scenario. First, social media platforms have been enabling ordinary black women to have their voice heard and amplified and, second, this disruptive digital technology is also empowering black Brazilian women to gain greater political independence.

In this context, social media is enabling black women to speak their mind freely, share lived experiences of racism and form a powerful network of like-minded women. In this process, they establish new grass-roots empowering communities aiming to deconstruct white supremacist discourses. Within that, praising the natural Afro hairstyle comprises a strong element in their discourse, embodying more than an aesthetic choice. In effect, it represents their political positioning in favour of a renewed perception of Brazilian blackness to deconstruct 'whitened' ideals.

Actually, making a concise counterpoint between the online racist derogatory discourses and the black empowering narratives, it is possible to identify one major characteristic on each side. The naturalisation of the 'hunter's tale' is based on constant repetition of derogatory depictions of black Brazilians over time. Conversely, the anti-racist narratives aim to legitimise the 'lion's voice', in an attempt to verbalise that the derogatory depiction does not represent them, they are inaccurate, out-of-date and out of place. In reality, black women are conveying a discourse that asserts that they are much more than the limited negative portrayals insist in naturalising. Consequently, this book has sought not only to bring to the surface a pressing contemporary social phenomenon that needs to be understood in its entirety, but also shed some light on its mechanisms, dynamics, and the real social impacts in people's lives. Finally, also to contribute towards raising general awareness and enrich the debate towards achieving the means to change the enduring blurred Brazilian racial landscape.

References

Acevedo, C.R. and Trindade, L.V.P. (2010) Imagens de indivíduos afrodescendentes em propagandas: análise da presença de estigmas e estereótipos nas formas de representações sociais, [Portrayal of Afro-descendant individuals on pieces of advertisements: analysis of stigmas and stereotypes on their social representation]. *Comunicação, Mídia e Consumo*, 7 (18), 55-82.

Acevedo, C.R. and Trindade, L.V.P. (2011) Análise de ausência de diversidade étnica nos telejornais brasileiros, [Analysis of the lack of ethnic diversity in Brazilian news programs]. *Alceu*, 11 (22), 90-108.

Adagba, S.M. (2006) "Until lions have their own historians, tales of the hunt shall always glorify the hunter", *African Proverbs, Sayings and Stories*, April, Hillsborough, NJ. Available from: http://www.afriprov.org/african-proverb-of-the-month/32-2006proverbs/224-april-2006-proverb-quntil-the-lion-has-his-or-her-own-storyteller-the-hunter-will-always-have-the-best-part-of-the-storyq-ewe-mina-benin-ghana-and-togo-.html

Adorno, S. (1991) Sistema penitenciário no Brasil: Problemas e desafios, [The Brazilian penitenciary system: problems and challenges]. *Revista USP*, (9), 65-78.

Agassiz, L. (1868) *A journey in Brazil*. Boston, MA: Ticknor and Fields.

Ajzenberg, E. (2012) A Semana de Arte Moderna de 1922, [The Modern Art Week of 1922]. *Revista de Cultura e Extensão da USP*, 7, 25-29.

Albuquerque, M. and Miguez, L. (1890) Hino da Proclamação da República, [Hymn to the Proclamation of Republic]. *Diário Oficial*, 21/01/1890, Rio de Janeiro, RJ. Available from: http://www2.planalto.gov.br/acervo/simbolos-nacionais/hinos/hino-da-proclamacao-da-republica

Alfonso, D.A. (2019) Bolsonaro's take on the 'absence of racism' in Brazil, *Race & Class*, 61 (3), 33-49.

Allan, J. (2001) Review of measurement of ethnicity: international concepts and classifications, *Statistics New Zealand*, September, Auckland, New Zeland, 44. Available from: http://archive.stats.govt.nz/~/media/Statistics/browse-categories/population/census-counts/review-measurement-ethnicity/international-main.pdf

Almeida, P.C. (2017) *O turismo no Rio de Janeiro durante a década de 1920 e 1930*, [Tourism in Rio de Janeiro during the 1920s and 1930s]. Paper presented at XXIX Simpósio de História Nacional, Brasília, DF, 24 to 28 July. Available from: https://www.snh2017.anpuh.org/resources/anais/54/1488645947_ARQUIVO_OTurismonoRiodeJaneiroduranteadecadade1920e1930.pdf

Alonso, A. (2014) O abolicionismo como movimento social, [Abolitionism as a social movement. *Novos Estudos - CEBRAP*, (100), 115-137.

Alves, J.E. (2018) Racismo e sexismo no Brasil em 2018, [Racism and sexism in Brazil in 2018]. *Instituto Humanitas Unisinos*, 14/09/2018, São Leopoldo, RS.

Available from: http://www.ihu.unisinos.br/78-noticias/582726-racismo-e-sexismo-no-brasil-em-2018

Alvez, E. (2017) Minha coroa são meus cachos, [My crown is my curly hair]. *Solilóquios*, 01/05/2017, Fortaleza, CE. Available from: http://meusoliloquios.blogspot.co.uk/2017/05/minha-coroa-sao-meus-cachos.html

Anderson, E. (2015) "The White Space", *Sociology of Race and Ethnicity*, 1 (1), 10-21.

Andrade, M.M.F. (2012) *Negritude em rede: discursos de identidade, conhecimento e militância - um estudo de caso da comunidade Negros do Orkut (2004-2011)*, [Online blackness: discourses of identity, knowledge and militancy - A case study of the community Negros (Black People) at Orkut (2004- 2011)]. Masters' Dissertation, July, USP - Universidade de São Paulo. Faculty of Education

Andrade, O. (1928) Manifesto Antropófago, [Anthropophagic Manifesto]. *Revista de Antropofagia*, (1), 3-7.

Andrews, G.R. (1991) *Blacks & Whites in São Paulo, Brazil, 1888-1988*. Madison, Wisconsin: University of Wisconsin Press.

Andrews, G.R. (1996) Brazilian racial democracy, 1900-90: an American counterpoint, *Journal of Contemporary History*, 31 (3), 483-507.

Andrews, G.R. (1997) Slavery and race relations in Brazil, *The Brazilian curriculum guide specialized biography. Series II*, Latin American Institute at the University of New Mexico; Mexico City, Mexico, 1-37. Available from: http://repository.unm.edu/handle/1928/7708

Ang, P.H. (1997) *How countries are regulating internet content*, Paper presented at 7th Annual Conference of the Internet Society, Kuala Lumpur, Malasya, 24 to 27 June. Available from: https://www.isoc.org/inet97/proceedings/B1/B1_3.HTM

Angioleto, M. (2017) Intolerância nas redes sociais cresce em ritmo preocupante, [Bigotry on social media grows at worrisome pace]. *Diário do Grande ABC*, 02/05/2017, Santo André, SP. Available from: http://www.dgabc.com.br/Noticia/2670456/intolerancia-nas-redes-sociais-cresce-em-ritmo-preocupante

Anistia (2017) Vidas Negras Importam!, [Black Lives Matter]. *Anistia Internacional, Brasil*, Rio de Janeiro, RJ. Available from: http://mobiliza.anistia.org.br/jnv/11-2525

Anthias, F. (2012) Intersectional what? Social divisions, intersectionality and levels of analysis, *Ethnicities*, 13 (1), 3-19.

Anthony, S. (2016) Brazilian Beauty Queen Says She Was Dethroned For Being 'Too Black', *Huffington Post US Edition*, 12/02/2016, New York, NY. Available from: http://www.huffingtonpost.com/entry/brazilian-beauty-queen-says-she-was-dethroned-for-being-too-black_us_56be13b6e4b08ffac124e66e

Antonieta, M. (2013) A difícil trajetória de vida das mulheres negras na sociedade brasileira, [The difficult life trajectory of black women in Brazilian society]. IN: Nova, A.V. and Dos Santos, E.A. (eds.) *Mulheres Negras: histórias de resistência, de coragem, de superação e sua difícil trajetória de vida na sociedade brasileira*. Duque de Caxias, RJ: Creative Commons, 19-20.

Arango, E.A. (2013) Racismo y discurso en la era digital: el caso de la revista Hola y los discursos en las redes sociales, [Racism and discourse in the digital era: the case of Hola Magazine and the discourses in social networks]. *Discurso & Sociedad*, 7 (4), 617-642.

Arantes, N. (2013) Pequena história do Carnaval no Brasil, [Brief history of carnival in Brazil]. *Revista Portal de Divilgação*, 29 (3), 6-20.

Araujo, A.L. (2019) Dandara e Luisa Mahin são consideradas heroínas no Brasil: o problema é que elas nunca existiram, [Dandara and Luisa Mahin are considered Brazilian heroes: the problem is that they have never existed]. *The Intercept Brasil*, 04/06/2019, São Paulo, SP. Available from: https://theintercept.com/2019/06/03/dandara-luisa-mahin-panteao-patria/

Araújo, J.Z. (2000) *A negação do Brasil: o negro na telenovela brasileira*, [The denial of Brazil: Blacks on Brazilian soap operas]. São Paulo, SP: Editora SENAC.

Araujo, L. (2015) Facebook tira do ar comunidade racista após denúncias, [Facebook terminates racist community after complaints]. *Opera Mundi*, 16/02/2015, São Paulo, SP. Available from: http://operamundi.uol.com.br/conteudo/samuel/39536/facebook+tira+do+ar+comunidade+racista+apos+denuncias.shtml

Araújo, L.E. (1999) Sargentelli traz de volta o ziriguidum, [Sargentelli brings back the ziriguidum]. *ISTOÉ Gente*, 15/11/1999, São Paulo, SP. Available from: http://www.terra.com.br/istoegente/15/reportagens/rep_sargenteli.htm

Araújo, P. (2015) Police identifies 30 people in investigation of internet racism against popular actress – but black Brazilians are called "monkey" everyday: what will they do about this when the victim isn't famous?, *Black Women of Brazil*, 06/11/2015, São Paulo, SP. Available from: http://wp.me/p1XDuf-6Qv

Araújo, T. (2015) Após Facebook tirar do ar, páginas com o termo 'Eu não mereço mulher preta' voltam à rede social, [Soon after Facebook had terminated the racist community 'I do not deserve Black woman', it returned to social media]. *Hufpost Brasil*, 22/02/2015, São Paulo, SP. Available from: http://www.brasilpost.com.br/2015/02/22/eu-nao-mereco-mulher-preta_n_6730230.html

Arraes, J. (2015) Quando me descobri negra: a descoberta de todos nós, [When I discovered myself black: the discovery of all of us]. *Revista Forum*, 29/10/2015, São Paulo, SP. Available from: http://www.revistaforum.com.br/semanal/quando-descobri-negra-descoberta-de-todos-nos/

Artes, A. and Ricoldi, A.M. (2015) Acesso de Negros no ensino superior: o que mudou entre 2000 e 2010, [Black's access to higher education: what has changed between 2000 and 2010]. *Cadernos de Pesquisa*, 45 (158), 858-881.

Assis, E. (2013) Saímos do Facebook, [We have come out from Facebook]. *Observatório da Imprensa*, 02/07/2013, São Paulo, SP. Available from: http://observatoriodaimprensa.com.br/jornal-de-debates/_ed753_saimos_do_facebook/

Atkins, J. (1735) *Voyage to Guinea, Brazil and The West Indies*. London, UK: Caesar Ward and Richard Chandler.

Azevedo, A.M. (2018) Samba: um ritmo negro de resistência, [Samba: a black rhythm of resistance]. *Revista do Instituto de Estudos Brasileiros*, (70), 44-58.

Back, L. and Solomos, J. (2000) *Theories of race and racism: a reader*. London, UK: Psychology Press.

Bailey, S.R. (2004) Group Dominance and the Myth of Racial Democracy: Antiracism Attitudes in Brazil, *American Sociological Review*, 69 (5), 728-747.

Balmer, C. (2017) Top Italian official says Facebook must do more against hate speech, *Reuters*, 12/02/2017, Rome, Italy. Available from: https://www.reuters.com/article/us-italy-boldrini-facebook/top-italian-official-says-facebook-must-do-more-against-hate-speech-idUSKBN15R0J1

Barbato, L.F.T. (2014) A construção da identidade nacional brasileira: necessidade e contexto, [The construction of Brazilian national identity: needs and context]. *Revista Eletrônica História em Reflexão*, 8 (15), 1-15.

Barbosa, L.C. (2004) *As situações de racismo e branquitude representadas na telenovela "Da cor do pecado"*, [The situations of racism and whitening at the soap opera "Shades of Sin"]. Paper presented at XXVII Congresso Brasileiro de Ciências da Comunicação, Porto Alegre, RS.

Baronov, D. (2000) *The abolition of slavery in Brazil: the "liberation" of Africans through the emancipation of capital*. London, UK: Greenwood Press.

Barros, R.P., Henriques, R. and Mendonça, R. (2000) Desigualdade e pobreza no Brasil: retrato de uma estabilidade inaceitável, [Inequality and poverty in Brazil: portrait of an unacceptable stability]. *Revista Brasileira de Ciências Sociais*, 15 (42), 123-142.

Barrucho, L. (2016) Ex-empregada doméstica lança campanha nas redes sociais para denunciar abusos de patrões, [Ex-maid launches social media campaign to report abuse of bosses]. *BBC News Brasil*, 21/07/2016, Rio de Janeiro, RJ. Available from: http://www.bbc.com/portuguese/salasocial-36857963

Bartel, C.E. (2014) Manifestações de Racismo e de Intolerância no Brasil Contemporâneo, [Expressions of Racism and Intolerance in Contemporary Brazil]. *História Unicap*, 1 (1), 104-118.

BBC (2005) Brazil's Lula 'sorry' for slavery, *BBC News*, 14/04/2005. Available from: http://news.bbc.co.uk/1/hi/world/americas/4446647.stm

BBC (2015) Campaigners target online trolls by putting their comments on billboards, *BBC News*, 30/11/2015, London, UK. Available from: http://www.bbc.co.uk/news/blogs-trending-34945756

BBC (2017) Social media warned to crack down on hate speech, *BBC News*, 29/09/2017, London, UK. Available from: http://www.bbc.co.uk/news/technology-41442958

Beaglehole, E., Comas, J., Pinto, L.A.C., Frazier, F., Ginsberg, M., Kabir, H., Lévi-Strauss, C. and Montagu, A. (1950) Fallacies of racism exposed: Unesco publishes declaration by world's scientis, *The Unesco Courier*, July-August, Paris, France, 1; 8-9. Available from: http://unesdoc.unesco.org/images/0008/000814/081475eo.pdf#nameddest=81475

Bechara, M. (2017) Blackface: "Brincar com a raça é privilégio de brancos", diz sociólogo francês, [Blackface: "Playing with the race is the privilege of whites," says French sociologist]. *Radio France internationale | Édition Brésil*, 21/12/2017, São Paulo, SP. Available from: http://br.rfi.fr/franca/20171221-blackface-brincar-com-raca-e-privilegio-de-brancos-diz-sociologo-frances

Belloni, L. (2016) O passado misógino, racista e homofóbico de Biel no Twitter é assustador, [Biel's misogynist, racist and homophobic past on Twitter is scary]. *HuffPost, Brazil Edition*, 02/08/2016, São Paulo, SP. Available from: https://www.huffpostbrasil.com/2016/08/02/o-passado-misogino-racista-e-homofobico-de-biel-no-twitter-e-as_a_21695077/

Bento, M.A.S. (2014) *Branqueamento e branquitude no Brasil*, [Whitening and whiteness in Brazil]. Paper presented at Racismo Institucional: Fórum de Debates - Educação e Saúde, Belo Horizonte, MG. Available from: http://www.cehmob.org.br/wp-content/uploads/2014/08/Caderno-Racismo.pdf#page=5

Bergland, C. (2017) The Neuroscience of Contagious Laughter, *Psychology Today*, 29/09/2017, New York, NY. Available from: https://www.psychologytoday.com/us/blog/the-athletes-way/201709/the-neuroscience-contagious-laughter

Bergson, H. (1914) *Laughter: An Essay on the Meaning of the Comic*. France, Paris: Revue de Paris.

Bertoni, E. (2018) 'Tudo é coitadismo', diz Bolsonaro sobre negros, mulheres e nordestinos, ['Everything becomes the subject of complaint', says Bolsonaro about blacks, women and northeasterners]. *Veja*, 24/10/2018, São Paulo, SP. Available from: https://veja.abril.com.br/politica/tudo-e-coitadismo-diz-bolsonaro-sobre-negros-mulheres-e-nordestinos/

Besse, S.K. (2005) Defining a "national type": Brazilian beauty contests in the 1920s, *Estudios Interdisciplinarios de América Latina y el Caribe*, 16 (1), 95-117.

Bessi, A., Zollo, F., Del Vicario, M., Puliga, M., Scala, A., Caldarelli, G., Uzzi, B. and Quattrociocchi, W. (2017) The Surprising Speed with Which We Become Polarized Online, *Kellogg Insight*, 06/04/2017, Evanston, IL. Available from: https://insight.kellogg.northwestern.edu/article/the-surprising-speed-with-which-we-become-polarized-online

Bethel, L. (1984) *Colonial Brazil*. New York, NY: Cambridge University Press.

Bilac, O. (1895) Fantasio na Exposição II: A Redempção de Cham, [Ham's Redemption]. *Gazeta de Notícias*, 05/09/1895, Anno XXI, N. 247, Rio de Janeiro, RJ, Front page. Available from: http://memoria.bn.br/DocReader/DocReader.aspx?bib=103730_03

Billig, M. (2001) Humour and hatred: the racist jokes of the Ku Klux Klan, *Discourse & Society*, 12 (3), 267-289.

Bittencourt, J. (2017) Estudo da Folha aponta que estudantes cotistas têm bom desempenho na universidade, [Folha's study points out that quota students perform well at the university]. *Revista Fórum*, 10/12/2017, São Paulo, SP. Available from: https://revistaforum.com.br/politica/estudo-da-folha-aponta-que-estudantes-cotistas-tem-bom-desempenho-na-universidade/

Boehm, C. (2018) Discursos de ódio e pornografia infantil são principais desafios da internet, [Hate speech and child pornography are major internet challenges]. *EBC - Empresa Brasil de Comunicação*, 06/02/2018, Brasília, DF. Available from: http://agenciabrasil.ebc.com.br/pesquisa-e-inovacao/noticia/2018-02/discursos-de-odio-e-pornografia-infantil-sao-principais-desafios

Boffey, D. (2018) EU threatens to crack down on Facebook over hate speech, *The Guardian*, 11/04/2018, London, UK. Available from: https://www.theguardian.com/technology/2018/apr/11/eu-heavy-sanctions-online-hate-speech-facebook-scandal

Bogle, D. (2001) *Toms, Coons, Mulattoes, Mammies, and Bucks: an interpretative history of Blacks in American films*, 4th ed.: Bloomsbury Publishing.

Bolsonaro, J.M. (2019) Lei Nº 13.616: Inscreve os nomes de Dandara dos Palmares e de Luiza Mahin no Livro dos Heróis e Heroínas da Pátria, [Law Number 13,816: Adds the names of Dandara dos Palmares and Luiza Mahin in the Book of Heroes and Heroines of the Nation]. *Presidência da República | Casa Civil*, 24/04/2019, Brasília, DF. Available from: http://www.planalto.gov.br/ccivil_03/_Ato2019-2022/2019/Lei/L13816.htm

Bonilla-Silva, E. (2001) *White supremacy and racism in the post-civil rights era*. New York, NY: Lynne Rienner Publishers.

Bonilla-Silva, E. (2006) *Racism without racists: Color-blind racism and the persistence of racial inequality in the United States*. Rowman & Littlefield Publishers.

Borrelli, I. (2015) O que as mulheres querem: o garoto da casa ao lado ou o deus grego?, [What do women want: the boy next door or the Greek god?]. *Tão Feminino*, 30/03/2015, São Paulo, SP. Available from: http://www.taofeminino.com.br/bombando-na-internet/pesquisa-revela-o-homem-ideal-s1313626.html

Bosi, A. (1992) *Dialética da Colonização*, [Dialectics of Colonization]. São Paulo, SP: Companhia das Letras.

Botero, J.C., Agrast, M.D., Ponce, A., Evandelides, A., Gryskiewicz, A., Patiño, C.G., Hamze, M., Harman, M., Hernández, R., Levine-Drizin, J., Long, S.C., Martinez, J., Pratt, C.S., Roberts, K., Walker, Q., Aramayo-Lipa, L., Bere, L., Coto, A., Duffy, M., Mujeeb, M., Neshati, N., Randall, A., Rotich, F., Sandino, R., Sepama, M., Severancce, A., Smith, J. and Treacy, N. (2016) *World Justice Project: Rule of Law Index 2016*, Washington, DC, World Justice Project. Available from: http://worldjusticeproject.org/sites/default/files/media/wjp_rule_of_law_index_2016.pdf

Boxman-Shabtai, L. and Shifman, L. (2015) When ethnic humor goes digital, *New Media & Society*, 17 (4), 520-539.

boyd, d.m. (2015) Social Media: A Phenomenon to be Analyzed, *Social Media + Society*, 1 (1), 1-2.

boyd, d.m. and Ellison, N.B. (2007) Social Network Sites: Definition, History, and Scholarship, *Journal of Computer-Mediated Communication*, 13 (1), 210-230.

Braga, A.B. (2011) *Dispositivos de uma beleza negra no Brasil*, [Aspects of black beauty in Brazil]. Paper presented at Simpósio Internacional de Letras e Lingüística, Uberlândia, MG. Available from: http://www.ileel.ufu.br/anaisdosilel/wp-content/uploads/2014/04/silel 2011_628.pdf

Brah, A. and Phoenix, A. (2004) 'Ain't I a Woman? Revisiting Intersectionality' *Journal of International Women's Studies*, 5 (3), 75-86.

Brandino, G. (2019) Quais as medidas concretas de Damares como ministra, [What are Damares' concrete measures as human rights minister]. *Nexo Jornal*, 25/10/2019, São Paulo, SP. Available from: https://www.nexojornal.com.br/expresso/2019/10/25/Quais-as-medidas-concretas-de-Damares-como-ministra

Brito, B. and Nascimento, V. (2013) *Negras (in)confidências: bullying não. Isto é racismo : mulheres negras contribuindo com as reflexões sobre a Lei 10639/03*, [Black (in)confidences: not bullying. This is Racism: Black Women Contributing to Reflections on Law 10639/03]. São Paulo, SP: Mazza Edições.

Brito, M.D. (2018) *Não. Ele não está*, [No. He is not at home]. Curitiba, PR: Editora e Livraria Appris.

Brown, A. (2017) What is so special about online (as compared to offline) hate speech?, *Ethnicities*, 18 (3), 297-326.

Bulmer, M. and Solomos, J. (1999) *Racism*. Oxford, UK: Oxford University Press.

Bulmer, M. and Solomos, J. (2004) *Researching race and racism*. New York, NY: Psychology Press.

Burdick, J. (1998) *Blessed Anastacia: Women, Race and Popular Christianity in Brazil*. New York, NY: Routledge.

Butler, K.D. (1998) *Freedoms Given, Freedoms Won: Afro-Brazilians in Post-abolition, São Paulo and Salvador*. New York, NY: Rutgers University Press.

Cabral, P. (2005) No Senegal, Lula pede perdão pela escravatura, [In Senegal, Lula apologizes for slavery]. *BBC News Brasil*, Brasília Available from: http://www.bbc.co.uk/portuguese/reporterbbc/story/2005/04/050414_lula pcmla.shtml

Caers, R., De Feyter, T., De Couck, M., Stough, T., Vigna, C. and Du Bois, C. (2013) Facebook: A literature review, *New Media & Society*, 15 (6), 982-1002.

Caetano, R. (2004) *A publicidade e a imagem do produto Brasil e da mulher brasileira como atrativo turístico*, [Advertising, Brazil's image as a product, and the Brazilian woman as tourist attraction]. Paper presented at Congresso Brasileiro de Ciências da Comunicação, Porto Alegre, RS. Available from: http://docplayer.com.br/12743019-A-publicidade-e-a-imagem-do-produto-brasil-e-da-mulher-brasileira-como-atrativo-turistico-1.html

Caldwell, K.L. (2000) Fronteiras da diferença: raça e mulher no Brasil, [Racialized Boundaries: Women's Studies and the Question of 'Difference' In Brazil]. *Estudos Feministas*, 8 (2), 91-108.

Caldwell, K.L. (2003) "Look at Her Hair": The Body Politics of Black Womanhood in Brazil, *Transforming Anthropology*, 11 (2), 18-29.

Camargo, O. (1988) The long struggle for liberation: reflections on the abolition of slavery in Brazil, *The Unesco Courier*, June, Paris, France, 36-38. Available from:

http://unesdoc.unesco.org/images/0007/000797/079702eo.pdf#nameddest =79711

Campos, A.C. (2017) População brasileira é formada basicamente de pardos e brancos, mostra IBGE, [Brazilian population consists basically of pardos and whites, shows IBGE]. *Agência Brasil*, 24/11/2017, Brasília, DF. Available from: http://agenciabrasil.ebc.com.br/economia/noticia/2017-11/populacao-brasileira-e-formada-basicamente-de-pardos-e-brancos-mostra-ibge

Campos, E.S. (2003) *Lei No 10.678, de 23 de maio de 2003*, [Law Number 10,678, 23 May 2003]. Brasília, DF. Available from: http://www.planalto.gov.br/ccivil_03/MPV/Antigas_2003/111.htm

Cann, A., Dimitriou, K. and Hooley, T. (2011) Social Media: A guide for researchers, *Research Information Network*, February, Leicster, UK, 48. Available from: http://www.rin.ac.uk/social-media-guide

Cardoso, F.H. (1962) *Capitalismo e escravidão no Brasil Meridional*, [Capitalism and Slavery in Southern Brazil]. São Paulo, SP: Difusão Européia do Livro.

Cardoso, F.H. (1996) Lei nº 9.315: Inscreve o nome de Zumbi dos Palmares no "Livro dos Heróis da Pátria", [Law Number 9,315: Adds the name of Zumbi dos Palmares in the "Book of Heroes of the Nation"]. *Presidência da República | Casa Civil*, 20/11/1996, Brasília, DF. Available from: http://www.planalto.gov.br/ccivil_03/Leis/L9315.htm

Cardoso, F.H. (1998) Construindo a Democracia Racial, [Building racial democracy]. *Secretaria de Comunicação Social da Presidência da República*, Brasília, DF, 1-49. Available from: http://www.biblioteca.presidencia.gov.br/presidencia/ex-presidentes/fernando-henrique-cardoso/publicacoes/construindo-a-democracia-racial

Cardoso, R. (2012) The Brazilianness of Brazilian Art: Discourses on Art and National Identity, c 1850–1930, *Third Text*, 26 (1), 17-28.

Carneiro, S. (2003) Mulheres em movimento, [Women on the move]. *Estudos Avançados*, 17 (49), 117-133.

Carone, I. (2003) Breve histórico de uma pesquisa psicossocial sobre a questão racial brasileira, [Brief history of a psychosocial research on the Brazilian racial question]. IN: Carone, I. and Bento, M.A.S. (eds.) *Psicologia social do racismo: estudos sobre branquitude e branqueamento no Brasil*, 2nd ed. São Paulo, SP: Vozes, 13-23.

Castells, M. (2010) The Information Technology Revolution, IN: Castells, M. (ed.) *The Rise of the Network Society*. New York, NY: Wiley-Blackwell, 28-76.

Castillo, M. (2018) Zuckerberg tells Congress Facebook is not a media company: 'I consider us to be a technology company', *CNBC*, 11/04/2018, Englewood Cliffs, NJ. Available from: https://www.cnbc.com/2018/04/11/mark-zuckerberg-facebook-is-a-technology-company-not-media-company.html

Castro, C. (2016) SUS, população negra e racismo: para promover saúde é preciso reconhecer e eliminar o preconceito, [SUS, black population and racism: to promote health, it is necessary to recognize and eliminate prejudice]. *Pense SUS*, 02/12/2016, Rio de Janeiro, RJ. Available from: https://pensesus.fiocruz.br/sus-popula%C3%A7%C3%A3o-negra-e-racismo-para-promover-sa%C3%BAde-%C3%A9-preciso-reconhecer-e-eliminar-o-preconceito

Castro, H.M.M. (1998) *Das cores do silêncio: Os significados da liberdade no sudeste escravista, Brasil século XIX*, [The colors of silence: The meanings of freedom in the slave southeast, Brazil 19th century]. 2nd ed. Rio de Janeiro, RJ: Nova Fronteira.

Castro, L.T. (1889) Questões e problemas: ódio entre as raças, [Issues and problems: hate between races]. *A Província de São Paulo*, 06/02/1889, São Paulo, SP, Front page. Available from: http://acervo.estadao.com.br/pagina/#!/18890206-4154-nac-0001-999-1-not/busca/castro

Castro, P.R.S. (2014) A Liberdade de Expressão e a incitação ao ódio racial, [Freedom of Expression and incitement to racial hatred]. *Âmbito Jurídico*, XVII (130), 1-4.

Castro, R. (2008) Para principiantes, [For beginners]. *Folha de S. Paulo*, 22/03/2008, São Paulo, SP. Available from: https://www1.folha.uol.com.br/fsp/opiniao/fz2203200805.htm

Cavalcanti, I.T.N., Andrade, C.M., Tiryaki, G.F. and Costa, L.C.C. (2019) Desempenho acadêmico e o sistema de cotas no ensino superior: evidência empírica com dados da Universidade Federal da Bahia, [Academic performance and the quota system in higher education: empirical evidence with data of the Federal University of Bahia]. *Avaliação: Revista da Avaliação da Educação Superior*, 24 (1), 305-327.

Cerqueira, D., Bueno, S., Lima, R.S., Neme, C., Ferreira, H., Alves, P.P., Marques, D., Reis, M., Cypriano, O., Sobral, I., Pacheco, D., Lins, G. and Armstrong, K. (2019) Atlas da Violência 2019, [2019 Atlas of Violence]. *IPEA - Instituto de Pesquisa Econômica Aplicada*, June, Brasília, DF. Available from: http://www.ipea.gov.br/atlasviolencia/download/12/atlas-2019

Cerqueira, D., Lima, R.S., Bueno, S., Valencia, L.I., Hanashiro, O., Machado, P.H.G. and Lima, A.S. (2017) *Atlas da Violência 2017*, [Atlas of Violence 2017]. Rio de Janeiro, RJ, Instituto de Pesquisa Econômica Aplicada - IPEA and Fórum Brasileiro de Segurança Pública - FBSP. Available from: http://www.ipea.gov.br/portal/images/170602_atlas_da_violencia_2017.pdf

Chan, R.C.L. (2015) Avante! A construção da indetiade nacional brasileira na modernidade, [Forward! The construction of Brazilian national identity in modernity]. *Letras Escreve*, 5 (2), 29-40.

Chapman, C.E. (1918) Palmares: The Negro Numantia, *Journal of Negro History*, 3 (January), 29-32.

Charão, C. (2011) *O longo combate às desigualdades raciais*, [The long fight against racial inequalities]. São Paulo, SP, IPEA Instituto Pesquisas Econômicas Aplicadas, Available from: http://www.ipea.gov.br/portal/images/stories/PDFs/120507_politicas_sociais.pdf

Charlton, C. (2015) Status - shamed: Racist messages on Facebook are turned into billboards near each writer's home after they are traced through geo-tagging, *Daily Mail*, 01/12/2015, London, UK. Available from: http://www.dailymail.co.uk/news/article-3340775/Status-shamed-Racist-messages-Facebook-turned-billboards-near-writer-s-home-traced-geo-tagging.html

Chasteen, J.C. (1996) The Prehistory of Samba: Carnival Dancing in Rio de Janeiro, 1840-1917, *Journal of Latin American Studies*, 28 (1), 29-47.

Chaykowski, K. (2017) Facebook Is Hiring 3,000 Moderators In Push To Curb Violent Videos, *Forbes*, 03/05/2017, New York, NY. Available from: https://www.forbes.com/sites/kathleenchaykowski/2017/05/03/facebook-is-hiring-3000-moderators-in-push-to-curb-violent-videos/#727f579a58cb

Child, D. (2018) Who is Jair Bolsonaro, Brazil's new far-right president?, *Al Jazeera*, 29/10/2018, London, UK. Available from: https://www.aljazeera.com/news/2018/10/jair-bolsonaro-brazil-presidential-candidate-181007020716337.html

Christo, M.C.V. (2009) Algo além do moderno: a mulher negra na pintura brasileira no início do século XX, [Something beyond the modern: the black woman in Brazilian painting in the early 20th century]. *19&20*, 4 (2), 1-8.

Cicalo, A. (2018) Goodbye 'Racial Democracy'? Brazilian Identity, Official Discourse and the Making of a 'Black' Heritage Site in Rio de Janeiro, *Bulletin of Latin American Research*, 37 (1), 73-86.

Citron, D.K. and Norton, H. (2011) Intermediaries and Hate Speech: Fostering Digital Citizenship for Our Information Age, *Boston University Law Review*, 91 (0), 1435-1484.

CNJ (2015) Conheça a diferença entre racismo e injúria racial, [Know the difference between racism and racial slur]. *Conselho Nacional de Justiça*, 08/06/2015, Brasília, DF. Available from: http://www.cnj.jus.br/noticias/cnj/79571-conheca-a-diferenca-entre-racismo-e-injuria-racial

Cobb, C. (2018) Editor's Introduction: Responding to the Cumulative Damage of Racism, *The American Journal of Economics and Sociology*, 77 (3-4), 581-644.

Collins, D., Efford, C., Elliott, J., Farrelly, P., Hart, S., Knight, J., Lucas, I.C., O'Hara, B., Pow, R., Stevens, J. and Watling, G. (2019) *Disinformation and 'fake news': Final Report*, London, UK, House of Commons Digital, Culture, Media and Sport Committee. Available from: https://publications.parliament.uk/pa/cm201719/cmselect/cmcumeds/1791/1791.pdf

Colonna, N. (2016) The challenges of being black and upper class in Brazil, *BBC News*, 10/08/2016, London, UK. Available from: http://www.bbc.co.uk/news/world-latin-america-37011638

Conrad, R.E. (1983) *Children of God's Fire: A Documentary History of Black Slavery in Brazil*. Princeton, NJ: Princeton University Press.

Corrêa, L.G. (2006) *De corpo presente: o negro na publicidade em revista*, [In person: Blacks in magazine advertising]. Masters' Dissertation, Abril, UFMG - Universidade Federal de Minas Gerais. Comunicação Social

Costa, E.V. (2013) *Abolition: from slavery fo free labour*. São Paulo, SP: Editora Unesp.

Costa, M.S. (2016) *Representacões de luta e resistência feminina na poesia popular*, [Representations of challenges and female resistance in the popular poetry]. Paper presented at III CONEDU - Congresso Nacional de Educação, João Pessoa, PB, 5 to 7 October. Available from: http://www.editorarealize.com.br/revistas/conedu/trabalhos/TRABALHO_EV056_MD1_SA9_ID4081_28052016001621.pdf

Crenshaw, K. (2000) Race, reform, and retrenchment: transformation and legitimization in antidiscrimination law, IN: Back, L. and Solomos, J. (eds.) *Theories of race and racism: a reader*. New york, NY: Routledge, 549-560.

Crenshaw, K. (2012) A Intersecionalidade na Discriminação de Raça e Gênero, [The intersectionality of Race and Gender Discrimination]. *Formação em Direitos Humanos*, 27/09/2012, São Paulo, SP, 7-16. Available from: http://www.acaoeducativa.org.br/fdh/wp-content/uploads/2012/09/Kimberle-Crenshaw.pdf

Criola (2015) Racismo virtual, as consequências são reais, [Virtual racism. Real consequences]. *ONG Criola*, 11/11/2015, Rio de Janeiro, RJ. Available from: https://www.youtube.com/watch?v=ED-p_nr1elA

Cunha, L.A. (2000) Ensino superior e universidade no Brasil, [Higher education and university in Brazil], IN: Lopes, E.M.T., Filho, L.M.F. and Veiga, C.G. (eds.) *500 anos de educação no Brasil*, 2nd ed. Belo Horizonte, MG: Autêntica, 151-204.

Czech, A. (2015) Para especialistas, gays e negros sempre se ofenderam com piadas de Didi, [Experts say that gays and blacks always took offense at Didi's jokes]. *UOL Notícias* 08/01/2015, São Paulo, SP. Available from: http://mulher.uol.com.br/comportamento/noticias/redacao/2015/01/08/para-especialistas-gays-e-negros-sempre-se-ofenderam-com-piadas-de-didi.htm

D'Oliveira, G.F. and Vergueiro, W. (2011) Humor na televisão brasileira: o interessante e inusitado caso do programa Os Trapalhões, [Humour on Brazilian television: the interesting and unusual case of the programme 'Os Trapalhões']. *Revista USP*, (88), 122-132.

Da Costa, A.E. (2014) Confounding Anti-racism: Mixture, Racial Democracy, and Post-racial Politics in Brazil, *Critical Sociology*, 42 (4-5), 495-513.

Daflon, V.T. (2014) *Tão longe, tão perto: pretos e pardos e o enigma racial brasileiro*, [So far, so close: blacks and browns and the Brazilian racial puzzle]. PhD Thesis, Universidade Estadual do Rio de Janeiro. Sociology

Daflon, V.T., Feres Júnior, J. and Campos, L.A. (2013) Race-based affirmative actions in Brazilian public higher education: an analytical overview, *Cadernos de Pesquisa*, 43, 302-327.

Dahia, S.L.M. (2008) A mediação do riso na expressão e consolidação do racismo no Brasil, [The laughter as a mediator of the expression and consolidation of racism in Brazil]. *Sociedade e Estado*, 23 (3), 697-720.

Dahia, S.L.M. (2010) Riso: uma solução intermediária para os racistas no Brasil, [Laughter: an intermediate solution to the racists in Brazil]. *Estudos e Pesquisas em Psicologia*, Ano 10 (2), 373-389.

DaMatta, R. (1986) *O Que faz o Brasil, Brasil?*, [What makes Brazil, Brazil?]. São Paulo, SP: Editora Rocco.

Daniels, J. (2009) *Cyber Racism: White Supremacy Online and the New Attack on Civil Rights*. Lanham, Maryland: Rowan & Littlefield Publishers, Inc.

Daniels, J. (2013) Race and racism in Internet Studies: A review and critique, *New Media & Society*, 15 (5), 695-719.

Database (2009) Timeline: Number of Captives Embarked and Disembarked per Year, *Voyages: The Trans-Atlantic Slave Trade Database*, Atlanta, GA. Available from: http://www.slavevoyages.org/assessment/estimates

Davies, C. (1990) *Ethnic humor around the world: a comparative analysis.* New York, NY: Indiana University Press.

Dávila, J. (2003) *Diploma of whiteness: race and social policy in Brazil, 1917-1945*. Durham, NC: Duke University Press.

Debetz, G.F. (1965) Biology looks at race, *The Unesco Courier*, April, Paris, France, 4-11. Available from: http://unesdoc.unesco.org/images/0007/000784/078423eo.pdf#nameddest=60308

Debret, J.B. (1839) *Voyage pittoresque et historique au Brésil ou, Séjour d'un Artiste Français au Brésil, depuis 1816 jusqu'en 1831 inclusivement (3 volumes)*, [Picturesque and Historical Trip to Brazil or, Stay of a French Artist in Brazil, from 1816 to 1831 inclusive (3 volumes)]. Paris, France: Firmin Didot Freres, Imprimeurs de L'Institut de France.

Deister, J. (2017) Projeto mostra as marcas do racismo na vida da população negra brasileira, [Project reveals the marks of racism in the life of the black Brazilian population]. *Brasil de Fato*, 15/09/2017, Rio de Janeiro, RJ. Available from: https://www.brasildefato.com.br/2017/09/15/projeto-mostra-as-marcas-do-racismo-na-vida-da-populacao-negra-brasileira/

Delacourt, J.T. (1997) The international impact of internet regulation, *Harvard International Law Journal*, 38 (1), 207-235.

Denissen, J.J.A., Neumann, L. and Van Zalk, M. (2010) How the internet is changing the implementation of traditional research methods, people's daily lives, and the way in which developmental scientists conduct research, *International Journal of Behavioral Development*, 34 (6), 564-575.

Dias, T. (2017) Quando a tinta preta é ofensiva: o maracatu e o debate sobre blackface, [When black ink is offensive: maracatu and the debate about blackface]. *Nexo Jornal*, 01/02/2017, São Paulo, SP. Available from: https://www.nexojornal.com.br/expresso/2017/02/01/Quando-a-tinta-preta-%C3%A9-ofensiva-o-maracatu-e-o-debate-sobre-blackface

Diniz, K. (2015) Brasil: onde o racismo se esconde por trás da própria lei, [Brazil: where racism lurks behind the law itself]. *Fato Online*, 20/11/2015, Brasília, DF. Available from: http://fatoonline.com.br/conteudo/12671/brasil-onde-o-racismo-se-esconde-por-tras-da-propria-lei?or=rss

Domingues, P. (2007) Movimento Negro Brasileiro: alguns apontamentos históricos, [Brazilian Black movement: some historical notes]. *Tempo*, 12 (23), 100-122.

Douglas, M. (1968) The Social Control of Cognition: Some Factors in Joke Perception, *Man*, 3 (3), 361-376.

Du Bois, W.E.B. (1903) *The Souls of Black Folk*. Chicago, IL: A. C. McClurg & Co.

Duchet, M., Franco, J.L., Pinto, F.L.V., Kake, I.B., Ogot, B.A., Gerbeau, H., Carreira, A., Conti, L., Curtin, P.D., Fouchard, J., Harris, J.E., Rego, W., Rodney,

W., Talib, Y. and Turne, J.M. (1979) *The African slave trade from the fifteenth to the nineteenth century*. Paris, France: UNESCO.

Dunham, J. (2016) *Freedom of the press 2016*, Washington, D.C., Freedom House. Available from: https://freedomhouse.org/sites/default/files/FH_FTOP_2016Report_Final_04232016.pdf

Dzidzienyo, A. (1971) *The position of blacks in Brazilian society*. Sacramento, CA: Minority Rights Group.

Edmonds, A. (2007) Triumphant Miscegenation: Reflections on Beauty and Race in Brazil, *Journal of Intercultural Studies*, 28 (1), 83-97.

Eltis, D. (2007) A Brief Overview of the Trans-Atlantic Slave Trade, *Voyages: The Trans-Atlantic Slave Trade Database*, Atlanta, GA. Available from: http://www.slavevoyages.org/assessment/essays#

Erdely, M.F. (2017) Brasil dobra número de presos em 11 anos, diz levantamento; de 726 mil detentos, 40% não foram julgados, [Brazil doubles number of prisoners in 11 years, says survey; of 726,000 detainees, 40% did not face trial]. *G1*, 08/12/2017, Rio da Janeiro, RJ. Available from: https://g1.globo.com/politica/noticia/brasil-dobra-numero-de-presos-em-11-anos-diz-levantamento-de-720-mil-detentos-40-nao-foram-julgados.ghtml

Esporte, G. (2019) No Dia da Consciência Negra, Fluminense explica origem do "pó-de-arroz": "Time de todos", [On Black Consciousness Day, Fluminense explains the origin of "face powder": "Everybidy's team"]. *Globo Esporte*, Rio de Janeiro, RJ. Available from: https://globoesporte.globo.com/futebol/times/fluminense/noticia/no-dia-da-consciencia-negra-fluminense-explica-origem-do-termo-po-de-arroz-time-de-todos.ghtml

Essed, P. (1991) *Understanding everyday racism: an interdisciplinary theory*. New York, NY: Sage Publications, Inc.

Ewbank, T. (1856) *Life in Brazil; or, a journal of a visit to the land of the cocoa and the palm*. New York, NY: Harper & Brothers.

Extra (2014) Jogadores da seleção grega conquistam internautas brasileiras: 'Deuses', [Players of the Greek team conquer female Brazilian Internet users: 'Gods']. *Extra*, 14/06/2014, Rio de Janeiro, RJ. Available from: https://extra.globo.com/esporte/copa-2014/jogadores-da-selecao-grega-conquistam-internautas-brasileiras-deuses-12861758.html

Fairclough, N. (1989) *Language and power*. Harlow, UK: Longman.

Fanon, F. (1986) *Black skin, white masks*. London, UK: Pluto Press.

Farias, L.D.M. (2018) *Marchas e manifestos contra a colonialidade da história: movimentos indígenas diante das comemorações oficiais dos 500 anos (1998-2000)*, [Demonstrations and manifestos against the coloniality of history: indigenous movements before the official celebrations of Brazil's 500th anniversary (1998-2000)]. Masters' Dissertation, Universidade de Brasília. Instituto de Ciências Humnas - História

Fernandes, A. (2016) Encontramos o Jacson do Samu, "Deus Grego" que salvou dona Marluci, [We have found the paramedic Jacson, the "Greek God" who saved Mrs Marluci]. *Campo Grande News*, 28/04/2016, Campo Grande, MS.

Available from:
https://www.campograndenews.com.br/lado-b/comportamento-23-08-2011-08/encontramos-o-jacson-do-samu-deus-grego-que-salvou-dona-marluci

Fernandes, F. (1965) *A integração do negro na sociedade de classes*, [The Negro in Brazilian Society]. São Paulo, SP: Dominus Editôra.

Fernandes, F. (1972) *O Negro no mundo dos Brancos*, [The Negro in the White's world]. São Paulo, SP: Difusão Européia do Livro.

Fernandes, M. and Martinelli, A. (2019) Nilma Lino Gomes: 'Estão em risco todas as políticas de combate à discriminação racial e de gênero', [Nilma Lino Gomes: 'All social policies to tackle racial and gender discrimination are at risk']. *Huffpost Brasil*, 20/11/2019, São Paulo, SP. Available from: https://www.huffpostbrasil.com/entry/nilma-lino-gomes-consciencia-negra_br

Ferrari, B. and Finco, N.(2016) Tchau, querido, [Bye bye, my dear]. *Época*, Rio de Janeiro, RJ. 08/08/2016, 64-66

Ferrari, M. (2016) The fight for abolition, *Revista Pesquisa Fapesp*, (240), 1-6.

Ferreira, C. (2016) *Mulheres negras e (in)visibilidade: imaginários sobre a intersecção de raça e gênero no cinema brasileiro (1999-2009)*, [Black women and (in) visibility: imaginary about the intersection of race and gender in Brazilian cinema (1999-2009)]. PhD Thesis, August, 2016, Universidade de Brasília. Comunicação Social

Ferreira, R.A. (2018) O sistema de cotas étnico-raciais adotado pela USP, [The ethnic-racial quota system adopted by USP]. *Jornal da USP*, 05/01/2028, São Paulo, SP. Available from: https://jornal.usp.br/artigos/o-sistema-de-cotas-etno-raciais-adotado-pela-usp/

Ferreira, R.F. (2002) O brasileiro, o racismo silencioso e a emancipação do afro-descendente, [The Brasilian, the silent racism and the afro descendant emancipation]. *Psicologia & Sociedade*, 14 (1), 69-86.

Fico, C. (2015) *História do Brasil Contemporâneo: Da Morte de Vargas Aos Nossos Dias*, [History of Contemporary Brazil: From Vargas' Death to Our Days]. São Paulo, SP: Editora Contexto.

Fields, K.E. and Fields, B.J. (2012) *Racecraft: The Soul of Inequality in American Life*. London, UK: Verso.

Figueiredo, A.L.S. (2004) Fora do jogo: a experiência dos negros na classe média brasileira, [Out of the game: brazilian black middle class experiences]. *Cadernos Pagu*, (23), 199-228.

Filho, J.S. (2007) *O turismo na era Vargas e o Departamento de Imprensa e Propaganda*, [Tourism in the Vargas era and the Press and Propaganda Department]. Paper presented at 9th SIT - Seminário Internacional de Turismo, Buenos Aires, Argentina, November. Available from: https://www.efdeportes.com/efd114/o-turismo-na-era-vargas-e-o-departamento-de-imprensa-e-propaganda.htm

Filho, M. (1947) *O negro no foot-ball brasileiro*, [Blacks in Brazilian football]. Rio de Janeiro, RJ: Irmãos Pongetti Editores.

Filipak, S.T. and Pacheco, E.F.H. (2017) A democratização do acesso à educação superior no Brasil, [The democratization of access to higher education in brazil]. *Revista Diálogo Educacional*, 17 (54), 1241-1268.

Fiorin, J.L. (2009) A construção da identidade nacional brasileira, [The construction of the Brazilian national identity]. *Bakhtiniana: Revista de Estudos do Discurso*, 1 (1), 115-126.

Fitzpatrick, J.A. (1932) Rio The Magnificent, *A Fitzpatrick Traveltalk*, Rio de Janeiro, RJ. Available from:
http://www.travelfilmarchive.com/item.php?id=11956

Fleming, C.M. and Morris, A. (2015) Theorizing Ethnic and Racial Movements in the Global Age: Lessons from the Civil Rights Movement, *Sociology of Race and Ethnicity*, 1 (1), 105-126.

Flor, K. (2019) Racismo e machismo mantêm mulheres negras no grupo de menores salários do país, [Racism and sexism make black women the lowest-paid group in Brazil]. *Brasil de Fato*, 19/11/2019, Rio de Janeiro, RJ. Available from:
https://www.brasildefato.com.br/2019/11/19/racismo-e-machismo-mantem-mulheres-negras-no-grupo-de-menores-salarios-do-pais/

Fonseca, D.J. (1994) *A piada - discurso sutil da exclusão: um estudo do risível no racismo à brasileira*, [The joke - subtle discourse of exclusion: A laughable study on Brazilian racism]. Masters' Dissertation, PUC-SP. Ciências Sociais

Fonseca, D.J. (2012) *Você Conhece Aquela? A Piada, o Riso e o Racismo À Brasileira*, [Do You Know That One? The Joke, Laughter and the Brazilian Racism]. São Paulo, SP: Selo Negro Edições.

Ford, T.E. and Ferguson, M.A. (2004) Social consequences of disparagement humor: a Prejudiced Norm Theory, *Personality and Social Psychology Review*, 8 (1), 79-94.

Freire, S. (2016) "A Casa Grande já surta quando a Senzala aprende a ler, imagine quando vira médica", ["The Big House already snaps when the Senzala learns to read, imagine when it engages into mecicine"]. *UNEafro Brasil*, 13/08/2016, São Paulo, SP. Available from:
http://uneafrobrasil.org/casa-grande-ja-surta-quando-senzala-aprende-ler-imagine-quando-vira-medica/

Freud, S. (1963) *Jokes and their Relation to the Unconscious*. Oxford, UK: W. W. Norton.

Freyre, G. (1977) The Afro-Brazilian experiment, *The Unesco Courier*, August-September, Paris, France, 13-18. Available from:
http://unesdoc.unesco.org/images/0007/000748/074814eo.pdf#nameddest=46680

Freyre, G. (1987) *The masters and the slaves: a study in the development of Brazilian civilization*, 2nd ed. New York, NY: University of California Press.

Frisina, A. and Hawthorne, C. (2018) Italians with veils and Afros: gender, beauty, and the everyday anti-racism of the daughters of immigrants in Italy, *Journal of Ethnic and Migration Studies*, 44 (5), 718-735.

Fry, P., Maggie, Y., Monteiro, S. and Santos, R.V. (2007) *Divisões Perigosas: Políticas Raciais no Brasil Contemporâneo*, [Dangerous Divisions: Racial Policies in Contemporary Brazil]. São Paulo, SP: Editora Civilização Brasileira.

Fuchs, C. (2008) *Internet and Society: Social Theory in the Information Age*. New York, NY: Routledge.

Funari, P. (2003) Conflict and the Interpretation of Palmares, a Brazilian Runaway Polity, *Historical Archaeology*, 37 (8), 81-92.

G1 (2013) Facebook rejeita denúncias de racismo em foto na rede social, [Facebook rejects allegations of racism in photo published on its platform]. *G1*, 20/08/2013, São Paulo, SP. Available from: http://g1.globo.com/tecnologia/noticia/2013/08/facebook-rejeita-denuncias-de-racismo-em-foto-na-rede-social.html

G1 (2015) 'Grupo queria ficar famoso', diz suspeito de cometer crime de racismo, ['The group aspired to become famous', says suspect of online racism]. *G1*, 10/12/2015, Rio de Janeiro, RJ. Available from: http://g1.globo.com/sao-paulo/sorocaba-jundiai/noticia/2015/12/suspeito-de-ter-cometido-crime-de-racismo-presta-depoimento.html

G1 (2017) Em 30 anos, apenas 244 processos de racismo e injúria racial chegaram ao fim no RJ, [In 30 years, only 244 cases of racism and racial insult came to an end in RJ]. *G1*, 06/12/2017, Rio de Janeiro, RJ. Available from: https://g1.globo.com/rj/rio-de-janeiro/noticia/em-30-anos-apenas-244-processos-de-racismo-e-injuria-racial-chegaram-ao-fim-no-rj.ghtml

Giacomini, S.M. (2006) Mulatas profissionais: raça, gênero e ocupação, [Professional Mulatas: Race, Gender and Occupation]. *Estudos Feministas*, 14 (1), 85-101.

Gillam, R. (2017) Representing Black Girlhood in Brazil: Culture and Strategies of Empowerment, *Communication, Culture & Critique*, 10, 609-625.

Gilroy, P. (1998) Race ends here, *Ethnic and Racial Studies*, 21 (5), 838-847.

Glezerman, G. (1973) Science, society and racism: the unequal development of people of different races is a product of history not of nature, *The Unesco Courier*, October, Paris, France, 12; 32. Available from: http://unesdoc.unesco.org/images/0007/000749/074906eo.pdf#nameddest=51825

Goldstein, D.M. (2003) *Laughter out of place: race, class, violence, and sexuality in Rio shantytown*. Los Angeles, CA: University of California Press.

Gomes, K. (2015) Quando a liberdade de expressão na internet vira crime, [When freedom of expression on the internet becomes a crime]. *Deutsch Welle Brasil*, 30/10/2015, São Paulo, SP. Available from: http://www.dw.com/pt-br/quando-a-liberdade-de-express%C3%A3o-na-internet-vira-crime/a-18817509

Gomes, L. (2007) *1808: Como uma rainha louca, um príncipe medroso e uma corte corrupta enganaram Napoleão e mudaram a História de Portugal e do Brasil*, [1808: The Flight of the Emperor - How a Weak Prince, a Mad Queen, and the British Navy Tricked Napoleon and Changed the New World]. São Paulo, SP: Editora Planeta.

Gomes, L. (2019) *Escravidão, volume 1: do primeiro leilão de cativos em Portugal até a morte de Zumbi dos Palmares*, [Slavery, volume 1: from the first auction of captives in Portugal to the death of Zumbi dos Palmares]. Rio de Janeiro, RJ: Globo Livros.

Gomes, M.S. (2010) A (des)(re)construção do Brasil como um paraíso de mulatas, [The (re)construction of Brazil as a Mulatto Paradise]. *Revista Eletrônica de Turismo Cultural*, 4 (2), 48-70.

Gomes, N.L. and Santos, É.O.L. (2016) *Promovendo a igualdade racial: para um Brasil sem racismo*, [Promoting racial equality: for a Brazil without racism]. Brasília, DF, Secretaria Especial de Políticas de Promoção da Igualdade Racial. Available from: http://www.seppir.gov.br/central-de-conteudos/noticias/ministerio-lanca-publicacao-sobre-a-politica-nacional-de-promocao-da-igualdade-racial-dos-ultimos-13-anos

Gonzaga, V. (2019) 20 de novembro: conheça a história do dia da Consciência Negra, [November 20: discover the history of Black Awareness Day]. *Brasil de Fato*, 20/11/2019, Recife, PE. Available from: https://www.brasildefatope.com.br/2019/11/20/20-de-novembro-conheca-a-historia-do-dia-da-consciencia-negra

Gonzalez, L. and Hasenbalg, C.A. (1982) *Lugar de Negro*, [Black's place]. Rio de Janeiro: Editora Marco Zero.

Gordon, D. (2013) A beleza abre portas: Beauty and the racialised body among black middle-class women in Salvador, Brazil, *Feminist Theory*, 14 (2), 203-218.

Guimarães, A.S.A. (1995) Racismo e anti-racismo no Brasil, [Racism and anti-racism in Brazil]. *Novos Estudos*, 1 (43), 26-44.

Guimarães, A.S.A. (2003) Racial insult in Brazil, *Discourse & Society*, 14 (2), 133-151.

Guimarães, A.S.A. (2004) Preconceito de cor e racismo no Brasil, [Colour prejudice and racism in Brazil]. *Revista de Antropologia - USP*, 47 (1), 9-43.

Haag, F.R. (2014) Mário Filho e 'O negro no futebol brasileiro': uma análise histórica sobre a produção do livro, [Mário Filho and 'The Negro in Brazilian Football': a historical analysis of the book's production]. *Esporte e Sociedade*, 9 (23), 1-23.

Hage, G. (1998) *White nation: Fantasies of white supremacy in a multicultural society*. New York, NY: Psychology Press.

Halfeld, P.C. (2013) A produção do humor na rede social Facebook, [Production of humor on Facebook]. *Revista Soletras*, (26), 219-236.

Hall, S. (1990) Cultural identity and diaspora, IN: Rutherford, J. (ed.) *Identity: Community, Culture, Difference*. London, UK: Lawrence & Wishart, 222-237.

Hansen, M.B.N. (2006) *Bodies in Code: Interfaces with Digital Media*. New York, NY: Routledge.

Harnois, C.E. and Ifatunji, M. (2011) Gendered Measures, Gendered Models: Toward an Intersectional Analysis of Interpersonal Racial Discrimination, *Ethnic & Racial Studies*, 34 (6), 1006-1028.

Harris, L. and Harrigan, P. (2015) Social Media in Politics: The Ultimate Voter Engagement Tool or Simply an Echo Chamber?, *Journal of Political Marketing*, 14 (3), 251-283.

Hasenbalg, C.A. (1979) *Discriminação e desigualdades raciais no Brasil*, [Race relations in post-abolition Brazil: the smooth preservation of racial inequalities]. 1st ed. São Paulo, SP: Graal.

Hawthorne, W. (2010) *From Africa to Brazil: culture, identity, and an Atlantic slave trade, 1600-1830*. New York, NY: Cambridge University Press.

Hébrard, J.M. (2013) Slavery in Brazil: Brazilian scholars in the key interpretive debates, *Translating the Americas*, 1, 47-95.

Help (2017) Community Standards, *Facebook, Inc.*, Menlo Park, CA. Available from: https://www.facebook.com/communitystandards#hate-speech

Henriques, R. (2001) *Desigualdade racial no Brasil: evolução das condições de vida na década de 90*, [Racial inequality in Brazil: evolution of living conditions in the 1990s]. Rio de Janeiro, RJ, IPEA, Instituto Pesquisas Econômicas Aplicadas. Available from: http://www.ipea.gov.br/portal/index.php?option=com_content&view=articl e&id=4061

Heringer, R. (2020) The future of affirmative action policies in Brazil, *Society for Cultural Anthropology*, 28/01/2020, New York, NY. Available from: https://culanth.org/fieldsights/the-future-of-affirmative-action-policies-in-brazil

Hern, A. (2019) Facebook to integrate Instagram, Messenger and WhatsApp, *The Guardian*, 25/01/2019, London, UK. Available from: https://www.theguardian.com/technology/2019/jan/25/facebook-integrate-instagram-messenger-whatsapp-messaging-platforms

Hill, K. (2014) Why Facebook's New 'Anonymous Login' Matters, *Forbes*, 30/04/2014, New York, NY. Available from: https://www.forbes.com/sites/kashmirhill/2014/04/30/why-facebooks-new-anonymous-log-in-matters/#5b71068f7e33

Hirata, H. (2014) Gênero, classe e raça: Interseccionalidade e consubstancialidade das relações sociais, [Gender, class and race: Intersectionality and consubstantiality of social relations]. *Tempo Social, Revista de Sociologia da USP*, 26 (1), 61-73.

Hogan, L. (2018) Myanmar groups criticise Zuckerberg's response to hate speech on Facebook, *The Guardian*, 06/04/2018, London, UK. Available from: https://www.theguardian.com/technology/2018/apr/06/myanmar-facebook-criticise-mark-zuckerberg-response-hate-speech-spread

Holanda, S.B. (2012) *Roots of Brazil*. Notre Dame, IN: University of Notre Dame Press.

Holston, J. (2014) "Come to the Street!": Urban Protest, Brazil 2013, *Anthropological Quarterly*, 87 (3), 887-900.

Hopkins, N. (2017) Revealed: Facebook's internal rulebook on sex, terrorism and violence, *The Guardian*, 21/05/2017, London, UK. Available from: https://www.theguardian.com/news/2017/may/21/revealed-facebook-internal-rulebook-sex-terrorism-violence

Howitt, D. and Owusu-Bempah, K. (2005) Race and ethnicity in popular humour, IN: Lockyer, S. and Pickering, M. (eds.) *Beyond a joke: the limits of humour*. New York, NY: Palgrave MacMillan, 45-62.

Htun, M. (2004) From "Racial Democracy" to Affirmative Action: Changing State Policy on Race in Brazil, *Latin American Research Review*, 39 (1), 60-89.

Hughes, T. (2015) Country Report: Brazil's Marco Civil da Internet, *Article 19*, 05/11/2015, London, UK. Available from: https://www.article19.org/resources.php/resource/38175/en/country-report:-brazil's-marco-civil-da-internet

Hughey, M.W. and Daniels, J. (2013) Racist comments at online news sites: a methodological dilemma for discourse analysis, *Media, Culture & Society*, 35 (3), 332-347.

Ianni, O. (1962) *As Metamorfoses do Escravo: Apogeu e Crise da Escravatura no Brasil Meridional*, [The Metamorphoses of the Slave: Apogee and the Crisis of Slavery in Southern Brazil]. São Paulo, SP: Difusão Européia do Livro.

IBGE (2010) *População presente e residente, por cor ou raça*, [Brazil's current population, by colour or race]. Rio de Janeiro, RJ. Available from: http://seriesestatisticas.ibge.gov.br/series.aspx?no=10&op=0&vcodigo=POP106&t=populacao-presente-residente-cor-raca-dados

IBGE (2012) *SIS 2012: acesso de jovens pretos e pardos à universidade triplicou em dez anos*, [SIS 2012: access of Black and Brown youth to university has tripled in ten years]. Rio de Janeiro, RJ, IBGE. Available from: http://cod.ibge.gov.br/2DQWS

IBGE (2017) PNAD 2016: população idosa cresce 16,0% frente a 2012 e chega a 29,6 milhões, [PNAD 2016: elderly population grows 16.0% compared to 2012 and reaches 29.6 million]. *Agência de Notícias IBGE*, 24/11/2017, Brasília, DF. Available from: https://agenciadenoticias.ibge.gov.br/agencia-sala-de-imprensa/2013-agencia-de-noticias/releases/18263-pnad-2016-populacao-idosa-cresce-16-0-frente-a-2012-e-chega-a-29-6-milhoes

IBGE (2019) Desigualdades sociais por cor ou raça no Brasil, [Social inequalities by race or colour in Brazil]. *IBGE Estudos e Pesquisas - Informações Demográficas e Socioeconômicas*, Rio de Janeiro, RJ. Available from: https://biblioteca.ibge.gov.br/visualizacao/livros/liv101681_informativo.pdf

Ingram, M. (2016) Sorry Mark Zuckerberg, But Facebook Is Definitely a Media Company, *Fortune*, 30/08/2016, New York, NY. Available from: http://fortune.com/2016/08/30/facebook-media-company/

Ingrams, A. (2017) Connective action and the echo chamber of ideology: Testing a model of social media use and attitudes toward the role of government, *Journal of Information Technology & Politics*, 14 (1), 1-15.

Isaac, M. (2019) Zuckerberg Plans to Integrate WhatsApp, Instagram and Facebook Messenger, *The New York Times*, 25/01/2019, New York, NY. Available from: https://www.nytimes.com/2019/01/25/technology/facebook-instagram-whatsapp-messenger.html

Isis, L. (2015) Projeto Cansei, [I am fed up Project]. *Contra Plano*, November, São José dos Campos, SP. Available from: http://www.porlarissaisis.com/cansei

Jaccoud, L., Osório, R.G. and Soares, S. (2008) *As políticas públicas e a desigualdade racial no Brasil 120 anos após a abolição*, [Public policies and racial inequality in Brazil 120 years after abolition]. 1st ed. Rio de Janeiro, RJ: IPEA

Jacomino, S. (2010) Penhor de escravos e queima de livros de registro, [Pledge of slaves and burning log books]. *Observatório do Registro*, 25/01/2010. Available from: https://cartorios.org/2010/01/25/penhor-de-escravos-e-queima-de-livros-de-registro/

Jane, E.A. (2017) *Misogyny Online: A Short (and Brutish) History*. London, UK: Sage Publications Ltd.

Janes, L.M. and Olson, J.M. (2000) Jeer pressure: The behavioral effects of observing ridicule of others, *Personality and Social Psychology Bulletin*, 26 (14), 474-485.

Jesus, C.M. (1960) *Quarto de despejo: diário de uma favelada*, [Child of the Dark: The Diary of Carolina Maria de Jesus]. São Paulo, SP: Franciso Alves.

Johnson, O.A. (2018) Racial Representation and Brazilian Politics: Black Members of the National Congress, 1983–1999, *Journal of Interamerican Studies and World Affairs*, 40 (4), 97-118.

Johnson, T.A. (2004) The enduring function of caste: colonial and modern Haiti, Jamaica, and Brazil: The economy of race, the social organization of caste, and the formulation of racial societies, *Comparative American Studies*, 2 (1), 61-73.

Johnson, T.A. and Bankhead, T. (2014) Hair It Is: Examining the Experiences of Black Women with Natural Hair, *Open Journal of Social Sciences*, (2), 86-100.

Jorge, J.P. (2015) Renato Aragão: uma conversa franca com o homem por trás de Didi Mocó, [Renato Aragão: a honest conversation with the man behind Didi Mocó]. *Revista VIP*, 26/02/2015, São Paulo, SP. Available from: http://vip.abril.com.br/renato-aragao-uma-conversa-franca-com-o-homem-por-tras-de-didi-moco/

Jorgensen, M. and Phillips, L.J. (2002) *Discourse analysis as theory and method*. Sage Publications.

Joseph, T.D. (2013) How does racial democracy exist in Brazil? Perceptions from Brazilians in Governador Valadares, Minas Gerais, *Ethnic and Racial Studies*, 36 (10), 1524-1543.

Junges, M. (2011) "O poder Judiciário é exemplar quando o criminoso é pobre", ["Judicial system is exemplary when the criminal is poor"]. *Revista Instituto Humanitas Unisinos*, XI (383), 1-4.

Júnia, R. (2016) Semana da Consciência Negra: desigualdade entre negros e brancos na saúde em debate, [Black Consciousness Week: inequality between blacks and whites in health debate]. *Fundação Oswaldo Cruz (Fiocruz)*, 25/11/2016, Rio de Janeiro, RJ. Available from: https://portal.fiocruz.br/pt-br/content/na-semana-da-consciencia-negra-desigualdade-no-acesso-saude-entre-negros-e-brancos-e-tema-de

Justwan, F., Baumgaertner, B., Carlisle, J.E., Clark, A.K. and Clark, M. (2018) Social media echo chambers and satisfaction with democracy among Democrats and Republicans in the aftermath of the 2016 US elections, *Journal of Elections, Public Opinion and Parties*, 1-19.

Kajihara, K.A. (2010) A imagem do Brasil no exterior: Análise do material de divulgação oficial da Embratur, desde 1966 até 2008, [Brazil's image abroad:

Analysis of official images's advertising of Embratur, from 1966 until 2008]. *Observatório de Inovação do Turismo*, 5 (3), 2-30.

Kehl, R.F. (1920) *Eugenia e medicina social: problemas da vida*, [Eugenics and social medicine: life's problems]. Rio de Janeiro, RJ: Livraria Franciso Alves.

Kehl, R.F. (1931) The first eugenics movements in Brazil, *Boletim de Eugenia*, Abril 1931, Rio de Janeiro, RJ. Available from: http://old.ppi.uem.br/gephe/BE/BEAno3N28Abr1931.pdf

Kelly, M.L. (2018) Media Or Tech Company? Facebook's Profile Is Blurry, *NPR - National Public Radio*, Washington, D.C. Available from: https://www.npr.org/2018/04/11/601560213/media-or-tech-company-facebooks-profile-is-blurry?t=1550139791618

Kelly, S., Truong, M., Shahbaz, A. and Earp, M. (2016) *Freedom on the Net 2016*, New York, NY, Freedom House. Available from: https://freedomhouse.org/sites/default/files/FOTN_2016_BOOKLET_FINAL.pdf

Kemp, S. (2019) Digital 2019: Essential insights into how people around the world use the internet, mobile devices, social media and e-commerce, *We are Social*, 30/01/2019, New York, NY, 1-221. Available from: https://www.slideshare.net/DataReportal/digital-2019-global-digital-overview-january-2019-v01?from_action=save

Kent, E.E. (1965) Palmares: an African state in Brazil, *Journal of African History*, 6 (2), 161-175.

Kettrey, H.H. and Laster, W.N. (2014) Staking Territory in the "World White Web": An Exploration of the Roles of Overt and Color-Blind Racism in Maintaining Racial Boundaries on a Popular Web Site, *Social Currents*, 1 (3), 257-274.

Kirk, C. (2013) The Most Popular Swear Words on Facebook, *Slate*, 11/09/2013, New Yor, NY. Available from: http://www.slate.com/blogs/lexicon_valley/2013/09/11/top_swear_words_most_popular_curse_words_on_facebook.html

Klein, H.S. (1969) The Colonial Freedman in Brazilian Slave Society, *Jorunal of Social History*, 3 (1), 30-52.

Klein, H.S. (1986) *African slavery in Latin America and the Caribbean*. New York, NY: Oxford University Press.

Klineberg, O. (1954) 32 Social Scientists Testify Against Segregation, *The Unesco Courier*, Paris, France, 24-33. Available from: http://unesdoc.unesco.org/images/0006/000699/069962eo.pdf#nameddest=69955

Kling, R., Lee, Y.-C., Teich, A. and Frankel, M.S. (1999) Assessing Anonymous Communication on the Internet: Policy Deliberations, *The Information Society*, (15), 79-90.

Koebler, J. and Cox, J. (2018) The Impossible Job: Inside Facebook's Struggle to Moderate Two Billion People, *Motherboard*, 23/08/2018, New York, NY. Available from: https://motherboard.vice.com/en_us/article/xwk9zd/how-facebook-content-moderation-works

Koffler, S. (1968) Statement on race and racial prejudice, *The Unesco Courier*, May, Paris, France, 30-32. Available from:

http://unesdoc.unesco.org/images/0005/000589/058953eo.pdf#nameddest
=58962

Kolko, B.E., Nakamura, L. and Rodman, G.B. (2000) *Race in Cyberspace*. New York, NY: Routledge.

Kosinski, M., Matz, S.C., Gosling, S.D., Popov, V. and Stillwell, D. (2015) Facebook as a research tool for the social sciences: Opportunities, challenges, ethical considerations, and practical guidelines, *American Psychologist*, 70 (6), 543-556.

Koster, H. (1816) *Travels in Brazil*. London, UK: Longman, Hurst, Rees, Orme & Brown, Paternoster-Row.

Kuchler, H. (2017) Facebook to hire 3,000 more moderators to check content, *Financial Times*, 03/05/2017, London, UK. Available from: https://www.ft.com/content/400414f8-300e-11e7-9555-23ef563ecf9a? mhq5j=e5

Kuipers, G. (2002) Media culture and Internet disaster jokes: bin Laden and the attack on the World Trade Center, *European Journal of Cultural Studies*, 5 (4), 450-470.

Lacerda, J.B. (1911) The 'metis', or half-breeds, of Brazil, IN: Spiller, G. (ed.) *First Universal Races Congress*, London, UK, 26-29 July. London, 377-382. Available from: http://etnolinguistica.wdfiles.com/local--files/biblio%3Alacerda-1911-metis/lacerda_1911_metis.pdf

Lacombe, A.J. (1986) *Obras completas de Rui Barbosa: Atos Legislativos, Decisões Ministeriais e Circulares - Volume XVII, Tomo II*, [Complete Works of Rui Barbosa: Legislative Acts, Ministerial and Circular Decisions - Volume XVII, Number II]. Rio de Janeiro, RJ: Fundação Casa Rui Barbosa.

Lagôa, T. (2018) Alunos cotistas se destacam em 95% dos cursos da UFMG, [Quota students perform better in 95% of UFMG's courses]. *O Tempo*, 22/11/2018, Belo Horizonte, BH. Available from: https://www.otempo.com.br/cidades/alunos-cotistas-se-destacam-em-95-dos-cursos-da-ufmg-1.2070583

Lagorio-Chafkin, C. (2018) Facebook's 7,500 Moderators Protect You From the Internet's Most Horrifying Content. But Who's Protecting Them?, *Inc.*, 26/09/2018, New York, NY. Available from: https://www.inc.com/christine-lagorio/facebook-content-moderator-lawsuit.html

Lane, J. (2005) *Blackface Cuba, 1840-1895*. Philadelphia, PA: University of Pennsylvania Press.

Lankaster-Owen, B., Douglas, B., Philips, C. and Riddel, J. (2016) The Brazilian carnival queen deemed 'too black' - video, *The Guardian Documentary*, 09/02/2016, London, UK. Available from: https://www.theguardian.com/news/video/2016/feb/09/brazilian-carnival-queen-too-black-nayara-justino-video

Laudone, S. (2010) *Facebook: A "Raced" Space or "Post-Racial"?*, Paper presented at American Sociological Association Annual Meeting, Atlanta, GA, 14 August. Available from: http://citation.allacademic.com/meta/p_mla_apa_research_citation/4/0/9 /6/6/p409664_index.html

Leaver, B. and Costa, M. (2018) Jair Bolsonaro's provocative views in six clips - video, *The Guardian*, 29/10/2018, London, UK. Available from: https://www.theguardian.com/world/video/2018/oct/29/jair-bolsonaros-views-on-homosexuality-torture-and-more-video

Lemos, R. (2007) Internet brasileira precisa de marco regulatório civil, [Brazilian Internet needs a civil regulatory framework]. *UOL*, 22/05/2007, São Paulo, SP. Available from: https://tecnologia.uol.com.br/ultnot/2007/05/22/ult4213u98.jhtm

Lempp, S. (2019) Jair Bolsonaro and affirmative action: political rupture or escalation?, *Allegra Lab*, 03/04/2019, New York, NY. Available from: https://allegralaboratory.net/jair-bolsonaro-and-affirmative-action-political-rupture-or-escalation/

Lever (1930) Concurso de Belleza realizado no Rio de Janeiro, [International Beauty Contest in Rio de Janeiro - Official Brochure]. *Album Oficial*, Rio de Janeiro, RJ, 30. Available from: https://web.archive.org/web/20080716061207/http://brazilpostcard.com:80/especial/beauty01.html

Levine, R.M. (1973) The First Afro-Brazilian Congress: Opportunities for the Study of Race in the Brazilian Northeast, *Race & Class*, 15 (2), 185-193.

Lévy, P. (2001) *Cyberculture*. Saint Paul, MN: University of Minnesota Press.

Lichtman, M. (2010) *Qualitative Research in Education: A User's Guide*. London, UK: Sage Publications.

Lima, J.D. (2017) Por que a USP foi a última a adotar cotas, segundo esta pesquisadora, [Why USP was the last to adopt quotas, according to this researcher]. *Nexo Jornal*, 06/07/2017, São Paulo, SP. Available from: https://www.nexojornal.com.br/expresso/2017/07/05/Por-que-a-USP-foi-a-%C3%BAltima-a-adotar-cotas-segundo-esta-pesquisadora

Lima, K. (2016) Meu cabelo, minha coroa, [My hair, my crown]. *Alma Preta*, 24/12/2016, Bauru, SP. Available from: https://www.almapreta.com/editorias/o-quilombo/meu-cabelo-minha-coroa

Lima, L. (2015) O cabelo crespo é a coroa da mulher negra, [Curly hair is the crown of the black woman]. *Nós Mulheres de Periferia*, 24/07/2015, São Paulo, SP. Available from: http://nosmulheresdaperiferia.com.br/noticias/o-cabelo-crespo-e-a-coroa-da-mulher-negra/

Lima, M. (2010) Apenas uma frase no muro, [Only a sentence on the wall]. *Recanto das Letras*, 04/12/2010, São Paulo, SP. Available from: http://www.recantodasletras.com.br/contos/2653869

Lima, N.C. and Lessa, M. (2017) Com 'telecoteco e ziriguidum', Oswaldo Sargentelli inventou o 'show de mulatas', [With 'telecoteco and ziriguidum', Oswaldo Sargentelli invented the '*mulata* show']. *O Globo*, 06/04/2017, Rio de Janeiro, RJ. Available from: http://acervo.oglobo.globo.com/em-destaque/com-telecoteco-ziriguidum-oswaldo-sargentelli-inventou-show-de-mulatas-21170942

Lockhart, J. and Schwartz, S.B. (1983) *Early Latin American: a history of colonial Spanish America and Brazil*. Cambridge, UK: Cambridge University Press.

Lockyer, S. and Pickering, M. (2008) You must be joking: the sociological critique of humour and comic media, *Sociology Compass*, 2 (3), 808-820.

Lopes, N. (2014) *Enciclopédia brasileira da diáspora africana*, [Brazilian Encyclopedia of the African Diaspora]. São Paulo, SP: Selo Negro.

Lopes, V. and Ricci, L. (2016) Crença no anonimato e impunidade favorecem racismo na internet, [Belief in anonymity and impunity contributes towards online racism]. *Estado de Minas*, 31/12/2016, Belo Horizonte, MG. Available from: https://www.em.com.br/app/noticia/gerais/2016/12/31/interna_gerais,836 174/crenca-no-anonimato-e-impunidade-favorecem-racismo-na-internet.shtml

Lorenz, S. (2008) Processos de purificação: expectativas ligadas à migração alemã para o Brasil (1880-1918), [Purification processes: expectations linked to the German migration to Brazil (1880-1918)]. *Espaço Plural*, 9 (19), 29-37.

Machado, C. (2006) O patriarcalismo possível: relações de poder em uma região do Brasil escravista em que o trabalho familiar era a norma, [The possible patriarchalism: relations of power in a region of slavery Brazil in which family work was the norm]. *Revista Brasileira de Estudos de População*, 23 (1), 167-186.

Machado, E.S. and Muniz, K.S. (2013) *Humor, Identidade Negra e Estereótipo: Análise de Personagens e Piadas sobre negros em programas humorísticos*, [Humor, Black Identit and Stereotype: Analysis of Characters and Jokes about Blacks in TV commedy shows]. Paper presented at XXI SEIC - Seminário de Iniciação Científica da UFOP, Ouro Preto, MG. Available from: http://www.encontrodesaberes.ufop.br/gerar_pdf.php?id=4067

Machado, M.R.A., Lima, M. and Neris, N. (2016) Racismo e insulto racial na sociedade brasileira: Dinâmicas de reconhecimento e invisibilização a partir do direito, [Racism and Racial Insults in Brazilian Society: The Dynamics of Law-Based Recognition and Invisibilization]. *Novos Estudos - CEBRAP*, 35 (3), 11-28.

Madrigal, A.C. (2018) Inside Facebook's Fast-Growing Content-Moderation Effort, *The Atlantic*, 07/02/2018, Boston, MA. Available from: https://www.theatlantic.com/technology/archive/2018/02/what-facebook-told-insiders-about-how-it-moderates-posts/552632/

Madureira, T. (2019) Protagonistas em campo, negros são relegados dos cargos de gestão de clubes da Série A, [Protagonists in the field, blacks are relegated from the management positions of Serie A clubs]. *Superesportes*, 25/04/2019, Belo Horizonte, BH. Available from: https://www.mg.superesportes.com.br/app/noticias/futebol/futebol-nacional/2019/04/25/noticia_futebol_nacional,580597/protagonistas-em-campo-negros-sao-excluidos-dos-cargos-de-gestao.shtml

Maier, F. (2006) Racismo cordial: qual é a sua cor predileta?, [Friendly racism: what is your favourite colour?]. *Mídia sem Máscara*, 23/11/2006, São Paulo, SP. Available from: http://www.midiasemmascara.org/arquivos/5687-racismo-cordial-qual-e-a-sua-cor-predileta.html

Maio, M.C. (1997) *A história do projeto Unesco: estudos raciais e ciências sociais no Brasil*, [The history of the UNESCO project: racial studies and social sciences in Brazil]. PhD Thesis, Instituto Universitário de Pesquisas do Rio de Janeiro (IUPERJ)

Malmqvist, K. (2015) Satire, racist humour and the power of (un)laughter: On the restrained nature of Swedish online racist discourse targeting EU-migrants begging for money, *Discourse & Society*, 26 (6), 733-753.

Manfred, T. (2012) Why is the internet so racist?, *Business Insider*, 24/05/2012, New York, NY. Available from: http://www.businessinsider.com/internet-racism-2012-5?IR=T

Maraire, J.N. (2015) "Until the lion learns how to write, every story will glorify the hunter.", *Goodreads*, San Francisco, CA. Available from: https://www.goodreads.com/quotes/8058892-until-the-lion-learns-how-to-write-every-story-will

Marcondes, M.M., Pinheiro, L., Queiroz, C., Querino, A.C. and Valverde, D. (2013) *Dossiê mulheres negras: retrato das condições de vida das mulheres negras no Brasil*, [Black women's dossier: portrait of black women's living conditions in Brazil]. Brasília, DF: Instituto de Pesquisa Econômica Aplicada - IPEA.

Mari, A. (2014) Brazil passes groundbreaking Internet governance Bill, *ZD Net*, 26/03/2014, London, UK. Available from: http://www.zdnet.com/article/brazil-passes-groundbreaking-internet-governance-bill/

Maringoni, G. (2011) O destino dos negros após a Abolição, [The Blacks' destiny after the Emancipation]. *Desafios do Desenvolvimento*, 29/12/2011, Brasília, DF. Available from: http://www.ipea.gov.br/desafios/index.php?option=com_content&id=2673%3Acatid%3D28&Itemid=23

Marinho, A., Cardoso, S. and Almeida, V. (2011) Desigualdade racial no Brasil: um olhar para a saúde, [Racial inequality in Brazil: a look at health conditions]. *Desafios do Desenvolvimento*, 8 (70), 44-46.

Marques, J. (2017) Negra, pobre e da rede pública fica em 1º em curso mais concorrido da Fuvest, [Black, poor and coming from public school rreaches 1st place in the most competitivve undergraduate admission exame]. *Folha de S. Paulo*, 06/02/2017, São Paulo, SP. Available from: https://www1.folha.uol.com.br/educacao/2017/02/1856050-negra-pobre-e-da-rede-publica-fica-em-1-em-curso-mais-concorrido-da-fuvest.shtml

Martins, S.D.S., Medeiros, C.A. and Nascimento, E.L. (2004) Paving Paradise: The Road from "Racial Democracy" to Affirmative Action in Brazil, *Journal of Black Studies*, 34 (6), 787-816.

Mattos, S.S.(2013) O grito das ruas, [The shouting coming from the streets]. *Sociologia*, São Paulo, SP, n. 48. agosto/setembro, 58-61

Máximo, J. (1999) Memórias do futebol brasileiro, [Memories of Brazilian football]. *Estudos Avançados*, 13 (37), 179-188.

Mccoy, D.B. (1959) Education in Brazil, *Peabody Journal of Education*, 37 (1), 39-43.

McPherson, M., Smith-Lovin, L. and Cook, J.M. (2001) Birds of a Feather: Homophily in Social Networks, *Annual Review of Sociology*, 27 (1), 415-444.

Mello e Souza, M. (2006) *África e Brasil Africano*, [Africa and African Brazil]. São Paulo, SP: Ática.

Melo, M. (1922) Corografia de Pernambuco, [Pernambuco's Chrographia]. *Revista do Instituto Archeológico, Histo´rico e Geogra´phico Pernambucano*, 24 (115-118), 1-148.

Mendonça, M.(2009) A volta do cabelo crespo, [The return of curly hair]. *Época* Rio de Janeiro, RJ. 12/10/2009, 114-117

Metcalf, A.C. (2005) *Go-betweens and the colonization of Brazil, 1500-1600*. Austin, TX: University of Texas Press.

Métraux, A. (1951) Brazil: land of harmony for all races?, *The Unesco Courier*, April, Paris, France, Available from: http://unesdoc.unesco.org/images/0007/000735/073516eo.pdf#nameddest =73516

Métraux, A. (1952) An inquiry into race relations in Brazil, *The Unesco Courier*, August-September, Paris, France. Available from: http://unesdoc.unesco.org/images/0007/000711/071135eo.pdf#71109

Mikulak, M.L. (2011) The Symbolic Power of Color: Constructions of Race, Skin-Color, and Identity in Brazil, *Humanity & Society*, 35 (1-2), 62-99.

Mills, J. (2005) *Charles Miller: O pai do futebol brasileiro*, [Charles Miller: the father of Brazilian football]. São Paulo, SP: Panda Books.

Miranda, S.F. (2016) Da base da pirâmide social à "elite" do sistema: um estudo de caso sobre as diversas incursões de uma mulher negra, nordestina e militante, [From the bottom of the social pyramid to the "elite" of the system: a case study about the varied incursions of a black woman, northeastern and militant]. *Pesquisas e Práticas Psicossociais*, 11 (1), 100-117.

Misoch, S. (2015) Stranger on the internet: Online self-disclosure and the role of visual anonymity, *Computers in Human Behavior*, 48, 535-541.

Moehlecke, S. (2002) Ação afirmativa: história e debates no Brasil, [Affirmative Action: History and debates in Brazil]. *Cadernos de Pesquisa*, (117), 197-217.

Moraes, E. (1924) Expansão de um preconceito, [Expansion of a prejudice]. *O Getulino*, 10/02/1924, Campinas, SP. Available from: http://www2.assis.unesp.br/cedap/cat_imprensa_negra/verbetes/getulino.html

Motta, F.C.P. and Alcadipani, R. (1999) Jeitinho brasileiro, controle social e competição, [Brazilian 'jeitinho', social control and competition]. *RAE - Revista de Administraçãao de Empresas*, 39 (1), 6-12.

Moura, C. (1988) *Sociologia do negro brasileiro*, [Sociology of Brazilian Negro]. São Paulo, SP: Editora Ática.

Moura, C. (2004) *Dicionário da Escravidão Negra no Brasil*, [Dictionary of Black Slavery in Brazil]. São Paulo, SP: Edusp - Editora da Universidade de São Paulo.

Mulher (2018) Onde encontrar famosos no Rio de Janeiro, [Where to find the famous in Rio de Janeiro]. *Via Mulher*, 07/11/2018, Rio de Janeiro, RJ. Available from: https://vilamulher.com.br/famosos/mundo-da-fama/onde-encontrar-famosos-no-rio-de-janeiro-6-1-80-760.html

Nabuco, J., Patrocínio, J. and Rebouças, A. (1880) *Manifesto da Sociedade Brasileira contra a Escravidão*, [Manifesto of the Brazilian Society against Slavery]. Rio de Janeiro, RJ: Sociedade Brasileira contra a Escravidão.

Nacked, R.C. (2012) Identidades em diáspora: o movimento Black no Brasil, [Diaspora identities: the Black movement in Brazil]. *Revista Desenredos*, IV (12), 1-11.

Nascimento, E.L. (1980) Aspects of Afro-Brazilian experience, *Journal of Black Studies*, 11 (2), 195-216.

Nascimento, S. (2017) BlackFace: A "homenagem" que nunca dá certo, [BlackFace: The "compliment" that never works]. *Mundo Negro*, 01/06/2017, São Paulo, SP. Available from: https://mundonegro.inf.br/blackface-america/

Nascimento, S.L. and Alves, W.J.M. (2011) Racismo: Desigualdades entre Negros e Brancos no Brasil, [Racism: Inequalities between Blacks and Whites in Brazil]. *Revista Acadêmica Espaço da Sophia*, (43), 107-120.

Neponucemo, E.B. (2013) Paradoxos carnavalescos: a presença feminina em carnavais da primeira república (1889-1910), [Carnival paradoxes: the female presence in carnivals of the First Republic (1889-1910)]. *Clio: Revista de Pesquisa Histórica*, 31 (1), 1-15.

Neto, A.P. and Lettry, E. (2013) Só o discurso não é suficiente para acabar com o racismo, diz Kabengele Munanga, [Discourse only is not enough to end racism, says Kabengele Munanga]. *Instituto de Estudos Brasil Europa*, 20/03/2013, São Paulo, SP. Available from: http://www.ibe.usp.br/index.php/pt/noticias/185-o-racismo-nao-acaba-so-com-discurso-garante-kabengele-munanga

Nkosi, D.F. (2014) O pênis sem o falo: algumas reflexões sobre homens negros, masculinidades e racismo, [The penis without the phallus: some reflections on black men, masculinities and racism]. IN: Blay, E.A. (ed.) *Feminismos e masculinidades: novos caminhos para enfrentar a violência contra a mulher*. São Paulo, SP: Cultura Acadêmica, 75-104.

Noble, S.U. (2018) *Algorithms of Oppression: How Search Engines Reinforce Racism*. New York, NY: New York University Press.

Nogueira, L.F.V. (2011) Expectativa de vida e mortalidade de escravos: Uma análise da Freguesia do Divino Espírito Santo do Lamim - MG (1859-1888), [Life expectancy and mortality of slaves: An analysis of the Freguesia do Divino Espírito Santo do Lamim - MG (1859-1888)]. *Histórica - Revista Eletrônica do Arquivo Público do Estado de São Paulo*, (51), 1-7.

Nogueira, O. (2007) Preconceito racial de marca e preconceito racial de origem: sugestão de um quadro de referência para a interpretação do material sobre relações raciais no Brasil, [Mark and origin: a framework for the analysis of racial prejudice in Brazil]. *Tempo Social*, 19 (1), 287-308.

Nogueira, S.G. (2013) Ideology of white racial supremacy: colonization and de-colonization processes, *Psicologia & Sociedade*, 25, 23-32.

Nova, A.V. and Santos, E.A. (2013) *Mulheres Negras: histórias de resistência, de coragem, de superação e sua difícil trajetória de vida na sociedade brasileira*, [Black Women: resistance stories of courage, resilience and their difficult life course in the Brazilian society]. 1st ed. Duque de Caxias, RJ: Creative Commons.

O'Maley, D.P. (2015) *Networking democracy: Brazilian internet freedom activism and the influence of participatory democracy.* PhD Thesis, Vanderbilt University. School of Anthropology

Olinto, M.T.A. and Olinto, B.A. (2000) Raça e desigualdade entre as mulheres: um exemplo no sul do Brasil, [Race and inequality among women: an example in southern Brazil]. *Caderno de Saúde Pública*, 16 (4), 1137-1142.

Oliva, A.R. (2003) A História da África nos bancos escolares: Representações e imprecisões na literatura didática, [The African History in the school benches: Representations and inaccuracies on textbooks]. *Estudos Afro-Asiáticos*, 25 (3), 421-461.

Oliveira, C. (2018) Is Neymar Black? Brazil and the Painful Relativity of Race, *The New York Times*, 30/06/2018, New York, NY. Available from: https://www.nytimes.com/2018/06/30/opinion/is-neymar-black-brazil-and-the-painful-relativity-of-race.html

Oliveira, C.L.P. and Barreto, P.C.S. (2003) Percepção do racismo no Rio de Janeiro, [Perception of racism in Rio de Janeiro]. *Estudos Afro-Asiáticos*, 25 (2), 183-213.

Oliveira, D.C.N. (2016) Meu cabelo não é só estética, é também política: os movimentos sociais e as narrativas visuais, [My hair is not only aesthetic, it is also political: social movements and visual narratives]. *Revista da Associação Brasileira de Pesquisadores/as Negros/as (ABPN)*, 8 (20), 217-230.

Oliveira, S. (2017) Silenciamento racial: qual discurso o branco quer ouvir?, [Racial silencing: which discourse do the whites want to hear?]. *Teeto*, 04/12/2017, São Paulo, SP. Available from: https://teeteto.com.br/silenciamento-racial-qual-discurso-o-branco-quer-ouvir-3244a4c1de0d

Orser, C., E. (1992) *In search of Zumbi: preliminary archeological research at the Serra da Barriga, State of Alagoas, Brazil.* Normal, IL: Illinois State University.

Ortiz, F. (2011) Reduto de artistas e ponto turístico do Rio, Santa Teresa se prepara para receber três UPPs, [Hot point of artists and touristic attraction in Rio, Santa Teresa prepares to receive three UPPs]. *UOL Notícias*, 05/02/2011, Rio de Janeiro, RJ. Available from: https://noticias.uol.com.br/cotidiano/ultimas-noticias/2011/02/05/favelas-de-santa-teresa-serao-pacificadas.htm

Osorio, R.G. (2003) O sistema classificatório de "cor ou raça" do IBGE, [The IBGE's classification system of "color or race"]. *Texto para Discussão - IPEA*, (996), 1-50.

Owensby, B.P. (2005) Toward a history of Brazil's "cordial racism": Race beyond liberalism, *Comparative Studies in Society and History*, 47 (2), 318-347.

Pacheco, L.C. (2011) Racismo cordial: manifestação da discriminação racial à brasileira. O domínio público e o privado, [Cordial racism: the Brazilian way of discrimination manifestation: The public and private domains]. *Revista de Psicologia*, 2 (1), 137-144.

Pacheco, T., Cavalcanti, A.P. and Levi, D. (2016) Racismo no Brasil: "O crime perfeito". Entrevista com Djamila Ribeiro, [Racism in Brazil: "The perfect crime". Interview with Djamila Ribeiro]. *Combate Racismo Ambiental*, 07/02/2016, São Paulo, SP. Available from: http://racismoambiental.net.br/2016/02/07/racismo-no-brasil-o-crime-perfeito-entrevista-com-djamila-ribeiro/

Pakman, D. (2015) People's Racist Facebook Comments on Billboards Near Their Homes, *David Pakman Show*, 05/12/2015, Boston, MA. Available from: https://www.youtube.com/watch?v=7RVe7jYaIeg

Passarelli, H. (2019) 'Ideia de universidade para todos não existe', diz ministro da Educação, ['Idea of university for all does not exist', says minister of Education]. *Valor Econômico*, 28/01/2019, Brasília, DF. Available from: https://www.valor.com.br/brasil/6088217/ideia-de-universidade-para-todos-nao-existe-diz-ministro-da-educacao#

Pereira, B., Costa, C.T., Cespedes, F. and Jorge, S. (2016) Dossiê intolerâncias: visíveis e invisíveis no mundo digital, [Bigotry dossier: visible and invisible in the digital world]. *Associação Brasileira de Comunicação Pública*, São Paulo, SP, 59 pages. Available from: http://www.conexaopublica.com.br/wp-content/uploads/2016/08/dossie_intolerancia.pdf

Pereira, L.N.N. (2008) O ensino e a pesquisa sobre a África no Brasil e a Lei 10.639, [Teaching and research on Africa in Brazil and the Law 10.639]. IN: Becerra, M.J. (ed.) *Los estudios afroamericanos y africanos en América Latina : herencia, presencia y visiones del otro*. Córdoba; Buenos Aires: CLACSO, Consejo Latinoamericano de Ciencias Sociales, 253-276.

Perez, K. (2016) How to Make a Truly Anonymous Facebook Account Part I, *The Order of the White Rose*, 09/05/2016, New York, NY. Available from: https://www.whiterose.us/make-truly-anonymous-facebook-account/

Pérez, R. (2013) Learning to make racism funny in the 'color-blind' era: Stand-up comedy students, performance strategies, and the (re)production of racist jokes in public, *Discourse & Society*, 24 (2), 478-503.

Pérez, R. (2017) Racism without Hatred? Racist Humor and the Myth of "Colorblindness", *Sociological Perspectives*, 60 (5), 956-974.

Philippou, S. (2005) Modernism and National Identity in Brazil, or How to Brew a Brazilian Stew, *National Identities*, 7 (3), 245-264.

Philips, T. and Kaiser, A.J. (2019) Brazil must not become a 'gay tourism paradise', says Bolsonaro, *The Guardian*, 26/04/2019, London, UK. Available from: https://www.theguardian.com/world/2019/apr/26/bolsonaro-accused-of-inciting-hatred-with-gay-paradise-comment

Phillips, T. (2018) Trump of the tropics: the 'dangerous' candidate leading Brazil's presidential race, *The Guardian*, 19/04/2018, London, UK. Available from: https://www.theguardian.com/world/2018/apr/19/jair-bolsonaro-brazil-presidential-candidate-trump-parallels

Pinto, E.A. (1993) *Etnicidade, genero e educação : a trajetoria de vida de D. Laudelina de Campos Mello (1904-1991)*, [Ethnicity, gender and education: the life trajectory of D. Laudelina de Campos Mello (1904-1991)]. Masters' Dissertation, Unicamp

Pinto, M.C.C. and Ferreira, R.F. (2014) Relações raciais no Brasil e a construção da identidade da pessoa negra, [Race relations in Brazil and the construction of the identity of the black person]. *Pesquisas e Práticas Psicossociais*, 9 (2), 257-266.

Pinto, R.P. (1993) *O movimento negro em São Paulo: luta e identidade*, [The black movement in São Paulo: struggle and identity]. PhD Thesis, Universidade de São Paulo. Faculdade de Filosofia, Letras e Ciências Humanas - Antropologia

Poster, M. (2001) *What's the Matter with the Internet?* Saint Paul, MN: University of Minnesota Press.

Potter, J. (1996) *Representing Reality: Discourse, Rhetoric and Social Construction*. London, UK: Sage Publications, Inc.

Purkayastha, B. (2012) Intersectionality in a Transnational World, *Gender & Society*, 26 (1), 55-66.

Quadrado, B.F. (2015) Concurso Miss Mulata Rio Grande do Sul: o conflito da cor e a branquitude nos padrões estéticos, [Miss Mulata Rio Grande do Sul Beauty Contest: colour conflict and whiteness in aesthetic standards]. *RELACult - Revista Latino-Americana de Estudos em Cultura e Sociedade*, 1 (2), 144-155.

Quaresma, A.(2014) Cibergeração, [Cybergeneration]. *Sociologia*, São Paulo, SP, n. 50. February, 28-31

Queiroz, D.M. and Santos, C.M. (2016) As mulheres negras brasileiras e o acesso à educação superior, [Black Brazilian women and access to higher education]. *Revista da FAEEBA – Educação e Contemporaneidade*, 25 (45), 71-87.

Ramos, A.G. (1940) *O negro brasileiro, Volume 1 - Etnologia religiosa*, [The Brazilian Black, volume 1 - Religious ethnology]. 2nd ed. Rio de Janeiro, RJ: Companhia Editora Nacional.

Ramos, A.G. (1942) *A aculturação negra no Brasil*, [Black acculturation in Brazil]. 1st ed. São Paulo, SP: Companhia Editora Nacional.

Ramos, A.G. (1946) *As culturas negras no Novo Mundo: O negro brasileiro - III*, [The Black culture in the New World: The Brazilian Black - III]. 2nd ed. São Paulo, SP: Civilização Brasileira.

Rega, L.S. (2000) *Dando um jeito no jeitinho: Como ser ético sem deixar de ser brasileiro*, [Fixing the 'jeitinho': How to be ethical and still remain Brazilian]. 1st ed. São Paulo, SP: ABEC.

Reis, J.J. (2005) Batuque: African Drumming and Dance between Repression and Concession, Bahia, 1808-1855, *Bulletin of Latin American Research*, 24 (2), 201-214.

Rheingold, H. (2000) *The Virtual Community: Homesteading on the Electronic Frontier*. Cambridge, MA: MIT Press.

Ribeiro, M. (2014) Acostumados com famosos, moradores do Vidigal criticam gravações de novela, [Accustomed to celebrities, Vidigal residents criticize soap opera recordings]. *UOL*, 15/04/2014, Rio de Janeiro, RJ. Available from: https://televisao.uol.com.br/noticias/redacao/2014/04/15/acostumados-com-famosos-moradores-do-vidigal-criticam-gravacoes-de-novela.htm

Rocha, E.F. (2015) *O Negro no mundo dos ricos: um estudo sobre a disparidade racial de riqueza no Brasil com os dados do Censo Demográfico de 2010*, [The Negro in the world of the rich: a study on the racial disparity of wealth in Brazil with data from the 2010 Demographic Census]. PhD Thesis, Universidade de Brasília, Sociology

Rodrigues, F. (1995) Racismo cordial, [Friendly racism]. IN: Turra, C. and Venturi, G. (eds.) *Racismo cordial: a mais completa análise sobre o preconceito de cor no Brasil*. São Paulo, SP: Editora Ática, 11-56.

Rodrigues, J.C. (1988) *O Negro Brasileiro e o Cinema*, [The Brazilian Black and the Cinema]. Rio de Janeiro, RJ: Globo.

Rodrigues, M. (2015) Polícia Civil investiga ofensas racistas a jornalista do DF em rede social, [Civil Police investigates racist offenses against journalist on social media]. *G1*, 06/05/2015, Rio de Janeiro, RJ. Available from: http://g1.globo.com/distrito-federal/noticia/2015/05/policia-civil-investiga-ofensas-racistas-jornalista-do-df-em-rede-social.html

Rodrigues, N. (1994) *A pátria em chuteiras: Novas crônicas de futebol*, [The country in football boots: New football chronicles]. São Paulo, SP: Companhia das Letras.

Rodrigues, R.N. (1932) *Os africanos no Brasil*, [The Africans in Brazil]. Rio de Janeiro, RJ: Companhia Editora Nacional.

Rogerio, J. (2010) Homem bonito. Já ouviu falar em "Deus Grego"? Não? Então veja o Janice Fronimakis, [Handsome man. Ever heard of "Greek God"? No? Then meet Janice Fronimakis]. *TV Canal 7*, 24/09/2010, São Paulo, SP. Available from: http://tvcanal7.blogspot.co.uk/2010/09/homem-bonito-ja-ouviu-falar-em-deus.html

Romão, M. (2015) Facebook volta atrás e tira do ar página nazista que atacava mulheres negras, [Facebook steps back and blocks nazi page that attacked Black women]. *Mama Press*, 15/02/2017, São Paulo, SP. Available from: https://mamapress.wordpress.com/2015/02/15/facebook-volta-atras-e-tira-do-ar-pagina-neonazista-que-atacava-mulheres-negras/

Rosa, A.R. (2014) Relações Raciais e Estudos Organizacionais no Brasil, [Race Relations and Organizational Studies in Brazil]. *RAC - Revista de Administração Contemporânea*, 18 (3), 240-260.

Rose, A.M. (1958) The roots of prejudice: how children come to have racial bias, *The Unesco Courier*, August, Paris, France, 24-25. Available from: http://unesdoc.unesco.org/images/0006/000662/066266eo.pdf#nameddest=66274

Rosemberg, F., Bazilli, C. and Baptista Da Silva, P.V. (2003) Racismo em livros didáticos brasileiros e seu combate: uma revisão da literatura, [Racism in Brazilian textbooks and the struggle to change that: a literature review]. *Educação e Pesquisa*, 29 (1), 125-146.

Roshani, N. (2016) Grassroots Perspectives on Hate Speech, Race, & Inequality in Brazil & Colombia, *Berkman Klein Center for Internet & Society at Harvard University*, December, Cambridge, MA, 1-22. Available from: https://cyber.harvard.edu/publications/2016/GrassrootsPerspectives

Rossini, C., Cruz, F.B. and Doneda, D. (2015) *The Strengths and Weaknesses of the Brazilian Internet Bill of Rights: Examining a Human Rights*

Framework for the Internet, Ontario, Canada, Global Commission on Internet Governance. Available from: https://www.cigionline.org/sites/default/files/no19_0.pdf

Rousseff, D., Cardozo, J.E., Belchior, M., Silva, P.B. and Diniz, C.C. (2014) *Lei Nº 12.965, de 23 de abril de 2014*, [Law Number 12,965 - 23 April 2014]. Brasília, DF: Presidência da República. Available from: http://www.planalto.gov.br/ccivil_03/_ato2011-2014/2014/lei/l12965.htm

Ruffato, L. (2016) A educação como privilégio de classe, [Education as a Class Privilege]. *El País*, 09/11/2016, São Paulo, SP. Available from: https://brasil.elpais.com/brasil/2016/11/09/opinion/1478706940_890374.html

Safernet (2015) Indicadores da Central Nacional de Denúncias de Crimes Cibernéticos, [Indicators of the National Complaints Centre of Cyber Crimes]. *Safernet Brasil*, 10/01/2015, Salvador, BA. Available from: http://indicadores.safernet.org.br/

Sales Jr., R. (2006) Democracia racial: o não-dito racista, [Racial democracy: the unspoken racism]. *Tempo Social*, 18 (2), 229-258.

Salmons, J. and Woodfield, K. (2013) *Social Media, Social Science & Research Ethics*, Paper presented at Social Media in Social Research Conference: Ethnics of Social Media Research, London, UK. Available from: http://the-sra.org.uk/wp-content/uploads/salmons_woodfield.pdf

Sansone, L. (1996) Nem somente preto ou negro: o sistema de classificação racial no Brasil que muda, [Not only black or negro: the racial classification system in Brazil that changes]. *Afro-Ásia*, (18), 165-187.

Santana, B. (2015) *Quando me descobri Negra*, [When I discovered myself Negra]. São Paulo, SP: SESI Editora.

Santana, J.C. (2015) *Tem preto de jaleco branco? Ações afirmativas na Faculdade de Medicina da Universidade Federal de Alagoas*, [Are there Blacks wearing white coats? Affirmative actions at the Faculty of Medicine of the Federal University of Alagoas]. PhD Thesis, Universidade Federal de Alagoas. Programa de Pós-Graduação em Educação

Santos, A. (2019) O racismo da academia apagou a história de Dandara e Luisa Mahin, [The Academia's racism has erased the story of Dandara and Luisa Mahin]. *The Intercept Brasil*, 04/06/2019, São Paulo, SP. Available from: https://theintercept.com/2019/06/03/dandara-luisa-mahin-historia/

Santos, Í.D. (2011) A diferença entre o crime de racismo e a injúria qualificada, [The difference between the crime of racism and racial injury]. *PHMP Advogados*, 10/01/2011, Jaraguá do Sul, SC. Available from: http://phmp.com.br/noticias/a-diferenca-entre-o-crime-de-racismo-e-a-injuria-qualificada/

Santos, J.A. (2019) Lima Barreto: apontamentos sobre football e protagonismo negro no Brasil, [Lima Barreto: Football and black protagonism appoitments in Brazil]. *Revista Prâksis*, 16 (1), 103-122.

Santos, J.C.F. (2018) O Espetáculo da Mulher Negra Nua na Televisão: Um estudo de caso sobre a Globeleza, [The Spetacle of the Naked Black Woman on Television: A case study about the *Globeleza*]. *INICIACOM - Revista Brasileira de Iniciação Científica*, 7 (1), 1-11.

Santos, J.T. (2000) O negro no espelho: imagens e discursos nos salões de beleza étnicos, [The Black in the mirror: Images and speeches in ethnic beauty salons]. *Estudos Afro-Asiáticos*, (38), 1-14.

Santos, M.A. (2009) *Entre a sujeira e a fatal de (com)postura 1831-1845*, [Between dirt and lack of decency 1831-1845]. Masters' Dissertation, February, Universidade Federal de Pernambuco. Departamento de Letras e Ciências Humanas

Santos, M.M. (2004) O preço dos escravos no tráfico atlântico: hipóteses de explicação, [The price of slaves in Atlantic traffic: explanatory hypotheses]. *Africana Studia*, (7), 163-181.

Santos, R.A. and Barbosa E Silva, R.M.N. (2018) Racismo científico no Brasil: um retrato racial do Brasil pós-escravatura, [Scientific racism in Brazil: a racial portrait of post-slavery Brazil]. *Educar em Revista*, 34 (68), 253-267.

Santos, S.B. (2009) As ONGs de mulheres negras no Brasil, [Black Women's NGOs in Brazil]. *Sociedade e Cultura*, 12 (2), 275-288.

Schucman, L.V. (2012) *Entre o "encardido", o "branco" e o "branquíssimo": raça, hierarquia e poder na construção da branquitude paulistana*, ['Dirty-white', 'white' and 'extra-white': race, hierarchy and power in the construction of paulistano whiteness]. PhD Thesis, Universidade de São Paulo. Instituto de Psicologia

Schwarcz, L.K.M. (1994) Espetáculo da miscigenação, [Show of the miscegenation]. *Estudos Avançados*, 8 (20), 137-152.

Schwarcz, L.K.M. (2011) Previsões são sempre enganosas: João Baptista de Lacerda e seu Brasil branco, [Predictions are always deceptive: João Baptista de Lacerda and his white Brazil]. *História, Ciências, Saúde-Manguinhos*, 18 (1), 225-242.

Schwartz, S.B. (1974) The Manumission of Slaves in Colonial Brazil: Bahia, 1684-1745, *The Hispanic American Historical Review*, 54 (4), 603-635.

Schwartz, S.B. (1985) *Sugar Plantations in the Formation of Brazilian Society: Bahia, 1550-1835*. New York, NY: Cambridge University Press.

Schwarz-Bart, S. and Schwarz-Bart, A.É. (2001) *In Praise of Black Women: Heroines of the Slavery Era*. Madison, WI: University of Wisconsin Press.

Scolese, E. (2005) Lula pede perdão por negros que foram escravos no Brasil, [Lula apologises for Blacks who were slaves in Brazil]. *Folha de S. Paulo*, 15/04/2005, São Paulo. Available from: http://www1.folha.uol.com.br/fsp/brasil/fc1504200508.htm

Selka, S. (2007) *Religion and the Politics of Ethnic Identity in Bahia, Brazil*. Gainsville, FL: University Press of Florida.

Semana, R. (1921) Qual e a mais bella mulher do Brasil?, [Who is the most beautiful Brazilian woman?]. *Revista da Semana*, 24/09/1921, Rio de Janeiro, 12-13. Available from: http://memoria.bn.br/DocReader/DocReader.aspx?bib=025909_02&PagFis=793&Pesq=

Sheperd, V., Biswas, M., Fanon-Mendes-France, M., Najcevska, M. and Sahli, M. (2014) *Report of the Working Group of Experts on People of African Descent on its fourteenth session*, New York, NY, United Nations Human Rights Council, Un. Available from:

http://www.ohchr.org/EN/HRBodies/HRC/RegularSessions/Session27/Doc uments/A.HRC.27.68.Add.1_AUV.doc

Silva, A.C. (1999) *As transformações da representação social do negro no livro didático e seus determinantes*, [Changes in social representation of Blacks on textbooks and their determinant factors]. Paper presented at XXII Congresso Brasileiro de Ciências da Comunicação Rio de Janeiro, RJ. Available from: http://www.portcom.intercom.org.br/pdfs/2a80cecae02ccf0480b55db2e4f6 1cf6.PDF

Silva, E.A. (2018) Trajetórias das políticas públicas de ação afirmativa para a população negra brasileira, [Evolution of affirmative action policies for black Brazilian population]. *Revista de Políticas Públicas e Segurança Social*, 2 (2), 53-70.

Silva, E.G. (2017) *"Isso não é palavreado para uma mocinha": Analisando a avaliação do uso de palavrões por mulheres do gênero feminino*, ['This is not an appropriate vocabulary for a lady': Analyzing the evaluation of the use of swear words by women of the feminine gender]. Paper presented at XII Colóquio Nacional e V Colóquio Internacional do Museu Pedagógico, Itapetininga, BA, 26 to 29 September. Available from: http://periodicos.uesb.br/index.php/cmp/article/viewFile/6850/pdf_542

Silva, K.C. (2003) A nação cordial: uma análise dos rituais e das ideologias oficiais de "comemoração dos 500 anos do Brasil", [The cordial nation: an analysis of rituals and official ideologies of the "celebrations of Brazil's 500th anniversary"]. *Revista Brasileira de Ciências Sociais*, 18 (51), 141-194.

Silva, L.I.L. and Buarque, C.R.C. (2003) *Lei Federal Nº 10.639, de 09 de janeiro de 2003*, [Federal Law Number 10.639, 9 January, 2003]. Brasília, DF: Presidência da República. Available from: http://www.planalto.gov.br/ccivil_03/leis/2003/l10.639.htm

Silva, L.S. (2003) *"Também, olha a cor do indivíduo": a visibilidade dos conflitos raciais registrados no Rio Grande do Sul*, ["But look at the color of the individual": the visibility of the racial conflicts registered in Rio Grande do Sul]. Paper presented at V Reuniao de Antropologia do Mercosul, Florianópolis, SC, 30/11 to 3/12. Available from: http://www.antropologia.com.br/arti/colab/vram2003/a13-lssilva.pdf

Silva, M.C.C. (2011) A Redenção de Cam, [Ham's Redemption]. *Mare - Museu de Arte para a Pesquisa e Educação*, 21/02/2011, Campinas, SP. Available from: http://www.mare.art.br/detalhe.asp?idobra=3097

Silva, M.N. (2000) O negro no Brasil: um problema de raça ou de classe?, [The Negro in Brazil: a racial or a social class problem?]. *Mediações - Revista de Ciências Sociais*, 5 (2), 99-124.

Silva, T. (2019) *Racismo Algorítmico em Plataformas Digitais: microagressões e discriminação em código*, [Algorithmic Racism on Digital Platforms: Microaggression and Code Discrimination]. Paper presented at VI Simpósio Internacional Lavits | Assimestrias e (In)visibilidades: Vigilância, Gênero e Raça, Salvador, BA, 26-28 June. Available from: http://lavits.org/vi-simposio-internacional-lavits-salvador-26_28-de-junho-2019/?lang=pt

Silva, V. and Silva, R.S. (2015) Das infovias às ruas: O Facebook e as manifestaçõs sociais na perspectiva da teoria do caos/complexidade, [From the infovias to the streets: The Facebook and the social manifestations from the perspective of chaos/complexity theories]. *Revista Rua*, 2 (21), 285-302.

Silva, V.G. (2014) Religion and black cultural identity. Roman Catholics, Afro-Brazilians and Neopentecostalism, *Vibrant: Virtual Brazilian Anthropology*, 11 (2), 210-246.

Silva, Z.L. (2018) Mulheres negras nos carnavais paulistanos: quem são elas? (1921-1967), [Black Women in São Paulo Carnivals: Who Are They? (1921-1967)]. *Revista Estudos Feministas*, 26 (2), 1-16.

Silveira, D. (2017) População que se declara preta cresce 14,9% no Brasil em 4 anos, aponta IBGE, [Population declaring black grows 14.9% in Brazil in 4 years, says IBGE]. *G1*, 24/11/2017, Rio de Janeiro, RJ. Available from: https://g1.globo.com/economia/noticia/populacao-que-se-declara-preta-cresce-149-no-brasil-em-4-anos-aponta-ibge.ghtml

Silveira, D. (2019) Em sete anos, aumenta em 32% a população que se declara preta no Brasil, [In seven years, the population that declares itself black in Brazil increases by 32%]. *G1*, 22/05/2019, Rio de Janeiro, RJ. Available from: https://g1.globo.com/economia/noticia/2019/05/22/em-sete-anos-aumenta-em-32percent-a-populacao-que-se-declara-preta-no-brasil.ghtml

Skidmore, T.E. (1992) Fact and Myth: Discovering a Racial Problem in Brazil, *The Helen Kellog Institute for International Studies*, Working Paper #173, 1-23.

Skidmore, T.E. (1993) *Black into white: race and nationality in Brazilian thought*. New York, NY: Duke University Press.

Soares, K.G. (2016) "Globo, eu não sou tuas negas": uma análise da comunicação contra-hegemônica em rede no movimento de boicote a minissérie Sexo & As Negas, ["Globo, I am not your nigger": An analysis of the counter-hegemonic communication in net in the boycott movement to the miniserie Sex & The Blacks]. *Revista da Associação Brasileira de Pesquisadores/as Negros/as (ABPN)*, 8 (20), 86-102.

Soares, W. (2016) Denunciados por ofensas a Maju tinham 'verdadeiro exército', diz MP, [Individuals charged for offenses against Maju held 'an army', says the Public Ministry]. *G1*, 22/06/2016, Rio de Janeiro, RJ. Available from: http://g1.globo.com/sao-paulo/noticia/2016/06/denunciados-por-ofensas-maju-tinham-verdadeiro-exercito-diz-mp.html

Society (2016) Internet Governance, *Internet Society*, 26/04/2016, Reston, VA. Available from: http://www.internetsociety.org/what-we-do/internet-issues/internet-governance

Soihet, R. (2003) A sensualidade em festa: representações do corpo feminino nas festas populares do Rio de Janeiro na virada do século XIX para o XX, [Sensuality at party: representations of the female body at popular festivals in Rio de Janeiro at the turn of the 19th to the 20th century]. IN: Matos, M.I.S. and Sohiet, R. (eds.) *O corpo feminino em debate*. São Paulo, SP: Editora Unesp, 177-197.

Solagna, F. (2015) *A formulação da agenda e o ativismo em torno do Marco Civil da Internet*, [The formulation of the agenda and activism around the Internet Regulatory Framework]. Masters' Dissertation, Universidade Federal do Rio Grande do Sul, Sociologia

Solomos, J. and Back, L. (1996) *Racism and Society*. London, UK: Macmillan Press.

Solon, O. (2017) Underpaid and overburdened: the life of a Facebook moderator, *The Guardian*, 25/05/2017, London, UK. Available from: https://www.theguardian.com/news/2017/may/25/facebook-moderator-underpaid-overburdened-extreme-content

Sousa, C.B. (2014) Racismo na mídia: entre a negaçaõ e o reconhecimento, [Racism in the media: between denial and recognition]. *Observato´rio do Direito a` Comunicaça˜o*, 29/07/2014, São Paulo, SP. Available from: http://www.intervozes.org.br/direitoacomunicacao/?p=28778

Souza, A.P.D.Á. (2018) O movimento abolicionista no Brasil: história e historiografia, [The abolitionist movement in Brazil: history and historiography]. *Revista da Academia **Lagartense de Letras**, 2 (2), 65-87.

Souza, L. (1930) O jury internacional outorgou o titulo de "Miss Universo" a "Miss Brasil", [The international jury has granted the "Miss Universe" title to "Miss Brazil"]. *A Noite*, 08/09/1930 - Extraordinary Edition, Rio de Janeiro, RJ, Front cover. Available from: http://memoria.bn.br/DocReader/DocReader.aspx?bib=348970_03

Souza, M.D. (2020) Bolsonaro foca em medidas punitivas e mortes causadas por policiais crescem em 2019, [Bolsonaro focuses on punitive measures and deaths caused by police increases in 2019]. *Brasil de Fato*, 04/03/2020, São Paulo, SP. Available from: https://www.brasildefato.com.br/2020/03/04/bolsonaro-foca-em-medidas-punitivas-e-mortes-causadas-por-policiais-crescem-em-2019

Souza, N.R. (2015) *Aculturação e identidade: o caso do seriado "Sexo e as Negas"*, [Acculturation and identity: the case of the TV series 'Sex and the Black Women']. Paper presented at VI Congresso da Associação Brasileira de Pesquisadores em Comunicação e Política (VI COMPOLÍTICA), Rio de Janeiro, RJ, 22 to 24 April. Available from: http://www.compolitica.org/home/wp-content/uploads/2015/04/GT5-Souza.pdf

Souza, N.S. (1990) *Tornar-se Negro ou As Vicissitudes da Identidade do Negro Brasileiro em Ascensão Social*, [Becoming Negro or the vicissitudes of the Brazilian Negro's identity in upward social mobility]. 2nd ed. Rio de Janeiro, RJ: Graal.

Starks, H. and Trinidad, S.B. (2007) Choose Your Method: A Comparison of Phenomenology, Discourse Analysis, and Grounded Theory, *Qualitative Health Research*, 17 (10), 1372-1380.

Stauffer, C. (2013) Social media spreads and splinters Brazil protests, *Reuters*, 22/06/2013, São Paulo, SP. Available from: https://www.reuters.com/article/us-brazil-protests-socialmedia-idUSBRE95K18O20130621

Stephenson, R.M. (1951) Conflict and control functions of humor, *American Journal of Sociology*, 56 (6), 569-574.

Sue, C.A. and Golash-Boza, T. (2013) 'It was only a joke': how racial humour fuels colour-blind ideologies in Mexico and Peru, *Ethnic and Racial Studies*, 36 (10), 1582-1598.

Takikawa, H. and Nagayoshi, K. (2017) *Political polarization in social media: Analysis of the "Twitter political field" in Japan*, Paper presented at 2017 IEEE International Conference on Big Data, Ipswich, MA, 11-14 December. Available from: http://ieeexplore.ieee.org/stamp/stamp.jsp?tp=&arnumber=8258291

Tavae, M. (2019) For President Bolsonaro, "racism is a rare thing in Brazil"; also claims he isn't racist because he once saved a black man from drowning, *Black Women of Brazil*, 10/05/2019, Salvador, BA. Available from: https://blackwomenofbrazil.co/for-president-bolsonaro-racism-is-a-rare-thing-in-brazil-also-claims-he-isnt-racist-because-he-once-saved-a-black-man-from-drowning/

Tavares, T. (2018) Indicadores Safernet Brasil, [Indicators SaferNet Brazil]. *Dia da Internet Segura | Safe Internet Day*, São Paulo, SP, 06/02/2018. Safernet & European Comission. Available from: https://www.youtube.com/watch?v=ofE2cU0avqA

Tavolaro, S.B.F. (2008) 'Neither Traditional nor Fully Modern...': Two Classic Sociological Approaches on Contemporary Brazil, *International Journal of Politics, Culture & Society*, (19), 109-128.

Telles, E.E. (2003) Repensando as relações de raça no Brasil, [Rethinking Race Relations in Brazil]. *Teoria e Pesquisa*, 1 (42 & 43), 131-159.

Telles, E.E. (2006) *Race in another America: the significance of skin color in Brazil*. Princeton, NJ: Princeton University Press.

Telles, N. (1989) Rebeldes, escritoras, abolicionistas, [Rebels, writers, abolitionists]. *Revista de História USP*, (120), 73-83.

Thompson, A. (2006) Study: Laughter Really Is Contagious, *Live Science*, 12/12/2006, New York, NY. Available from: https://www.livescience.com/9430-study-laughter-contagious.html

Thompson, E.B.(1965a) Does amalgamation work in Brazil? | Part 1, *Ebony*, New York, NY, vol. 20, n. 9. July, 27-42

Thompson, E.B.(1965b) Does amalgamation work in Brazil? | Part 2, *Ebony*, New York, NY, vol. 20, n. 11. September, 33-42

Tiraboschi, J., Caetano, M. and Mesquita, R.V.(2016) Feminismo Negro: o poder da mulher, [Black Feminism: the woman's power]. *Planeta*, São Paulo, SP, 4. 32-41

Tokarnia, M. (2015) Estatuto da Igualdade Racial completa 5 anos com desafio de equiparar direitos, [Statute of Racial Equality completes five years but still with the challenge to reduce inequalities]. *EBC – Empresa Brasileira de Comunicação*, 19/07/2015, Brasília, DF. Available from: http://www.ebc.com.br/cidadania/2015/07/estatuto-da-igualdade-racial-completa-5-anos-com-desafio-de-equiparar-direitos

Travaglia, L.C. (1989) O que é engraçado? Categorias do risível e o humor brasileiro na televisão, [What is funny? Laughable categories and the Brazilian humour on TV]. *Estudos Lingüísticos e Literários*, 5 (6), 42-79.

Trindade, L.V.P. (2008) *Participação e representação social de indivíduos afro-descendentes retratados em anúncios publicitários de revistas: 1968-2006*, [Participation and social representation of Afro-descendant individuals portrayed on Brazilian magazine advertisements: 1968-2006]. Masters' Dissertation, Universidade Nove de Julho. Administração de Empresas

Trindade, L.V.P. (2018a) How the Brazilian Elite Delegitimize Demands for Greater Racial Equality, *Social Science Space | Sage Publishing*, 21/12/2018, California, US. Available from: https://www.socialsciencespace.com/2018/12/how-the-brazilian-elite-delegitimize-demands-for-greater-racial-equality/

Trindade, L.V.P. (2018b) *It is not that funny. Critical analysis of racial ideologies embedded in racialized humour discourses on social media in Brazil*. PhD Thesis, University of Southampton, Sociology

Trindade, L.V.P. (2019) Hate speech on social media undermines important UN declarations, *Social Science Space | Sage Publishing*, 22/04/2019, California, US. Available from: https://www.socialsciencespace.com/2019/04/hate-speech-on-social-media-undermines-important-un-declarations/

Trindade, L.V.P. (2020a) Mídias sociais e a naturalização de discursos racistas no Brasil, [Social media and the naturalisation of racial discourses in Brazil]. IN: Silva, T. (ed.) *Comunidades, algorítimos e ativismos digitais: olhares afrodiaspóricos*, 1ˢᵗ ed. São Paulo, SP: Literarua, 27-42.

Trindade, L.V.P. (2020b) The silent takeover of power by the far-right, *Annals of Social Sciences & Management Studies*, 5 (1), 5-7.

Trotta, F.C. and Santos, K.J.F.P. (2012) Respeitem meus cabelos, brancos: música, política e identidade negra, [Have some respect for my hair, whites: music, politics and black identity]. *Famecos*, 19 (1), 225-248.

Truz, I. (2013) Alforriados, negros ainda foram explorados como escravos, [Freedmen, blacks were still exploited as slaves]. *Agência USP de Notícias*, 28/02/2013, São Paulo, SP. Available from: http://www.usp.br/agen/?p=129240

Turkle, S. (1995) *Life on the Screen*. New York, NY: Simon and Schuster.

Twine, F.W. (1998) *Racism in a racial democracy: the maintenance of white supremacy in Brazil*. New York, NY: Rutgers University Press.

UN (2001) International Migration, Racism, Discrimination and Xenophobia. *World Conference against Racism, Racial Discrimination, Xenophobia and Related Intolerance*, August, Geneva, Switzeerland, 1-37. Available from: http://www.refworld.org/pdfid/49353b4d2.pdf

UN (2017) Pelo fim da violência contra a juventude negra no Brasil, [Ending violence against black youth in Brazil]. *Nações Unidas Brasil*, São Paulo, SP. Available from: https://nacoesunidas.org/campanha/vidas-negras/

Uneafro (2019) Uneafro-Brasil: Atlas da Violência 2019 mostra que genocídio da juventude e das mulheres negras continua, [Uneafro-Brasil: Atlas of Violence 2019 shows that genocide of youth and black women continues]. *Revista Fórum*, 27/06/2019, São Paulo, SP. Available from: https://revistaforum.com.br/rede/uneafro-brasil-atlas-da-violencia-2019-mostra-que-genocidio-da-juventude-e-das-mulheres-negras-continua/

Valenti, J. (2017) Facebook is too lenient on those peddling hate speech, *The Guardian*, 24/05/2017, London, UK. Available from: https://www.theguardian.com/commentisfree/2017/may/24/facebook-lenient-peddling-hate-speech?CMP=Share_iOSApp_Other van den Berghe, P. (1967) *Race and racism: a comparative perspective*. New York, NY: John Wiley & Sons, Inc.

van Dijk, T.A. (1992) Discourse and the denial of racism, *Discourse & Society*, 3 (1), 87-118.

Vargas, J.H.C. (2004) Hyperconsciousness of Race and Its Negation: The Dialectic of White Supremacy in Brazil, *Identities*, 11, 443-470.

Vasques, L.(2014) Como anda o sonho brasileiro?, [How's the Brazilian dream?]. *Sociologia*, São Paulo, SP. December, 16-23

Vieira, C.A., Costa, F.L. and Barbosa, L.O. (1982) O 'jeitinho' brasileiro como um recurso de poder, [The Brazilian 'jeitinho' as a power resource]. *Revista de Administração Pública*, 16 (2), 5-31.

Vieira, P.A.S. (2015) A cor das cotas nas universidades brasileiras: ação afirmativa, raça e sobrerepresentação de grupos sociais no ensino superior, [The quota's colour in Brazilian universities: affirmative action, race and over-representation of social groups in higher education]. *Revista da Associação Brasileira de Pesquisadores/as Negros/as (ABPN)*, 7 (17), 23-44.

Vitorino, H. (2018) Duas mães denunciam o racismo, mas só uma delas é levada a sério, [Two mothers denounce racism, but only one is taken seriously]. *Portal Raízes*, 18/12/2018, São Paulo, SP. Available from: https://www.portalraizes.com/maes-racismo/

von Spix, J.B., Von Martius, K.F.P. and Lloyd, H.E. (1824) *Travels in Brazil, in the years 1817-1820. Undertaken by command of His Majesty the King of Bavaria*. London, UK: Longman, Hurst, Rees, Orme & Brown, Paternoster-Row.

W3Haus (2016a) Mirros of Racism, *W3Haus*, 04/01/2016, São Paulo, SP. Available from: https://vimeo.com/150728678

W3Haus (2016b) Mirros of Racism. W3Haus for Criola NGO, *W3Haus*, 19/06/2016, São Paulo, SP. Available from: https://vimeo.com/171342627

Wade, P. (2010) *Race and Ethnicity in Latin America*. London, UK: Pluto Press.

Wagley, C. (1963) Race and class in rural Brazil, *UNESCO - Race and Society*, December, New York, NY, 172. Available from: http://unesdoc.unesco.org/images/0005/000545/054502eb.pdf

Wainer, J. and Melguizo, T. (2018) Políticas de inclusão no ensino superior: avaliação do desempenho dos alunos baseado no Enade de 2012 a 2014, [Inclusion policies in higher education: evaluation of student performance based on the Enade from 2012 to 2014]. *Educação e Pesquisa*, 44, 1-15.

Waiselfisz, J.J. (2007) *Mapa das desigualdades digitais no Brasil*, [Map of digital inequalities in Brazil]. Brasília, DF, Rede de Informação Tecnológica Latino-Americana, RITLA. Available from: https://www.faneesp.edu.br/site/documentos/mapa_desigualdades_digitai s.pdf

Watson, C. (2015) A Sociologist Walks into a Bar (and Other Academic Challenges): Towards a Methodology of Humour, *Sociology*, 49 (3), 407-421.

Watts, J. (2013) Brazil erupts in protest: more than a million on the streets, *The Guardian,* 21/06/2013, London, UK. Available from: http://www.theguardian.com/world/2013/jun/21/brazil-police-crowds-rio-protest

Weaver, S. (2010) Developing a rhetorical analysis of racist humour: examining anti-black jokes on the Internet, *Social Semiotics*, 20 (5), 537-555.

Weaver, S. (2011a) Jokes, rhetoric and embodied racism: a rhetorical discourse analysis of the logics of racist jokes on the internet, *Ethnicities*, 11 (4), 413-435.

Weaver, S. (2011b) *The rhetoric of racist humour: US, UK and global race joking.* Surrey, UK: Ashgate Publishing Ltd.

Weaver, S. (2013) A rhetorical discourse analysis of online anti-Muslim and anti-Semitic jokes, *Ethnic and Racial Studies*, 36 (3), 483-499.

White, Y.M. (2014) *Being Dark-Skinned and Poor in Brazil: The Intersectionality of Skin Color, Income, and Gender.* Masters' Dissertation, May, Vanderbilt University. Latin American Studies

Willems, E. (1970) Social Differentiation in Colonial Brazil, *Comparative Studies in Society and History*, 12 (1), 31-49.

Wimmer, A. (2015) Race-centrism: a critique and a research agenda, *Ethnic and Racial Studies*, 38 (13), 2186-2205.

Winant, H. (1999) Racial democracy and racial identity: comparing the United States and Brazil, IN: Hanchard, M. (ed.) *Racial politics in contemporary Brazil.* Durham, NC: Duke University Press, 98-115.

Winter, B. (2013) Analysis: Brazil's protests: Not quite a 'Tropical Spring', *Reuters*, 19/06/2013, São Paulo, SP. Available from: https://www.reuters.com/article/us-brazil-protests-impact-analysis-idUSBRE95I1LQ20130619

Witoslawski, H. (2005) Representações da brasilidade: o corpo como símbolo para o modernismo e para o varguismo (1920-1945), [Representations of the brazilian identity: the body to the modernism and to the government ot Getúlio Vargas (1920-1945)], *Revista Temas & Matizes*, 4 (7), 75-82.

Xavier, E. (2017) *Senti na pele: relatos*, [I have felt it on my skin: victims' reports]. Rio de Janeiro, RJ: Malê Edições.

Xavier, G. (2013) Segredos de penteadeira: conversas transnacionais sobre raça, beleza e cidadania na imprensa negra pós-abolição do Brasil e dos EUA, [Dressing-table secrets: transnational conversations on race, beauty and citizenship in post-abolition black press in Brazil and USA]. *Estudos Históricos, Rio de Janeiro*, 26 (52), 429-450.

Younge, G. (2012) Who thinks about the consequences of online racism?, *The Guardian*, 12/07/2012, London, UK. Available from: http://www.theguardian.com/commentisfree/2012/jul/12/consequences-of-online-racism

Zakabi, R. and Camargo, L. (2007) Gêmeos idênticos, Alex e Alan foram considerados pelo sistema de cotas como 'branco' e 'negro': É mais uma prova de que raça não existe, [Identical twins, Alex and Alan were considered by the quota system as 'white' and 'black': It's another evidence that race doesn't exist]. *Veja*, 40 (2011), 82-88.

Zampier, D. (2013) Barbosa diz que Justiça pune de forma desigual ricos e pobres, [Barbosa says Justice punishes unequally rich and poor]. *Agência Brasil*, 03/05/2013, Brasília, DF. Available from:

http://memoria.ebc.com.br/agenciabrasil/noticia/2013-05-03/barbosa-diz-que-justica-pune-de-forma-desigual-ricos-e-pobres

Zimmer, M. (2010) "But the data is already public": on the ethics of research in Facebook, *Ethics and Information Technology*, 12 (4), 313-325.

Zweig, S. (1941) *Brazil: Land of the Future*. New York, NY: The Viking Press.

Index

Lightning Source UK Ltd.
Milton Keynes UK
UKHW021257121120
373260UK00005B/286